D1257313

THE HASKINS SOCIETY JOURNAL

STUDIES IN MEDIEVAL HISTORY

The Charles Homer Haskins Society
Officers and Councillors for 2015

THE HASKINS SOCIETY JOURNAL

STUDIES IN MEDIEVAL HISTORY

EDITED BY LAURA L. GATHAGAN AND WILLIAM NORTH

Volume 27
2015

THE BOYDELL PRESS

First published 2016
The Boydell Press, Woodbridge

ISBN 978–1–78327–148–1

ISSN 0963–4959

The Boydell Press is an imprint of Boydell & Brewer Ltd
PO Box 9, Woodbridge, Suffolk IP12 3DF, UK
and of Boydell & Brewer Inc.
668 Mt Hope Avenue, Rochester, NY 14620–2731, USA
website: www.boydellandbrewer.com

A CIP catalogue record for this book is available
from the British Library

The publisher has no responsibility for the continued existence or accuracy of
URLs for external or third-party internet websites referred to in this book,
and does not guarantee that any content on such websites is,
or will remain, accurate or appropriate

Contents

Figures

Editors' Note

This volume of the Haskins Society Journal includes papers read at the 34th Annual Conference of the Charles Homer Haskins Society at Carleton College in November 2015, papers read at earlier Haskins conferences, and individual paper submissions. Martin Millett delivered the C. Warren Hollister Memorial Lecture and Katherine L. Hodges-Kluck's essay received the 2015 Bethell Prize, judged by Bruce O'Brien of Mary Washington University, Washington, DC.

This is the regular volume for 2015. The Editor and Associate Editor would like to offer thanks to the contributors, anonymous reviewers, and to Caroline Palmer and her excellent staff at Boydell & Brewer, Ltd. for their help and patience during the production of this volume.

The Haskins Society Journal is an international refereed journal, and its contents are not limited to papers read at the Society's own conference or at the sessions which it sponsors at Leeds, Kalamazoo, or other venues. Papers on topics in the many fields and periods of the medieval past to which Charles Homer Haskins contributed, including but not limited to Anglo-Saxon, Viking, Norman, and Angevin history as well as the history of the neighboring peoples and territories, are welcome from any scholar. Authors intending to submit are asked to consult the Society's website (www.haskinssociety.org) or write to the Editor (Dr. Laura Gathagan, Department of History, SUNY Cortland, P.O. Box 2000 Cortland, NY 13045–0900, USA; email: laura.gathagan@cortland.edu) or Associate Editor (Dr. William North, Department of History, Carleton College, 1 North College Street, Northfield, MN 55057, USA; email: wnorth@carleton.edu).

Laura L. Gathagan, Editor
William North, Associate Editor

Abbreviations

AASS	*Acta Sanctorum* (67 vols., Antwerp/Brussels/Paris 1643–1884)
AHR	*American Historical Review*
ANS	*Anglo–Norman Studies* (formerly *Proceedings of the Battle Conference on Anglo-Norman Studies*)
ASC	Anglo-Saxon Chronicle; normally cited from *Two of the Saxon Chronicles Parallel*, ed. Charles Plummer (2 vols., Oxford, 1892–9), with year and MS
ASE	*Anglo-Saxon England*
Bede, *EH*	Bede, *Ecclesiastical History of the English People*, ed. and trans. B. Colgrave and R.A.B. Mynors (Oxford, rev. ed. 1991)
Bk. of Fees	*Liber feodorum: the Book of Fees, commonly called Testa de Nevill* (3 vols., London, 1920–31)
BL	British Library, London
Bracton	*Bracton on the Laws and Customs of England*, ed. and trans. Samuel E. Thorne (4 vols., Cambridge, MA, 1968–77)
Bracton's Note Book	*Bracton's Note Book: a Collection of Cases decided in the King's Courts during the Reign of Henry the Third*, ed. F.W. Maitland (3 vols., London, 1887)
CCM	*Cahiers de Civilisation Médiévale*
Cal. Chart. R.	*Calendar of the Charter Rolls, 1226–1516* (6 vols., London, 1903–27)
Cal. Docs. France, ed. Round	*Calendar of Documents preserved in France illustrative of the History of Great Britain and Ireland, I: A.D. 918–1206*, ed. J.H. Round (London, 1899)
Cal. Lib. R.	*Calendar of the Liberate Rolls preserved in the Public Record Office* (6 vols., London, 1916–64)
Cal. Pat.	*Calendar of the Patent Rolls preserved in the Public Record Office* (London, 1891 and in progress)
Camb. Hist. Jnl.	*Cambridge Historical Journal*
CCCM	Corpus Christianorum, continuatio medievalis (Turnhout, 1971–)

CCSL	Corpus Christianorum, series latina (Turnhout, 1953–)
Close R.	*Close Rolls of the Reign of Henry III preserved in the Public Record Office* (14 vols., London, 1902–38)
Complete Peerage	G.E. C[okayne], *The Complete Peerage of England, Scotland, Ireland, Great Britain, and the United Kingdom, Extant, Extinct, and Dormant*, new edn. by V. Gibbs and others (12 vols. in 13, London, 1910–59)
Cur. Reg. R.	*Curia Regis Rolls preserved in the Public Record Office* (17 vols., in progress, London, 1922–)
DB	*Domesday Book, seu liber censualis Wilhelmi primi regis Angliae* [ed. Abraham Farley] (2 vols., London, 1783)
DNB	*Dictionary of National Biography*, ed. Leslie Stephen and Stephen Lee
Dudo, *History*	*Dudo of St Quentin: History of the Normans*, Eric Christiansen, trans. (Woodbridge, 1998)
EcHR	*Economic History Review*
EHD	*English Historical Documents, I: c. 500–1042*, ed. Dorothy Whitelock (2nd edn., London, 1979); *II: 1042–1189*, ed. David C. Douglas and George W. Greenaway (2nd edn., London, 1981); *III: 1189–1327,* ed. Harry Rothwell (London, 1975)
EHR	*English Historical Review*
EME	*Early Medieval Europe*
EYC	*Early Yorkshire Charters*, ed. W. Farrer and C.T. Clay (13 vols.: vols. i–iii, Edinburgh, 1914–16; index to vols. i–iii, and vols. iv–xii, Yorkshire Archaeological Soc. Record Ser. Extra Ser. 1–10 [1935–65])
FSI	*Fonti per la Storia d'Italia*
Gesta Stephani	*Gesta Stephani*, ed. K.R. Potter and revised R.H.C. Davis (Oxford, 1976)
Glanvill	*The Treatise on the Laws and Customs of the Realm of England commonly called Glanvill*, ed. and trans. G.D.G. Hall with guide to further reading by M.T. Clanchy (Oxford, rev. ed. 1993)
GND, ed. van Houts	*The Gesta Normannum Ducum of William of Jumièges, Orderic Vitalis, and Robert of Torigni*, ed. and trans. Elisabeth M.C. van Houts (2 vols., Oxford, 1992–5)
Henry of Huntingdon, *Historia*	Henry, Archdeacon of Huntingdon, *Historia Anglorum: the History of the English People*, ed. and trans. Diana Greenway (Oxford, 1996)
Hist. Res.	*Historical Research* (formerly *Bulletin of the Institute of Historical Research*)
HSJ	*Haskins Society Journal*
JEH	*Journal of Ecclesiastical History*
JMH	*Journal of Medieval History*

John of Worcester,	*The Chronicle of John of Worcester*, ed. and trans. R.R.
Chronicle	Darlington, P. McGurk, and J. Bray (3 vols., Oxford, 1995–)
MGH	Monumenta Germaniae Historica
AA	*Auctores Antiquissimi*
Epp.	*Epistolae*
LdL	*Libelli de Lite*
SS	*Scriptores in folio*
SSRG	*Scriptores Rerum Germanicarum, separatim editi*
SSRG, n.s.	*Scriptores Rerum Germanicarum, nova series*
MS./MSS.	Manuscript/Manuscripts
NA	The National Archives, Kew, London
OV	*The Ecclesiastical History of Orderic Vitalis*, ed. Marjorie Chibnall (6 vols., Oxford, 1969–80)
PBA	*Proceedings of the British Academy*
Pipe R.	*The Great Roll of the Pipe* (Pipe Roll Society), with regnal year
PL	*Patrologiae latinae cursus completus*, ed. J.-P. Migne (221 vols., Paris, 1844–64)
Rec. Com.	Record Commissioners
Recueil, ed. Fauroux	*Recueil des actes des ducs de Normandie de 911 à 1066*, ed. M. Fauroux (Caen, 1961)
Regesta	*Regesta regum Anglo-Normannorum, 1066–1154*, ed. H.W.C. Davis and others (4 vols., Oxford, 1913–69)
RHC	*Recueil des Historiens des Croisades*
Doc.Arm.	*Documents arméniens* (2 vols., Paris, 1869–1906)
Gr.	*Historiens Grecs* (2 vols., Paris, 1875–81)
Lois	*Lois* (2 vols., Paris, 1841–43)
Occid.	*Historiens Occidentaux* (5 vols. in 6, 1844–95)
Or.	*Historiens Orientaux* (5 vols., Paris, 1872–1906)
RIS	*Rerum Italicarum Scriptores*
Rot. de Lib.	*Rotuli de liberate ac de misis et praestitis, regnante Johanne*, ed. T.D. Hardy (London, 1844)
Rot. Hund.	*Rotuli hundredorum temp. Hen. III & Edw. I*, ed. W. Illingworth and J. Caley (2 vols., London, 1812–18)
Rot. Litt. Claus.	*Rotuli litterarum clausarum in turri Londinensi asservati, 1204–27*, ed. T.D. Hardy (2 vols., London, 1833–44)
Rot. Litt. Pat.	*Rotuli litterarum patentium in Turri Londinensi asservati (1201–16)*, ed. T.D. Hardy (London, 1835)
RS	Rolls Series
Sawyer, *Charters*	P.H. Sawyer, *Anglo-Saxon Charters: an Annotated List and Bibliography* (London, 1968), with charter number
s.a. (no italics)	*sub anno/annis* [under the year/-s]
ser.	series
Settimane	*Settimane di Studio del Centro Italiano di Studi sull'Alto Medioevo*

Soc.	Society
Stubbs, *Charters*	*Select Charters and Other Illustrations of English Constitutional History from the Earliest Times to the Reign of Edward the First*, ed. William Stubbs (9th edn., revised H.W.C. Davis, Oxford, 1913)
s.v. (no italics)	*sub verbo*
Symeon, *Opera*	*Symeonis monachi opera omnia*, ed. Thomas Arnold, RS 75 (2 vols., London, 1882–5)
TRHS	*Transactions of the Royal Historical Society*
Univ.	University
unpub.	unpublished
VCH	*The Victoria History of the Counties of England* (in progress), with name of county
William of Malmesbury, *GP*	William of Malmesbury, *Gesta Pontificum Anglorum*, ed. and trans. R.M. Thomson and M. Winterbottom (2 vols., Oxford, 2007)
William of Malmesbury, *GR*	William of Malmesbury, *Gesta regum Anglorum*, ed. and trans. R.A.B. Mynors, R.M. Thomson, and M. Winterbottom (2 vols., Oxford, 1998–1999)
William of Malmesbury, *HN*	William of Malmesbury, *Historia novella*, ed. K.R. Potter and E. King (Oxford, 1998)
William of Poitiers, *Gesta*	William of Poitiers, *The Gesta Gvillelmi of William of Poitiers*, ed. and trans. R.H.C. Davis and M. Chibnall (Oxford, 1998)

1

The Warren Hollister Memorial Essay

Rural Settlement in Roman Britain
and Its Significance for the Early Medieval Period

Martin Millett

Figure 1. Cowdery's Down excavation. General view of Structures A1, B4, C8 and associated fence-line from the south-east. (Photo: G. Huxley, Cowdery's Down Project)

It is now just over thirty years since the report on the excavation of a major early medieval settlement site at Cowdery's Down, Basingstoke was published (Figure1).[1] That publication was followed-up by a paper seeking to place the remarkable architectural evidence revealed at Cowdery's Down into a broader British and European context. In particular, we discussed how the settlement and architectural tradition related to the issue of continuity or discontinuity between Roman and early medieval Britain.[2] It is perhaps timely to stand back from the evidence provided by that site to consider how information about architecture and rural settlement now looks in relation to these broader debates. This is particularly worthwhile now since there has been a vast increase in the amount of evidence available from Britain, and a series of projects is underway that will soon produce a set of new syntheses of the evidence. As I hope to make clear, recent research raises a number of interesting issues but ones that are difficult to address both because of contrasting academic traditions and because of the different character of the data from the Roman and early medieval periods. It seems self-evident, therefore, that if we are to arrive at a better understanding of the transition between Roman and early medieval Britain, we need to create understandings that bridge this academic divide.

Although I do not want to discuss the evidence and interpretation of Cowdery's Down in detail in this paper, it is worth saying something about the nature of the evidence and outlining our conclusions about it. The early medieval phases of the site were found by chance during an excavation that had been designed to investigate features revealed by aerial photography in advance of building operations. The fifth- to seventh-century buildings lay to one side of an Iron Age and Romano-British settlement site, which itself overlay Bronze Age burial mounds and settlement features. The most remarkable feature of the early medieval phase was the quality of evidence for its architecture. Most of the sixteen timber halls excavated had their foundations cut into the white chalk bedrock, but the topsoil had a high clay content and a contrasting reddish brown colour. Thus, as the buildings had been constructed with large baulks of timber set into the ground and packed around with chalk rubble, 'ghosts' of the timbers were preserved when the wood had rotted and clay-rich topsoil had slipped into replace it (Figures 2A and B). As a result, not only did the excavation reveal nearly complete building plans but also timber-by-timber layouts of their structures.

Reviewing this exceptionally good quality architectural evidence, we were able to make a series of suggestions about the superstructures of the excavated buildings. We concluded from the Cowdery's Down evidence that the buildings were highly sophisticated and designed around the use of horizontal baulks of timber that had been carefully trimmed to provide rectangular cross-sections.

[1]   M. Millett with S.T. James, 'Excavations at Cowdery's Down, Basingstoke, 1978–81', *Archaeological Journal* 140 (1983), 151–279.
[2]   S.T. James, A. Marshall and M. Millett, 'An Early Medieval Building Tradition', *Archaeological Journal* 141 (1985), 182–215. Reprinted in *The Archaeology of Anglo-Saxon England*, ed. C.E. Karkov (New York, NY, 1999), 79–118.

Figures 2A & 2B. Cowdery's Down excavation. Timber ghosts in the walls of buildings: (A, left) as seen in plan in the south wall of Structure C12, (B, right) as seen in section in the wall of Structure C9. (Photos: G. Huxley, Cowdery's Down project)

These were held in place by vertical baulks, set either in post-holes or in continuous trenches, such that they created very heavy and robust walls on which the main weight of the roof was carried.[3] We concluded that a horizontal wall-plate laid along the tops of the walls provided the housing on which the roofing timbers stood, and that in order to counteract the turning motion created by the load of the roof, external raking timbers (which, when previously found, were erroneously considered to be 'buttresses') were placed round the outside walls of the buildings close up to the walls.[4] The roofs themselves were supported by timbers running along their ridges, which were, in turn, supported by posts along the building axis. All these features were clear from the evidence, and do not seem to have been questioned by subsequent scholars. More controversially, we suggested, first, that the largest of the buildings had raised timber floors, the joists of which were supported on horizontal baulks in the walls,[5] and that the timbers set against walls in the interior near the middle of each building housed crucks which rose to support the ridge.[6]

---

3   Millett, 'Excavations at Cowdery's Down', 227–233.
4   Millett, 'Excavations at Cowdery's Down', 242–243.
5   Millett, 'Excavations at Cowdery's Down', 240–242.
6   Millett, 'Excavations at Cowdery's Down', 236–240; 243–246.

Although there was some variation, the plans of the Cowdery's Down buildings were consistently laid-out on the basis of a module of two-squares with the doorways centrally placed in the long walls. In reviewing the evidence from other sites in Britain, we found both that this plan-form was widely repeated, and that the fragmentary evidence for the superstructures of the buildings was largely consistent with the model we had proposed for Cowdery's Down.[7]

In a critique of the Cowdery's Down reconstruction, N.W. Alcock and D. Walsh reject the suggested cruck construction for the roof,[8] although their alternative reconstruction of the roof nonetheless also relies on the heavy walls to support the roof load. They also questioned the use of a raised timber floor,[9] although in this case they do not seem to have fully engaged with the detailed archaeological evidence we presented. Helena Hamerow, too, doubts the evidence for timber floors,[10] although she does not address the evidence adduced for them but rather deploys a general argument based on their apparent absence from other sites. Irrespective of the debate about the interpretation of the details of this architectural tradition, it seems very clear that by the sixth to seventh centuries CE, a widespread and consistent architectural tradition was well established across southern and eastern England. Furthermore, the lavish use of substantial timbers in their construction represents a major outlay of scarce resources in the shape of very large oak trees. This sophisticated architecture thus represents a distinctive mode of élite social display complementing the evidence from the much more widely studied burials of the period.[11] Equally, differentiation in building size seems increasingly to have been used to mark social status through the period.[12] Like the burial evidence, this architecture should therefore be used to help us to understand the social structure and dynamics of this society.

On the basis of our broader survey we also concluded that this architectural tradition was different from that seen on the Continent during the same period. This conclusion supported ideas previously proposed on the basis of much more fragmentary evidence.[13] The principal difference noted was in the form of the building plans: although there were a few double-square buildings from sites in the Low Countries and Germany, in these areas the long-house or byre house was clearly dominant, whilst this type of building was wholly absent from Britain. Equally, whilst there were some possible links in the structural forms

---

[7]   James et al., 'An Early Medieval Building Tradition', 186–198. See also A. Marshall and G. Marshall, 'A Survey and Analysis of the Buildings of Early and Middle Anglo-Saxon England', *Medieval Archaeology* 35 (1991), 29–43; A. Marshall and G. Marshall, 'Differentiation, Change and Continuity in Anglo-Saxon Buildings', *Archaeological Journal* 150 (1993), 366–402.

[8]   N.W. Alcock and D. Walsh, 'Architecture at Cowdery's Down: A Reconsideration', *Archaeological Journal* 150 (1993), 403–09.

[9]   Alcock and Walsh, 'Architecture at Cowdery's Down', 408.

[10]   H. Hamerow, *Rural Settlements and Society in Anglo-Saxon England* (Oxford, 2012), 44.

[11]   R. Fleming, *Britain after Rome* (London, 2011), 65–75.

[12]   A. Marshall and G. Marshall, 'Differentiation, Change and Continuity', 399–400.

[13]   P. Dixon, 'How Saxon is a Saxon House?', in *Structural Reconstruction. Approaches to the Interpretation of the Excavated Remains of Buildings*, ed. P.J. Drury (Oxford, 1982), 275–86.

of roofs, the distinctive and lavish use of timber to create heavy load-bearing walls seen in Britain was largely absent from the continental examples.[14] At the same time we noted that elements of the British early medieval tradition were already present on some Romano-British sites. In particular, simple rectangular halls following a two-square module were reasonably widespread.[15] Although such buildings were largely built of stone rather than wood, they did exemplify a tradition in which the roof load was carried on heavily built walls. We concluded that such a widespread and unusually uniform tradition must have been a hybrid that developed in England starting in the fifth century that reached its *floruit* by the seventh century. The tradition was neither a wholly indigenous Romano-British one nor a wholly Germanic import. Rather it was either a product of Germanic immigrants adopting British building forms but re-conceptualizing them in timber, or the descendants of the Romano-British population continuing their building plans but adopting ascendant Germanic fashions in their execution.[16]

New sources of evidence

Before we turn to review how this evidence should be understood some three decades later, it is important to appreciate that in the interim there have been significant changes in the nature of the archaeological evidence available from Britain that have had an important impact on our understanding of both the Roman and early medieval periods. Archaeology in Britain underwent something of a revolution in 1990 when there were significant changes in the way that development planning was organized. In brief, a system was introduced whereby any building or infrastructure development in the United Kingdom had to be preceded by an assessment of its potential archaeological implications. Where such assessments provide evidence (through such methods as geophysical survey and trial trenching) that archaeological remains will be adversely affected or destroyed, developers have either to revise their plans to mitigate this impact or pay for excavation of the site.[17] This has led to something of an explosion in the amount of archaeological evidence available, the product of both site evaluations and larger scale excavations. Of particular importance is the fact that hitherto little-explored areas are now being investigated regularly as a by-product of developments so that we are obtaining information from a broader range of sites across the country, although the number is still far from a statistically valid random sample. Equally, the large-scale excavations that are

---

14   James et al., 'Early Medieval Building Tradition', 199–201.
15   James et al., 'Early Medieval Building Tradition', 201–205.
16   cf. Fleming, *Britain after Rome*, 48–49.
17   The policy was governed by *Planning Policy Guidance No. 16: Archaeology and Planning* (London, 1990). For discussion see P. Pickering, 'Learning from PPG16', *London Archaeologist* 10/3 (2002), 64–68.

now quite common provide information about a very much wider range of site types than had previously been examined for research purposes. Finally, the burgeoning of this new industry of developer-funded archaeology has led to an impressive increase in the standard of archaeological work and the quality of publication, at least on some sites.

There is, however, is a downside to this massive expansion of archaeological investigation, namely that although the top-quality work is done by the best excavators and contractors, the lack of any effective regulatory regime has nonetheless allowed some sites to be lost due to rather poor excavators, whilst the full and proper publication of archaeological projects has not commonly followed from fieldwork. Instead, many projects, especially evaluations, result in unpublished reports (generally called 'grey literature') which are usually deposited only in the archive of the local Planning Department, although such reports are now increasingly becoming available on-line.[18]

An increasing awareness of the shortcomings of the use of knowledge from this rich potential resource has led to a new trend, with various groups of archaeologists establishing projects to review systematically the available evidence and draw conclusions from it.[19] Although some key baseline information has been published from the first studies of this type,[20] it is too early to assess the impact of these projects in this paper, but it is possible to see some directions in which this evidence is leading.

It is also worth noting here that a further source of information has increasingly become available over the last few years as a product of the Portable Antiquities Scheme.[21] This scheme seeks to collate the evidence from occasional finds that are most often the product of work by metal-detector users rather than from archaeological projects. Whilst these data, too, have inherent biases, the systematic collection of vast volumes of material is providing a key new source of information from across the country which needs to be integrated with other kinds of evidence.[22]

The medieval perspective

When we return to the issue of how to understand the origins of the architectural tradition in fifth- to seventh-century Britain in the light of more recent work,

---

[18]   www.heritagegateway.org.uk.
[19]   R. Bradley 'Bridging the Two Cultures: Commercial Archaeology and the Study of Prehistoric Britain', *Antiquaries Journal* 86 (2006), 1–13; M.G. Fulford and N. Holbrook 'Assessing the Contribution of Commercial Archaeology to the Study of the Roman Period in Britain', *Antiquaries Journal* 91 (2011), 323–45.
[20]   J. Taylor, *An Atlas of Roman Rural Settlement in England* (York, 2007).
[21]   www.finds.org.uk.
[22]   T. Brindle, *The Portable Antiquities Scheme and Roman Britain* (London, 2014); P.J. Walton, *Rethinking Roman Britain: Coinage and Archaeology* (Wetteren, 2012).

there are three key lines of development. In a sequence of publications Helena Hamerow has provided a broad review of the settlement evidence, both from Britain and the continent. This work provides a new baseline for study, although it is important to appreciate that her work does not engage very closely with the details of the architectural tradition as exemplified at Cowdery's Down.[23] Looking primarily at building plans, she places most emphasis on Germanic influence despite the continued absence of the long-house from Britain. She rules out Romano-British influence on the two-square plan module of early medieval buildings on the basis that there are now more such buildings known in Germanic areas on the continent, although it remains clear that they were not dominant there but were so in Britain.[24] In concluding, she accepts some form of hybridization and tends to favour the view that there was some kind of process whereby the descendants of Romano-British inhabitants adopted Germanic traditions.

In several papers that were preparatory to the publication of his major synthesis of developer-funded work in England, John Blair clearly favours a model of hybridization to explain the origins of the architectural tradition. He gives some support to the views we expressed in 1984 but also and importantly identifies a revolution in settlement planning alongside its consolidation in southern and eastern England in the seventh century.[25] His work shows how excavation since the 1990s has reinforced the view that there was a very widespread and remarkably uniform pattern of building across this region. Pointing towards sites like Catholme,[26] he also identifies a trend towards the orthogonal planning of such rural sites, even suggesting the use of standard units of measurement.[27] This provides a fascinating complement to the sophisticated architectural tradition discussed above but also raises some interesting questions about its relationship to Roman Britain. Blair inclines towards the view that Romano-British influence was important, although this raises problems in the context of what we now know about settlements in Roman Britain (see below). Notwithstanding this caveat, it seems clear that he has taken the argument one stage further forward with his recognition of the relationship of a sophisticated architecture to a more uniform tradition of settlement planning.

Finally, following a different line of evidence, Steve Rippon has been undertaking a new study combining work on field-systems with a review of the environmental evidence.[28] This work suggests a strong pattern of continuity of

---

[23] H. Hamerow, *Early Medieval Settlements: The Archaeology of Rural Communities in NW Europe 400–900* (Oxford, 2002); H. Hamerow, *Rural Settlements and Society*
[24] Hamerow, *Early Medieval Settlements*, 48–50.
[25] J. Blair, *The British Culture of Anglo-Saxon Settlement (H.M. Chadwick Memorial Lecture no. 24)* (Cambridge, 2013).
[26] S. Losco-Bradly and G. Kinsley, *Catholme: An Anglo-Saxon Settlement on the Trent Gravels in Staffordshire* (Nottingham, 2002).
[27] J. Blair, 'Grid-Planning in Anglo-Saxon Settlements: The Short Perch and Four-Perch Module', *Anglo-Saxon Studies in Archaeology and History* 18 (2012), 18–61.
[28] S.Rippon, C. Smart, B. Pears and F. Fleming, 'The Fields of Britannia: Continuity and Discontinuity in the *Pays* and Regions of Roman Britain', *Landscapes* 14/1 (2013), 33–53.

land-use and fields across the whole country, with little evidence for the change in balance between arable, pasture, and woodland. Although this continuity forms part of a complex story that goes far beyond the scope of this paper, it is of great importance as it reinforces the view that any interpretation of the period must allow for not only continuity of land-use but also the production of an economic surplus that could be deployed by those controlling society. Such people thus had more economic power than is sometimes assumed.

The significance of the Romano-British past

It might seem an obvious point, but the consensus that the rural settlement pattern in early medieval England is the product of the hybridization of Germanic and Romano-British traditions presupposes that we have a strong understanding of both pre-existing societies. In the context of Roman Britain, surprisingly, I think we need to be very cautious in accepting this view in the light of current archaeological evidence. Whilst I am not sure that we yet have a clear understanding of the nature and variety of the Romano-British countryside, I suspect that many widely held traditional understandings are flawed.

Common views of rural settlement in Roman Britain remain dominated by the the Roman villa, villa landscapes, and villa estates, with implicit historical models based on the dominance of markets for the accumulation of wealth, and the expenditure of the money earned on symbols of *Romanitas*. This vision tends also to divide the landscape into a 'Romanized' versus and 'un-Romanized' sector, invoking the state and the army as major sources of both control and economic demand. In the most recent synthesis, this perspective has been transformed into David Mattingly's 'landscapes of opportunity' and 'landscapes of resistance'.[29] This is a complex subject, and here I do not have space to do more than draw out some some key themes which seem to me to undermine this view. By arriving at a better understanding of the Romano-British background, we can gain a clearer understanding of subsequent developments.

My first point is that the countryside of Roman Britain was very densely settled. Jeremy Taylor's evaluation of the data based on Historic Environment Records suggested that there are about 28,000 known rural settlement sites across Roman Britain, within which there are perhaps only 2,000 which can be classified as villas.[30] Even here we need to take care, as the term villa is used very loosely in the UK to refer to any rural house with aspirations towards Romanized architecture, so the majority are modest and would not have been recognized as élite residences by those from the Mediterranean. Taylor's estimates are not incompatible with my own suggestion that the population

[29]   D. Mattingly, *An Imperial Possession: Britain in the Roman Empire* (London, 2006); compare M. Millett 'Perceptions of the Imperial Landscape', *Journal of Roman Archaeology* 25 (2012), 772–75.
[30]   Mattingly, *An Imperial Possession,* 370.

was in the region of 3.6 million, with about 90 per cent of those living in the countryside.[31] Of that rural population probably fewer than 10 per cent lived in so-called villas, and many of those would have been the owners' dependents and workers, not themselves members of any social élite. Thus, although there was no doubt a highly cultured rural aristocracy, literate and familiar with Mediterranean culture,[32] they were comparatively few in number, and given what we know of the distribution of villas, they were unevenly spread across the landscape with many areas in the west and north lacking evidence for any such a population group.

The big current project looking at the recent evidence for Romano-British rural settlement from developer-funded archaeology is emphasizing not only the density of settlement but also its incredible diversity.[33] As yet it is too soon to see what patterns emerge from the project, but the scale of data available is indicated by the number of excavated sites that the project has examined. At the time of writing, over 3,200 sites have been analysed, revealing that the simple distinction between villa and non-villa gets nowhere near summarizing the complexity of the settlement system. One impression that I have from looking at some of the evidence is that simple rectangular halls like those discussed above are even more widespread than we had thought. Whilst some of these are distinctive and occasionally highly elaborate buildings with side aisles,[34] many were far simpler, and such structures may well have been the most common across the province (Figure 3) .

There is also abundant evidence, however, that the landscape of Roman Britain was highly regionally diverse with distinctive patterns of varied rural sites.[35] Such regional patterns are not simply a matter of economic differentiation but suggest complex patterns of varied social identity. In Roman Kent for instance,[36] there is enormous natural geographical variation, with the geology changing across a series of narrow east–west bands from the Thames estuary across the North Downs and into the Weald. Whilst this is to some extent reflected in the

[31] M. Millett, *The Romanization of Britain: An Essay in Archaeological Interpretation* (Cambridge, 1990), 183–186.

[32] Mattingly, *An Imperial Possession*, 457–71.

[33] See www.cotswoldarchaeology.co.uk/discover-the-past/ and www.reading.ac.uk/archaeology/research/roman-rural-settlement/ for work on this project that is still in progress.

[34] J.T. Smith, 'Romano-British Aisled Houses', *Archaeological Journal* 120 (1963), 1–30; A.C. King 'The South-East Façade of Meonstoke Aisled Building', in *Architecture in Roman Britain*, ed. P. Johnson and I. Haynes, (York, 1996), 56–69; B.W. Cunliffe *The Danebury Environs Roman Programme: A Wessex Landscape during the Roman Era* (2 vols., Oxford, 2008), i, 114–120.

[35] See, for instance, *The Impact of Rome on the British Countryside: A Conference Organized by the Royal Archaeological Institute, Chester, 11–13 October 2013*, ed. D. Breeze (Wetherby, 2014), and M. Millett, 'By Small Things Revealed: Rural Settlement and Society', in *The Oxford Handbook of Roman Britain* ed. M. Millett, L. Revell and A. Moore (Oxford, 2016), 697–717.

[36] M. Millett, 'Roman Kent', in *The Archaeology of Kent to AD 800*, ed. J.H. Williams (Woodbridge, 2007), 135–84; E.D. Blanning, 'Landscape, settlement and materiality: aspects of rural life in Kent during the Roman period', University of Kent Ph.D. thesis, 2015.

Figure 3. Rectangular stone-walled building of typical Romano-British type
under excavation at Thwing, East Yorks. (Photo: M. Millett, Thwing project).

settlement archaeology, there are even more striking differences in the patterns
between east and west, with the landscape in the Darent valley in the west of
the county characterized by a significant cluster of villas, whilst the east of
the county has fewer villas. This distinction is also visible in the patterns of
pottery use etc., suggesting a long-standing social distinction within the territory
of a single *civitas*. The patterns of settlement also have a complex relationship with the distribution of different types of artefact – for instance brooches
which represent styles of dress – also showing intricate regional patterns. In
summary at the interregional level there is in a sense no such a thing as 'Roman
Britain': the pattern of settlement varies constantly through both space and time.
Such large-scale regional variation contrasts very strongly with the much more
uniform patterns in settlement planning and building types of the early medieval
period as explored by John Blair (see above). This calls into question the extent
of any direct continuity between the periods, and suggests rather that if people
in the seventh century were looking to the Roman past for inspiration, this was
an idealized or imagined *Romanitas* rather than the real Roman Britain.[37]

Given this pattern of regional diversity, it is all too easy to ignore how
well-studied areas also show very considerable local variations across the rural
landscape. Much of my own fieldwork over the last quarter century has been
focused on an in-depth study of elements of the Roman landscape in East

[37] Fleming, *Britain after Rome,* 90–102.

Yorkshire,[38] and this work together with other projects in the region can be used to give greater texture to the national pattern. As in other parts of the United Kingdom, a variety of work has demonstrated sheer density of Iron Age and Romano-British settlement and landscape exploitation. Nowhere is this more clearly demonstrated than in Dominic Powlesland's work on the edge of the Vale of Pickering survey.[39] Here, the deployment of geophysics on a scale unknown elsewhere has revealed a heavily exploited landscape the character of which is unfamiliar elsewhere in Britain. It comprises discontinuous linear settlement following the route of a trackway, with innumerable fields, settlement enclosures, cemeteries, and features related to agricultural exploitation, all rooted in an Iron Age tradition. The nature of the buildings used to house this extensive population in this period is as yet unknown, but it must have involved timber structures. It may be no coincidence that Powlesland has also excavated a very extensive early medieval settlement in this area, at West Heslerton, at which he has revealed a large number of timber halls in the same tradition as seen at Cowdery's Down. His analysis of the dating of this site suggests that there was only a narrow gap if any between the foundation of this site and the 'ending of Roman Britain'.[40]

Our own work, mainly focused a little further to the south in the Vale of York, shows equally high densities of settlement and a great variety of site types and different patterns of interaction with the Roman state. Although there are a few modest villas just beyond our study area, in the immediate hinterland of Brough-on-Humber (*Petuaria Parisiorum*)[41] none is apparently dominant, and our landscape is characterized by a highly varied mass of small, mostly enclosed farms. These are comparatively poorly understood, but the combination of intensive survey using a range of techniques, with the collation of large numbers of metal-detector finds and selective excavation, shows that the landscape was highly differentiated. Some settlements were evidently engaged in intensive farming, others seem to have lain in areas of managed woodland by the wetlands, with the wood used to fuel large-scale pottery manufacture, albeit within a domestic context. Notably, there is much clustering of Roman-period settlement along the Roman road that runs from Brough-on-Humber to York, with large roadside settlements every 10 km or less. Two of these, at Shiptonthorpe and at Hayton, have been examined in our work. Differences in

---

38 *Rural Settlement and Industry: Studies in the Iron Age and Roman Archaeology of Lowland East Yorkshire*, ed. P. Halkon and M. Millett (Leeds, 1999); *Shiptonthorpe, East Yorkshire: Archaeological Studies of a Romano-British Roadside Settlement*, ed. M. Millett (Leeds, 2006); *Hayton, East Yorkshire: Archaeological Studies of the Iron Age and Roman Landscapes*, ed. P. Halkon, M. Millett and H. Woodhouse (Leeds, 2015).
39 https://thelrc.wordpress.com/2012/02/26/the-lrc-digital-atlas-of-the-archaeology-of-the-vale-of-pickering/ .
40 http://www.landscaperesearchcentre.org/html/the_anglian_settlement.html; D.J. Powlesland, 'West Heslerton – The Anglian Settlement: Assessment of Potential for Analysis and Updated Project Design', *Internet Archaeology* 5 (1998), http://intarch.ac.uk/journal/issue5/westhes_toc.html.
41 P. Ottaway, *Roman Yorkshire: People, Culture and Landscape* (Pickering, 2013), 170–175, 267.

landscape utilization, artefact and coin-use provide evidence for the complexity of economic and social relations. This can be illustrated with a few examples, although a discussion of the full details, traceable generation-by-generation, lies beyond the scope of this paper.[42]

At one extreme, there were communities (in the Holme-on-Spalding Moor area) that were largely isolated from receiving outside goods or influences, although they were evidently networked with the Roman world since they were producing large numbers of pottery vessels that achieved an extensive distribution through the Roman North.[43] It is not clear how or why this was happening, but it is in marked contrast to their close neighbours who lived alongside the Roman road, and those on the uplands of the Wolds to the north. The latter were themselves connected with the population beside the road via the seasonal movements of stock along routes between upland and lowland, probably linked to periodic fairs or markets. The sites of these are hinted at by a proliferation of metal finds from areas that are devoid of settlement features. It is tempting to see this evidence as bearing witness to the presence of gathering points for small producers who were trading into the networks supplying York and the Roman army beyond. At the far end of these routes, high on the Yorkshire Wolds, our more recent work at Thwing has shown the wide network of contacts and the remarkable accumulation of wealth retained by these farmers.[44]

The focus of all these interactions lay beside the Roman road, and work on sites here shows that they formed very significant places of innovation, connectivity, and hybridization. Although not particularly prepossessing sites, they have produced a very rich array of material, show consistent evidence for literacy and commerce, and reveal strong evidence for interactions which spread through and beyond Britain. Pottery evidence suggests that people migrated along the road and settled, whilst the array of metal-work includes evidence for a dynamic craft-tradition which was itself innovative.

Returning to our architectural theme, it is worth looking at the large timber hall (21m x 8m) excavated at Shiptonthorpe[45] and dating to the third to fourth century (Figure 4). In plan this is basically an aisled hall of the type that is widespread in Roman Britain. The basic structural principle of such a building is that its roof was supported on the superstructure of the aisle posts which extended up to carry arcade plates on which the middle of the roof pitch was supported. However, in this example, there is evidence for posts to support the ridge, both in the gable end walls and along the axis, providing evidence for a different roofing principle, whereby the roof load was supported by a ridge timber. This method of construction is of course that followed in the

42   Halkon et al., *Hayton, East Yorkshire*, 499–565.
43   Halkon and Millett, *Rural Settlement and Industry*, 226.
44   R. Ferraby, P. Johnson, M. Millett and L. Wallace, *Thwing, Rudston and the Roman-Period Exploitation of the Yorkshire Wolds* (Leeds, forthcoming).
45   M. Millett, *Shiptonthorpe*, 311–14.

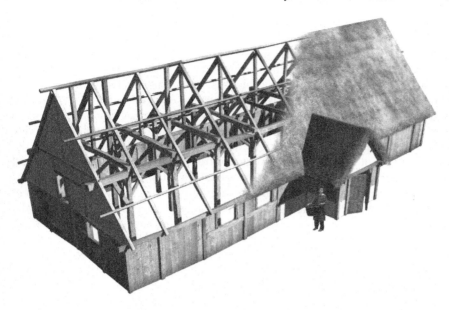

Figure 4. The late Roman aisled hall (Structure 3.3) at Shiptonthorpe, East Yorks. Reconstruction drawing by Mark Faulkner. (Shiptonthorpe project).

early medieval buildings discussed above, both in Britain and, as we have suggested, on the continent. The combination of structural methods used in the Shiptonthorpe structure thus suggests a hybrid, and it is very tempting to suggest that it represents a combination of the British aisled building tradition with influences from the Low Countries around the mouth of the Rhine. Such contacts across the North Sea are well-established through the pottery evidence from the region,[46] and it would seem highly likely that the movement of people and other traditions, such as ideas about building, were a commonplace as well through the Roman period. Since I would argue that this was a two-way process we should expect ideas to be passing in both directions, and hence one might question whether the minority of two-square building plans found on the continent could have been inspired by models brought from Roman or early medieval Britain. I would not wish to push the particularities of this argument too far, but I do think that it is worth exploring the extend to which contacts across the North Sea during the Roman period and later may have led to a greater exchange of ideas than is usually assumed for this would change our perspective on the processes of hybridization that happened in the following centuries.

---

[46] B. Sitch, 'Faxfleet B, a Romano-British Site near Broomfleet', in *Humber Perspectives: A Region through the Ages*, ed. S. Ellis and D.R. Crowther (Hull, 1990), 158–71 at 163.

So how then should we understand the bold and distinctive architectural tradition that was widespread in England in the fifth to seventh centuries CE? For me the origin of the tradition is still open for debate, but I think that we should now try to understand it as part of deliberate acts of hybridization rather than as an accidental by-product of other processes, as we interpreted it in the 1980s. Furthermore, it is clear that it was a tradition that evolved to reach its *floruit* in the seventh century alongside other elements of settlement planning that John Blair has identified. Although those in this period may have sought to recreate a form of *Romanitas* in the same way as they manipulated other aspects of the past,[47] there is nothing in the rural evidence from later Roman Britain to suggest that this was anything more than an imagined tradition.

Different elements of the early medieval tradition thus seem to have different origins. The plans of the buildings have a long ancestry in Roman Britain with the two-square plan increasingly seen in excavated sites. However, although these buildings often had heavily built walls on which the roof load could be carried, they were almost invariably built of stone rather than wood. Where we do have timber buildings, as in the hall at Shiptonthorpe, they lack the distinctive heavy walls that is typical of the later buildings. Such heavy timbered walls seem to be an innovation the development of which can be traced in England from the fifth century onwards, forming a distinctive and apparently insular mode of architectural display in wood. The choice of building élite houses in timber as opposed to stone is surely a Germanic import, and it is arguable that the form of the superstructure of the roofs, relying on a system of ridge-supports, was also continental in origin. I would therefore argue that we need to think about this process as one of constructing a new and distinctive early medieval form of architecture which, although drawing on earlier ideas, should be understood in the context of conscious acts of creation within the emergent societies of early medieval England rather than the product of passive reception either from Roman Britain or the Germanic continent.

---

[47] Fleming, *Britain after Rome,* 90–102.

Holy Relics, Authority, and Legitimacy in Ottonian Germany and Anglo-Saxon England[1]

Laura E. Wangerin

Holy relics played an important role in the political activities of both the Anglo-Saxon kings in England and the Ottonian kings and emperors in tenth-century Germany. Kings in both realms were active in the translation and acquisition of relics as both pious and symbolic political acts.[2] Relics were used as currency in diplomatic and formal gift-giving exchanges and were carried into battle for aid and protection. Rulers staged elaborate public ceremonies to solemnize translations of relics. Relics also provided opportunities for legitimation by foreign or contested kings in tenth-century Germany and England. This paper explores the idea that while the Ottonians and Anglo-Saxons both co-opted the symbolism of relics for the purpose of establishing legitimacy, the Ottonians used relics to establish an ideology – even a mythology – about their rule, as well as to reinforce the legitimacy of their claims to both the royal and imperial titles, in much the same way that they used ruler images to reflect their evolving ideology about kingship.[3]

This study will focus on the Holy Lance as one object of this program, looking at the tenth-century narrative sources that emphasize the role of the

[1]   An early version of this paper was presented at the Haskins Society Conference at Carleton College, 7–9 November 2014. I wish to thank those who offered comments at that time. Thanks are also extended to the *Haskins Society Journal* reviewers for their constructive feedback and suggestions.

[2]   See Jörg Oberste, 'Heilige und ihre Reliquien in der politischen Kultur der früheren Ottonenzeit', *Frühmittelalterliche Studien* 37 (2003), 73–98. Regarding the importance of public political rituals in the early Middle Ages, of which these translations of relics would have been a part, see Geoffrey Koziol, *Begging Pardon and Favor: Ritual and Political Order in Early Medieval France* (Ithaca, NY, 1992) and Gerd Althoff, *Spielregeln der Politik im Mittelalter. Kommunikation in Frieden und Fehde* (Darmstadt, 1997). Discussion of the importance of other political rituals specific to Ottonian Germany can be found in Philippe Buc, *The Dangers of Ritual: Between Early Medieval Texts and Social Scientific Theory* (Princeton, NJ, 2001), 15–50; and David A. Warner, 'Ritual and Memory in the Ottonian Reich: The Ceremony of Adventus', *Speculum* 76 (2001), 255–83.

[3]   Laura Wangerin, 'Tenth-Century Governance: A Comparative Study of the Ottonians and Anglo-Saxons', Ph.D. dissertation (University of Wisconsin-Madison, 2014), 249–266; Ernst H. Kantorowicz, *The King's Two Bodies: A Study in Mediaeval Political Theology* (rev. ed. Princeton, NJ, 1985; orig. pub. 1957), 65.

lance in establishing empire and authority for the Ottonian dynasty: Liudprand of Cremona's *Antapodosis,* written between 958 and 962; Widukind of Corvey's *Rerum gestarum Saxonicarum libri tres*, probably completed *c.* 967/968, with additional chapters added after Otto I's death in 973; and Thietmar of Merseburg's *Chronicon*, written between 1012 and 1018.[4]

These three chroniclers, important contemporary sources for Ottonian history, approached their narratives from distinctly different points of view. Liudprand of Cremona (*c.* 920–972) served at the court of Otto I after he fled Italy when he fell out of favor at the Italian court of Berengar II. He wrote his *Antapodosis*, meaning 'revenge' or 'retribution', to highlight examples of divine retribution in recent history as well as to serve as a personal revenge against those he felt had wronged him. His portrayals of the Ottonians are generally positive.[5] We know significantly less about Widukind of Corvey (*c.* 920–925?–after 973). A monk at the monastery of Corvey, his name and the focus on Saxony in his history suggests that he himself was a Saxon.[6] Although he states in a prologue that his *Rerum gestarum Saxonicarum libri tres*, 'Deeds of the Saxons', was written to record the achievements of the great Saxon princes, his dedication to Otto I's daughter Mathilda implies that this history was intended to celebrate the glorious deeds of Henry I and Otto I.[7] Thietmar of Merseburg (975–1018), the last of the three chroniclers to be considered here, belonged to an aristocratic Saxon

4   Liudprand of Cremona, *The Complete Works of Liudprand of Cremona*, ed. and trans. Paolo Squatriti (Washington, DC, 2007), 18; Widukind of Corvey, *Deeds of the Saxons*, ed. and trans. Bernard S. Bachrach and David S. Bachrach (Washington, DC, 2014), xxix; Thietmar of Merseburg, *Ottonian Germany: The Chronicon of Thietmar of Merseburg*, ed. and trans. David A. Warner (Manchester, 2001), 61. Among those sources that, notably, do not include any mention of the holy lance are Adalbert of Magdeburg's continuation of Regino of Prüm's *Chronicon*; the *Annales* of Flodoard of Reims; and the *Annales Corbeienses, Hildesheimenses, Quedlinburgenses*, and *Einsidlenses*.

5   For an overview of Liudprand's life and how it relates to his writings, see Paolo Squatriti's introduction, Liuprand, *Complete Works*, 3–37. See also Karl Leyser, 'Liudprand of Cremona: Preacher and Homilist', in   *The Bible in the Medieval World. Essays in Honour of Beryl Smalley*, ed. Katherine Walsh and Diana Wood, Studies in Church History, Subsidia 4 (Oxford, 1985), 43–60, and 'Ends and Means in Liudprand of Cremona', *Byzantinische Forschungen* 13 (1988), 119–43 (both reprinted in *Communications and Power in Medieval Europe: The Carolingian and Ottonian Centuries*, ed. Timothy Reuter (Rio Grande, OH, 1994), 111–24 and 125–42 respectively), for useful insights into Liudprand's life and career. For a more extensive study of Liudprand, see Jon N. Sutherland, *Liudprand of Cremona, Bishop, Diplomat, Historian: Studies of the Man and his Age* (Spoleto, 1988).

6   Raymund F. Wood, 'The Three Books of the Deeds of the Saxons by Widukind of Corvey, Translated with Introduction, Notes, and Bibliography', Ph.D. dissertation (University of California at Los Angeles, 1949), 38; Bernard S. Bachrach and David S. Bachrach, introduction to Widukind, *Deeds of the Saxons*, xiv.

7   Widukind of Corvey, *Widukindi Monachi Corbiensis: Rerum Gestarum Saxonicarum Libri Tres*, MGH SRG 60, 1–2. For more about Widukind's life and work, see Bachrach and Bachrach, xiii–xxxvii; and Sverre Bagge, *Kings, Politics, and the Right Order of the World in German Historiography c. 900–1150* (Leiden, 2002), 23–94. Whether or not the dedication to Mathilda was part of Widukind's original plan for his history has been a subject of debate; see Bagge, *Kings, Politics*, 25; Gerd Althoff, 'Widukind von Corvey: Kronzeuge und Herausforderung', *Frühmittelalterliche Studien* 27 (1993), 257–258.

family, and was bishop of Merseburg from 1009. His *Chronicon* is a curious combination of a history of his bishopric and a royal history.[8] While he relied on Widukind and others for earlier Saxon history, adulation of the Ottonian kings and emperors was not his goal. Rather, the kings who had helped Merseburg are praised – Otto I who established the bishopric, Henry II who restored it – while the acts of Otto II, who diminished the authority of his diocese, are described in decidedly less laudatory terms.[9]

When we take these three narratives and the varying points of view of the men who wrote them into account, an examination of the portrayal of the Holy Lance in these sources raises some interesting questions about the relationships between relics and authority, relics and texts, text and audience, the creation of an imperial ideology, and the opportunities for using and manipulating symbols. The differing and evolving presentation of the Holy Lance in these texts, all of which are very different kinds of works, offers clues about the way that the Ottonians were wielding symbols in the service of their dynastic legitimacy.

The Holy Lance described by these texts refers in actuality just to a lance head, which was affixed to a shaft for ceremonies or to carry into battle. Hollowed out in the middle to display a Holy Nail held in place by silver wire, it is a double relic – the lance head itself acting as a sort of reliquary to display the Holy Nail. Now in the collections of the Kunsthistorisches Museum in Vienna,[10] this relic remained an important component of the Holy Roman Imperial regalia throughout the centuries following the Ottonians.[11] One of several objects being claimed as holy lances in the tenth century, this particular lance head is Carolingian in origin and was associated at various times in its history with Constantine, St Maurice, and Longinus.[12] These associative transformations, as

---

8   Bagge, *Kings, Politics*, 96.
9   Bagge, *Kings, Politics*, 99, 106. For more comprehensive considerations of Thietmar and his work, see David A. Warner, 'Introduction: Thietmar, Bishop and Chronicler', in Thietmar, *Ottonian Germany*, trans. Warner, 1–64; and Bagge, *Kings, Politics*, 95–188.
10   Imperial Cross (Reichskreuz), Kunsthistorisches Museum Wien (XIII 21).
11   See Percy Ernst Schramm, 'Die "Heilige Lanze", Reliquie und Herrschaftszeichen des Reiches und ihre Replik in Krakau. Ein Überblick über die Geschichte der Königslanze', in *Herrschaftszeichen und Staatssymbolic: Beiträge zu ihrer Geschichte vom dritten bis zum sechzehnten Jahrhundert*, MGH Schriften 13 (3 vols., Stuttgart, 1954), ii, 492–537. For a comprehensive archaeological analysis of the Ottonian holy lance blade, see Mechthild Schulze-Dörrlamm, 'Die Heilige Lanze in Wien: Die Frühgeschichte des karolingisch-ottonischen Herrschaftszeichens aus archäologischer Sicht', *Jahrbuch des römische-germanischen Zentralmuseums* 58 (2011), 707–42. Essays treating the cultural history and significance of the Holy Lance can be found in *Die Heilige Lanze in Wien: Insignie – Reliquie – 'Schickalsspeer'*, ed. Franz Kirchweger (Vienna, 2005), with the medieval period treated in Gunther G. Wolf, 'Nochmals zur Geschichte der Heiligen Lanze bis zum Ende des Mittelalters', 23–51. Cynthia Hahn discusses the lance and its relationship to the cross reliquary that houses it in *Strange Beauty: Issues in the Making and Meaning of Reliquaries, 400–ca. 1204* (University Park, PA, 2012), 99–102.
12   Schramm, 'Heilige Lanze', ii, 534–537; Wolf, 'Nochmals zur Geschichte', 23–24. The blade itself had been broken at some point, probably weakened from being hollowed out to hold the Holy Nail. In the eleventh century the broken halves of the blade were held together by a strip of iron. An ornate collar of silver with gold bands was commissioned by Henry IV sometime

well as the physical alterations made to the blade in the course of its history, are consistent with the treatment of other medieval relics.[13]

Before we look at the Holy Lance and its treatment in contemporary texts, it is worth considering the role of relics in general in medieval society. Saints' cults in the early Middle Ages were an important part of the cultural landscape.[14] Their social role in creating a point of commonality in what could be 'violently fractious' communities has long been noted by scholars.[15] Peter Brown specifically addresses the importance of community shrines which housed saints' relics in dealing with local powers in the absence of royal administrative structures or imperial governance: 'the shrine became a fixed point where the solemn, necessary play of "clear power" – of *potentia* exercised as it should be – could be played out in acts of healing, exorcism, and rough justice.'[16] The active presence of a saint, via the enshrinement and veneration of his or her relics, thus provided a locus for power and community concord.[17] While Brown was referring to this role of saints' cults and relics in the context of the end of the Roman Empire, his assessment seems equally applicable to the situation in Europe in the wake of the Carolingian collapse. Patrick Geary links the importance of relics and saints' cults to periods of weak central government, with regard to the Roman Empire in the sixth century, and also in the eleventh century, when relics 'were prized not only for their thaumaturgic power but also for their ability to substitute for public authority, protect and secure the community, determine the relative status of individuals and churches, and provide for the community's economic prosperity'.[18] The acquisition of relics in Merovingian times as a way to strengthen aristocratic lordship as well as sanctify the donors was noted by Karl Leyser. These foundations thus became essential to the sense of community:

With the help of these wonder-working pledges (*pignora*) which assured the presence of the saints, aristocratic foundations could become important religious centers and they gave their fluctuating noble founding kins a chance to consolidate round their sanctuary.

---

between 1084 and 1105, inscribed with the legend: 'CLAVVS DOMINICVS + HEINRICVS D[EI] GR[ATI]A TERCIVS / ROMANO[RVM] / IMPERATOR AVG[VSTVS] HOC ARGEN / TVM IVSSIT / FABRICARI AD CONFIRMATIONE[M] / CLAVI D[OMI]NI ET LANCEE SANCTI MAVRI / CII // SANCTVS MAVRICIVS //'. Another collar made of gold was fit over the silver one during the reign of Karl IV (r. 1346–1378) inscribed: '+ LANCEA ET CLAVVIS DOMINI' (Wolf, 'Nochmals zur Geschichte', 23–24; Gude Suckale-Redlefsen, *Mauritius: Der heilige Mohr = The Black Saint Maurice* (Houston, TX, 1987), 35).

[13]   See Hahn, *Strange Beauty*, 6, 9.

[14]   See, for example, Hahn, *Strange Beauty*; and Charles Freeman, *Holy Bones, Holy Dust: How Relics Shaped the History of Medieval Europe* (New Haven, CT, 2011).

[15]   Patrick Geary, *Before France and Germany* (New York, NY, 1988), 136. See also Peter Brown, 'Relics and Social Status in the Age of Gregory of Tours', in *Society and the Holy in Late Antiquity* (Berkeley, CA, 1982), 222–50.

[16]   Peter Brown, *The Cult of the Saints: Its Rise and Function in Latin Christianity* (Chicago, IL, 1981), 105.

[17]   Brown, *Cult of Saints*, 97–98.

[18]   Patrick Geary, *Living with the Dead in the Middle Ages* (Ithaca, NY, 1994), 205–6.

The shrines also bound the surrounding rural population more closely to their lords' power. The Saxon nobility in the ninth century learned of these advantages from its Frankish teachers.[19]

Relic cults thus presented communities with a common purpose, and they also provided opportunities for divine intercession, a place to appeal for heavenly help when earthly matters were beyond comprehension or control. Additionally, the use of relics and their display as a kind of 'participatory aesthetic [that] constructed a particular sort of poetic or imaginative meaning' has been discussed by Cynthia Hahn.[20] She notes that the way in which relics were publicly presented was crucial to creating contexts and stories around them, and that the audience to which a relic was displayed was central to its validation and authentication, as well as its constructed meaning.[21] Thus, the public presentation of relics and the reliquaries that housed them were as important to the meaning of a saint's presence in a community as the relics themselves. The importance of relics in medieval Europe peaked in the ninth to eleventh centuries, precisely the period that concerns us here.[22] But while relics and their associated cults appealed to the sensibilities of lay and clerical Christians at all levels of society, to kings and nobles relics were an important diplomatic currency. Among their various roles in royal and imperial courts they served as ransoms and bribes, were given as gifts, and functioned as a surety to guarantee the integrity of oaths.[23] Thus, relics were often translated in the service of political goals.

Both Anglo-Saxon and Ottonian kings were active collectors of relics, and many of the translations of relics into their kingdoms resulted from this interest.[24] Æthelstan (895–939), the first king of England to rule over all of the various Anglo-Saxon kingdoms, actively sought to acquire relics from the continent to augment what saints' remains were available to him within his realm. Many of these were acquired through marriage, diplomatic exchanges or negotiations, or given as gifts by nobles currying favor, but Æthelstan was also

---

[19] Karl Leyser, *Rule and Conflict in an Early Medieval Society: Ottonian Saxony* (Bloomington, IN, 1979), 87.

[20] Hahn, *Strange Beauty*, 29.

[21] Hahn, *Strange Beauty*, 9, 17–18.

[22] Patrick Geary, *Furta Sacra: Thefts of Relics in the Central Middle Ages* (1978; Princeton, NJ, 1990), 27.

[23] For examples of relics as diplomatic gifts, see Eliza Garrison, 'A Curious Commission: The Reliquary of St. Servatius in Quedlinburg', *Gesta* 49 (2010), 17–29 at 28–29 note 47; J.J.M. Timmers, 'Byzantine Influences on Architecture and Other Art Forms in the Low Countries with Particular Reference to the Region of the Meuse', in *Byzantium and the Low Countries in the Tenth Century: Aspects of Art and History in the Ottonian Era*, ed. Victoria van Aalst and Krjnie N. Ciggaar (Hernen, 1985), 104–145 at 140. For an example of their use in oaths, see Adalbert of Magdeburg, *Adalberti Continuatio Regionis, sub anno* 964, in Regino of Prüm, *Regionis Abbatis Prumiensis Chronicon cum Continuatione Treverensi*, ed. F. Kurze, MGH *SRG* 50 (Hannover, 1890), 173–175 at 173.

[24] See David Rollason, 'Relic-Cults as an Instrument of Royal Policy *c.* 900–*c.* 1050', *ASE* 15 (1986), 91–103.

active in purchasing relics from relic merchants.[25] The Ottonians also acquired many of their relics through diplomatic exchange, but their conquest of Italy was particularly valuable to them because of its wealth in relics. Roman relics were carted away in huge numbers as spoils of conquest, and collection of these items 'was one of the marked preoccupations of German bishops and, not least of all, royal chaplains'.[26]

Translations of relics in both Anglo-Saxon England and Ottonian Germany were also spurred by frontier conflicts and invasions, though in distinctly different ways. In England, translation of relics accelerated with the Danish invasions. For example, Symeon of Durham, in his early twelfth-century history of the Church of Durham, reports that the relics of Cuthbert (*c.* 634–687), an important Northumbrian saint, were removed from Lindisfarne when the monks there fled in advance of Danish invasions in the mid-ninth century.[27] Cuthbert's relics were translated several times, finally arriving at Durham in the late tenth century, and were then translated into different churches at Durham before being placed in a permanent shrine.[28] Certain locations were designated as places where saints' relics could be kept safe from Danish invaders, such as Bradford-on-Avon.[29] And saints were believed to protect their shrines from their enemies, both local and foreign, adding to their perceived importance in times of invasion or conflict.[30] Anglo-Saxon kings as well as monks were engaged in the care and relocation of saintly remains. For example, Æthelred the Unready (r. 978–1013 and 1014–1016) took an interest in the remains of his murdered half-brother, Edward the Martyr (d. 978), and actively promoted his cult and the translation of his relics.[31] But an even more overtly political patronage, and yet another connection to the Danish invasions, can be found in the cult of St Edmund. While the cult originated after Edmund's martyrdom in 869, it

---

25   Geary, *Furta Sacra*, 49. See also Sarah Foot, *Æthelstan: The First King of England* (New Haven, CT, 2011), 188–198, regarding Æthelstan's personal relics collection.

26   Karl Leyser, 'Frederick Barbarossa, Henry II and the Hand of St James', *EHR* 90 (1975), 481–506. Here cited from *Medieval Germany and Its Neighbors 900–1250* (London, 1982), 215–43 at 221.

27   Symeon of Durham, *Libellus de exordio atque procursu istius, hoc est Dunhelmensis, ecclesie*, ed. David Rollason (Oxford, 2000), 101–103.

28   Symeon, *Libellus*, 148–150.

29   J. Kemble, *Codex diplomaticus aevi saxonici* (6 vols., London, 1839–1848), iii, 319: 'cum adiacente undique uilla humili deuotione offero coenobium quod uulgariter æt Bradeforda cognominatur, hoc mecum sub sapientum meorum testimonio tacite præiudicans, ut supradictum donum sancto semper subiaceat monasterio æt Sceftesbirio uocitato, ac ditioni uenerabilis familiæ sanctimonialium inibi degentium, quatenus aduersus barbarorum insidias ipsa religiosa congregatio cum beati martyris cæterorumque sanctorum reliquiis ibidem dea seruiendi impenetrabile optineat confugium.' See also Sawyer, *Charters*, 899.

30   This was the case, for example, with Edmund the Martyr at Bury St Edmunds. Frederick S. Paxton, 'Abbas and Rex: Power and Authority in the Literature of Fleury, 987–1044', in *The Experience of Power in Medieval Europe, 950–1350*, ed. Robert F. Berkhofer III, Alan Cooper, and Adam J. Kosto (Aldershot, 2005), 201.

31   *Passio et miracula sancti Eadwardi Regis et Martyris*, in Christine Fell, *Edward, King and Martyr* (Leeds, 1971), 12; Sawyer, *Charters*, 899.

took on a new dimension in light of the Danish conquest of 1016, when royal interest in the saint coalesced into St Edmund becoming what Susan Ridyard calls 'a symbol of political defiance and survival' in the face of the Danish invaders and attempts to reestablish Anglo-Saxon rule.[32] But, while St Edmund became a symbol of defiance in the face of foreign rulers, he did not become a legitimizing symbol for a single dynasty.

The Ottonians' co-opting of relics to serve political ends was no less overt than that of the Anglo-Saxons, but was expressed in different ways. Saints' relics, though sometimes translated to locations safe from invaders,[33] were often instead conducted to the front lines. Fortified monasteries were endowed along the borders with the Slavs and Magyars, and the Ottonians provided these foundations with saints' relics of political significance, relics intended to protect their kingdom from external invasions. Magdeburg is one such example of an Ottonian foundation intended to protect the eastern frontier. According to Thietmar of Merseburg,

> The emperor [Otto I] had precious marble, gold, and gems brought to Magdeburg. And he ordered that relics of saints should be enclosed in all of the columns … In the year 961 of the Incarnation and in the twenty-fifth year of his reign, in the presence of all the nobility, on the vigil of Christmas, the body of St Maurice was conveyed to him at Regensburg along with the bodies of some of the saint's companions and portions of other saints. Having been sent to Magdeburg, these relics were received with great honour by a gathering of the entire populace of the city and of their fellow countrymen. They are still venerated there, to the salvation of the homeland.[34]

Not only were relics incorporated into the architectural structure of the cathedral, but the body of St Maurice, a warrior saint adopted by Otto I as patron of his empire, was installed as part of a grandly staged translation. St Maurice was a well-known and widely venerated saint throughout the Middle Ages. As the leader of the Theban Legion, a group of Christian Roman soldiers martyred in the late third century, Maurice and his companions in arms would have had a

---

[32]   Susan J. Ridyard, *The Royal Saints of Anglo-Saxon England: A Study of West Saxon and East Anglian Cults* (Cambridge, 1988), 226.

[33]   See, for example, Flodoard of Reims, who notes, 'Corpus sancti Remigii et aliorum quorundam sanctorum pignera Hungarorum metu Remis a suis monasteriis sunt delata; inter quae sanctae quoque Walbergis reliquiae, ad quas nonnulla exercebantur miracula', *Annales, sub anno* 926, in MGH *SS* 3, ed. G. Pertz (Hannover, 1839), 376.

[34]   Thietmar of Merseburg, *Thietmari Mersebergensis Episcopi Chronicon* ii.17, ed. R. Holtzmann, MGH *SRG* n.s. 9 (repr. München, 1980): 'Preciosum quoque marmor cum auro gemmisque cesar precepit ad Magadaburc adduci. In omnibusque columnarum capitibus sanctorum reliquias diligenter includi iussit … Anno dominicae incarnationis DCCCCLXI., regni autem eius vicesimo Vᵒ, presentibus cunctis optimatibus, in vigilia nativitatis Domini corpus sancti Mauricii et quorundam sociorum eius cum aliis sanctorum porcionibus Ratisbone sibi allatum est. Quod maximo, ut decuit, honore Parthenopolim transmissum unanimi indigenarum et comprovincialium conventu ibidem susceptum est et ad salutem patriae tocius hactenus veneratum est', (Thietmar, *Ottonian Germany*, trans. Warner, 104). For the importance of the actual translation ceremony, which Peter Brown asserts 'counted far more than the mere fact of its presence' in a city, see Brown, *Cult of Saints*, 92–93; Geary, *Furta Sacra*, 120; Buc, *Dangers of Ritual*, 60.

natural appeal for a Christian warrior king.[35] St Maurice had strong connections as well with Burgundy and the Burgundian court, which might have furthered Ottonian interest in the saint as they sought to expand their sphere of interest into Italy.[36] The important connection that the Ottonian court sought to establish with St Maurice is illustrated on a contemporary ivory relief depicting Otto the Great presenting a model of the cathedral he founded at Magdeburg to Christ (Figure 1).[37] Otto dedicated the cathedral to St Maurice, and on the plaque, St Maurice stands behind Otto as he presents the cathedral to Christ. It creates, in essence, a pictorial representation of Otto's power and protection of his realm.[38] St Maurice was a warrior saint, and the cathedral at Magdeburg was founded 'as the ecclesiastical focus of [Otto the Great's] wars against the Slavs ... the military resources of heaven would be harnessed to his shrine at Magdeburg'.[39]

---

[35] For the cult of St Maurice in the Middle Ages, see Maurice Zufferey, 'Der Mauritiuskult im Früh- und Hochmittelalter', *Historisches Jahrbuch* 106 (1986), 23–58; David A. Warner, 'The Cult of Saint Maurice: Ritual Politics and Political Symbolism in Ottonian Germany', Ph.D. dissertation (University of California at Los Angeles, 1989); and Adalbert J. Herzberg, *Der Heilige Mauritius: Ein Beitrag zur Geschichte der deutschen Mauritiusverehrung* (Dusseldorf, 1936). Although its primary focus is the history of the pictorial representation of blacks from the thirteenth to the sixteenth centuries, Suckale-Redlefsen's *Mauritius* does situate the origins of Maurice's cult and legend in its historic context (28–37), and provides a catalogue of later medieval images of St Maurice that further demonstrate his martial character. For the vita of St Maurice, see Eucherius of Lyon, *Passio Acaunensium martyrum*, ed. Bruno Krusch, in MGH *SRM* 3 (Hannover, 1896), 20–41.

[36] Warner, 'Cult of Saint Maurice', 77. The affiliation of St Maurice with the Burgundian court was paralleled by the Ottonian emperors' adoption of the saint as a special patron in their own court rituals. For example, Ottonian coronation rituals included a vigil kept in the chapel of St Maurice in Aachen cathedral (Suckale-Redlefsen, *Mauritius*, 36–37). See also Warner, 'Cult of Saint Maurice', 296–306, for a discussion of the significance of the altar of St Maurice in imperial coronation ceremonies.

[37] 'Plaque with Otto I presenting the Cathedral of Magdeburg [Ottonian]' (41.100.157). New York: The Metropolitan Museum of Art. Discussed in Henry Mayr-Harting, *Ottonian Book Illumination: An Historical Study* (2 volumes, London, 1991; repr. 1999), i, 180–181; in Percy Ernst Schramm and Florentine Mütherich, *Denkmale der deutschen Könige und Kaiser* (Munich, 1962), 141–142, 282 (Plate 68); and Hermann Fillitz, *Die gruppe de Magdeburger Elfenbeintafeln* (Mainz, 2001), 29–31. There has been debate over whether this ivory depicts Otto I or Otto II; for an overview of the arguments in this debate as well as further justification for accepting it as a representation of Otto I, see Charles T. Little, 'The Magdeburg Ivory Group: A Tenth Century New Testament Narrative Cycle', Ph.D. dissertation (New York University, 1977), 111–17. Schramm and Mütherich (*Denkmale*, 141–142) identified it as a depiction of Otto I.

[38] In Mayr-Harting, *Ottonian Illumination* i, 180. See also Fillitz, *Magdeburger Elfenbeintafeln*, 29–31.

[39] Mayr-Harting, *Ottonian Illumination* i, 12. This martial affiliation of St Maurice was attractive to other royal houses as well. In a later example that shows both this appeal of the saint as well as how public rituals could be used to create a royal association between saint and king, Louis IX (1214–1270) founded a house of Augustinian canons at Senlis in 1261 to house the relics of St Maurice and twenty-three of his companions that he had acquired. Anne Lester argues that Louis' failure in the Seventh Crusade gave the Maurice legend a personal meaning for him – the adventus Louis arranged for the translation of these relics created a deliberate parallel between Louis' knights and the Roman legionnaires who were martyred with Maurice, and that thus, 'in his death, in the popular imagination, and for those who knew him, Louis became one of the companions of Saint Maurice, draped in red as one of the martyrs'. Anne E. Lester, 'Confessor

Figure 1. Plaque with Christ receiving Magdeburg Cathedral from Emperor
Otto I, Ivory, c. 962–968 (courtesy of The Metropolitan Museum of Art)

Thus, the translation of relics of St Maurice to Magdeburg would have been an
important and significant event, carefully choreographed – an imperial reception
of the saint into his new home.

These types of translations where saints were formally and publicly
received into a community were conscious emulations of an imperial *adventus*
which, with its origins as a Roman imperial ritual, was a key public ritual of
the Ottonians.[40] A translation of the kind described by Thietmar would have
given the relics additional immediate parallels for its audience, connecting the
Roman Empire and the Ottonians.[41] Thietmar specifies, too, that the veneration

King, Martyr Saint: Praying to Saint Maurice at Senlis', in *Center and Periphery: Studies on
Power in the Medieval World in Honor of William Chester Jordan*, ed. Katherine L. Jansen, G.
Geltner, and Anne E. Lester (Leiden, 2013), 195–210 at 199 and 210.

[40] Warner, 'Ritual and Memory', 261.

[41] Warner, 'Ritual and Memory'; Buc, *Dangers of Ritual*, 39; Brown, *Cult of Saints*, 98. See also Ildar
H. Garipzanov, *The Symbolic Language of Authority in the Carolingian World (c. 751–877)* (Leiden,

of St Maurice and his companions, also warriors, is a protective act for the kingdom. What is clear is that this was not the royal establishment of a local cult that was intended to serve a small community – the installation of St Maurice at Magdeburg was meant to protect Otto's larger interests on the eastern frontiers.[42]

The abbey at Quedlinburg was another important foundation in the Ottonian wars on the eastern frontiers. Like Magdeburg, the Ottonians fortified Quedlinburg with relics of military significance. Relics of St Denis, whose aid was said to be summoned in times of war, were given to Quedlinburg by Henry I, and the relics of St Servatius were translated to Quedlinburg by Otto I.[43] The Ottonian kings customarily celebrated feast days at the same places along their *iter* every year; the royal itinerary was one of their highly visual symbols of power, especially the custom of celebrating certain feast days at the same places each year.[44] They normally kept the Eastertime feasts, which preceded a summer of military engagements along their borders, at Quedlinburg.[45] The Ottonians, through their acquisitions of these saints, also acquired their protection and intercessory powers. The public translations and celebration of feast days would renew those associations between saintly intercessory powers and the king, and would have 'enhanced his political credit'.[46]

Relics, both their acquisition and their translation, were thus important aspects of tenth-century kingship. The Holy Lance serves as an example of how the Ottonians took a relic and remastered its symbolism to create a powerful tool that asserted their legitimacy as kings and emperors. Much like the sword Excalibur in Arthurian legend, the Holy Lance became almost mythical in its ability to confer legitimacy upon its holder, so much so that even after the demise of the Ottonians and their Salian successors, even into the twentieth century under Emperor Wilhelm II, the idea of a connection between the Holy Lance and German imperial legitimacy was alive and well.[47] That mythology

---

2008), 220, 222, regarding the Carolingian use of Roman imperial symbols on their seals as a way of communicating Carolingian authority.

[42] Leyser, *Rule and Conflict*, 87–88. This intent can be further divined from events at the monastery of Lure, where the author of the tenth-century *Life of Deicolus* unambiguously attributes the rescue of that monastery from Magyar raids to the saint installed there, not to the early tenth-century Burgundian lords or Ottonians who repelled them. Hans J. Hummer, *Politics and Power in Early Medieval Europe: Alsace and the Frankish Realm, 600–1000* (Cambridge, 2005), 239; *Ex Vita S Deicoli* c. 11, ed. G. Waitz, MGH *SS* 15.2 (Hannover, 1888), 677.

[43] Garrison, *Curious Commission*, 17, 26.

[44] Henry Mayr-Harting, *Church and Cosmos in Early Ottonian Germany: The View from Cologne* (Oxford, 2007), 4; John Bernhardt, *Itinerant Kingship and Royal Monasteries in Early Medieval Germany c. 936–1075* (Cambridge, 1993), 51.

[45] Garrison, *Curious Commission*, 17; Bernhardt, *Itinerant Kingship*, 140–141.

[46] Leyser, *Rule and Conflict*, 88. Leyser notes as well the importance of relics as royal gifts in enhancing Ottonian authority throughout their realm.

[47] Howard L. Adelson, 'The Holy Lance and the Hereditary German Monarchy', *The Art Bulletin* 48, no. 2 (1966), 177–92 at 177. The parallel drawn with Excalibur is in fact more complex than this simile might suggest. Swords, often conveyed in dream visions, served a function similar to

had its inception in the narrative sources of the Ottonian era. The Ottonians were masters at using ruler images to reflect changing ideas about a developing ideology of kingship, a change that took place mainly during the reigns of the three Ottos – Henry I was not yet working to develop an imperial ideology, and Henry II was an able manipulator of images but was mainly working from what was then established practice under the Ottos.[48] Looking at the Holy Lance, we can see how the Ottonians also used relics to establish an ideology of rulership, as well as to reinforce the legitimacy of their claims to both the royal and imperial titles.

A key difference between the polities of Anglo-Saxon England and the Ottonian Empire was the relative ease with which Anglo-Saxon kings could be replaced with non-Anglo-Saxon rulers. Once they had effectively established that they were there to stay, foreign kings who ruled in England such as Cnut (r. 1016–1035), Cnut's sons Harold (r. 1035–1040) and Harthacnut (r. 1040–1042), and William the Conqueror (r. 1066–1087) do not seem to have had any great difficulties in establishing a sense of their legitimacy.[49] This is an important distinction that manifests itself in the kinds of historical writings that we see in each realm. The *Anglo-Saxon Chronicle*, for example, stresses continuity, a historical thread that extends into the past.[50] We do not see this interest in linking the present to a historic past with the key Ottonian chroniclers Widukind, Liudprand, and Thietmar, who seem to have had little interest in the Carolingian past of East Francia, or in creating a connection between the Ottonian kings and their Carolingian predecessors. This is particularly intriguing since the Ottonian kings consciously emulated the Carolingians in many aspects of their rulership.

that of the lance for the Ottonians, conferring legitimacy to the rightful ruler. See Geary, *Living with the Dead*, 61–64 and 71–73.

[48] This transformation is described in detail in Wangerin, 'Tenth-Century Governance', 249–266. One example of this type of portraiture is 'The Emperor Otto Seated in Majesty', Liuthar Gospels (Aachen Gospels), *c.* 996, Aachen Cathedral Treasury, fol. 16, discussed at length by Kantorowicz in *The King's Two Bodies*, 61ff, as well as by Schramm and Mütherich, *Denkmale*, 103; Hagen Keller, *Ottonische Königsherrschaft* (Darmstadt, 2002), 173–176; Mayr-Harting, *Ottonian Illumination* I, 59–60; Christopher de Hamel, *A History of Illuminated Manuscripts* (London, 1986; repr. 1994), 60; and Eliza Garrison, *Ottonian Imperial Art and Portraiture: The Artistic Patronage of Otto III and Henry II* (Burlington, VT, 2012), 39. Other ruler images include ivories, such as the ivory of the presentation of the cathedral of Magdeburg discussed above (at note 37), 'Otto II and Theophanu crowned by Christ', *c.* 982–983 (Paris, Musée de Cluny), and 'Ivory Plaque with Family of Emperor Otto', *c.* 965/983 (Milan, Collections of the Castello Sforzesco). Schramm and Mütherich discuss both of these objects (*Denkmale*, 144).

[49] Timothy Reuter, 'The Making of England and Germany, 850–1050: Points of Comparison and Difference', in *Medieval Polities and Modern Mentalities*, ed. Janet Nelson (Cambridge, 2006), 284–99 at 290.

[50] Reuter, 'The Making of England', 290. The *Anglo-Saxon Chronicle* likely was begun toward the end of the ninth century. Beginning with a genealogy of King Alfred from fifth century, it was intended to be a continuous chronicle, 'supplemented and maintained, either systematically year on year, or sometimes … at intervals in sporadic bursts of activity', *The Anglo-Saxon Chronicle*, ed. and trans. Michael Swanton (New York, 1998), xviii–xxi.

Timothy Reuter has suggested that this key difference in how the Anglo-Saxons and Ottonians conceptualized kingship necessitated the use of symbols by the Ottonians that we just do not see in England.[51] Imperial ruler images were one such way that we can see the Ottonians developing and utilizing symbolic representation to communicate a developing ideology of rulership. Their use of holy relics was another. Relics are unique in the way that they act as symbols, largely because their meaning is conferred upon them by a community: 'Unlike other objects, the bare relic – a bone or a bit of dust – carries no fixed code or sign of its meaning as it moves from one community to another or from one period to a subsequent one.'[52] Whereas a text or a picture communicates specific ideas, the only importance that relics had when moved from one context to another – that is, when relics were translated to a new location – was whatever that new society attributed to them.[53] Thus, relic acquisitions provided opportunities for creating political meaning and reinventing symbolic associations. Patrick Geary, in his work on relic thefts, suggests that stories about relic thefts, whether real or invented, were deliberately perpetrated and circulated by pious monks, sometimes even perhaps just to create a memorable story that would capture the imagination of parishioners and pilgrims.[54] It is not such a stretch to imagine contemporary chroniclers exercising similar poetic license to emphasize special relationships between particular relics and their kings. Additionally, Cynthia Hahn has observed that reliquaries – how relics were displayed or presented to an audience – in essence created stories. Although her observation is specifically in reference to late antique pilgrimages, the suggestion that 'stories (and their material equivalent, reliquaries) are essential. Context and story arouse the interest of the audience and make contact with the relic significant and wondrous' resonates with the idea that Ottonian authors were contextualizing the Holy Lance by creating stories.[55]

It was during the course of the reigns of the three Ottos that a new philosophy of rulership developed. Over the course of their dynasty, the Ottonians developed an ideology of sacral kingship that was demonstrated and promoted through rituals, ruler images, and the manipulation of symbols such as the Holy Lance. When the Ottonians first came to power, dynastic succession was anything but assured. Henry I and Otto I, especially, were dealing not only with the Magyar attacks on their borders but also with internal competition from others aspiring

---

51 Reuter, 'The Making of England', 290–291.

52 Geary, *Furta Sacra*, 5.

53 Geary, *Furta Sacra*, 6–7.

54 Geary, *Furta Sacra*, 57, 84. Geary also argues that religious sentiment was changeable, and that monasteries attempting to create traditions of *furta sacra*, whether or not their relics had actually been stolen, 'were forced by changing fashions in saints to acquire the remains of a new patron more attractive to popular tastes' (74). It seems no large stretch to consider that a similar strategic adoption might be made by a king or emperor. For a discussion of how texts might have been used to elaborate or enhance the symbolic meaning of relics, see Thomas Head, 'Art and Artifice in Ottonian Trier', *Gesta* 36 (1997), 65–82.

55 Hahn, *Strange Beauty*, 17–18.

to the throne. Thus, asserting their legitimacy as a dynasty was a critical part of their program. It is in this milieu that the first efforts to create a sense of sacrality developed.[56] That idea evolved over the course of the reigns of the three Ottos but had its inception during the reign of Otto I.

When Henry I died in 936, Otto I was formally crowned in an elaborate coronation ceremony, signaling a change in how he was conceptualizing the idea of kingship. Henry I had forgone the rituals of unction and a formal coronation ceremony, ostensibly out of humility.[57] At the time Henry became king, a formal coronation and divine unction were not yet essential to confer legitimation of power. It certainly added prestige, and perhaps suggested divine support for the king, but Germanic kingship was still conferred by election of the nobility. Under Otto I, these ceremonies were two of many ways that sacralization of the empire began to take shape.[58] When Otto succeeded his father as duke of Saxony and king of Germany, the coronation ceremony was staged at Aachen, a location with strong Roman and Carolingian imperial associations, and at the banquet afterward he was attended at table by the dukes of the four other duchies of the kingdom.[59] While the precise meaning of many of the nuances of these ceremonies are no doubt lost to us today, it is clear that the coronation was performed in a symbolic idiom that would have been understood by contemporary audiences and made explicit to them the claims that this king was making with regard to his reach, authority, and legitimacy.[60]

---

[56] Leyser, *Rule and Conflict*, 84.

[57] Sverre Bagge, *Kings, Politics*, 34, 90. See Widukind of Corvey, *Rerum gestarum Saxonicarum libri tres* ii, 26, MGH *SRG* 60 (Hannover, 1935), 39: 'Cumque ei offerretur unctio cum diademate a summo pontifice, qui eo tempore Hirigerus erat, non sprevit, nec tamen suscepit: "Satis", inquiens, "michi est, ut pre maioribus meis rex dicar et designer, divina annuente gratia ac vestra pietate; penes meliores vero nobis unctio et diadema sit: tanto honore nos indignos arbitramur". Placuit itaque sermo iste coram universa multitudine, et dextris in caelum levatis nomen novi regis cum clamore valido salutantes frequentabant.'

[58] Other ways in which the idea of sacral kingship was reinforced by the Ottonians were through various highly visual symbols of power, such as public crown wearings and the collection and display of relics. See Mayr-Harting, *Church and Cosmos*, 4. The imperial use of the holy lance by the Ottonians would be representative of this trend.

[59] For a description of the coronation ceremony, see Widukind, *Rerum gestarum* ii.1, 63–66. The feast is described in the following section, where 'duces vero ministrabant. Lothariorum dux Isilberhtus ... omnia procurabat; Evurhardus mensae preerat, Herimannus Franco pincernis, Arnulfus equestri ordini et eligendis locandisque castris preerat ...' (ii. 2, 66–67). Widukind is careful to point out that the palace at Aachen is near Julo, a place known to have been founded by Julius Caesar: 'Est autem locus ille proximus Iulo, a conditore Iulio Caesare cognominato' (i.1, 63). The architectural complex and chapel at Aachen were constructed by Charlemagne to be his main residence, and the chapel became the focus for coronation ceremonies of Roman Emperors (W. Eugene Kleinbauer, 'Charlemagne's Palace Chapel at Aachen and its Copies', *Gesta* 4 (1965), 2–11 at 2). Charlemagne was interred there after his death – Thietmar reports that Otto III discovered and opened Charlemagne's tomb (Thietmar, *Chronicon*, iv.47; see also Timothy Reuter, 'The Ottonians and Carolingian Tradition', in *Medieval Polities and Modern Mentalities*, ed. Janet Nelson (Cambridge, 2006), 268–83 at 279).

[60] See note 2, above, regarding the importance of public rituals.

And Otto I went even further. He began to reinterpret and practice rites of the late Carolingian rulers, and to consciously adopt Byzantine motifs as the foundation for a specific kind of representation of his kingship, for example, adopting a basileus style for his representation on seals and coins.[61] It is important to note that Otto's succession was not uncontested – his younger brother Henry, duke of Bavaria, whose candidacy was supported by their mother, Mathilda, challenged Otto's rule, and the Battle of Birten was fought as a part of this contest.[62] In trying to legitimize his new and tenuous claim to imperial and dynastic authority, Otto I recognized the ability of symbols to create and perpetuate an image of power and stability. And one of the symbols most important to this developing idea of sacrality was being crowned Roman Emperor by the pope.[63] There was still tension throughout the Ottonian period between the traditional Germanic emphasis on interpersonal relationships between the ruler and his magnates and this new ruler philosophy based on sacral kingship, evidenced in the narratives of contemporary chroniclers such as Widukind of Corvey.[64] It would not be until the Salian period that this ideology of a 'Christian doctrine of royal government and the people's duty of obedience' was next presented in writing as well as in imagery, indicating its full assimilation.[65] But it must be remembered that it was the program of the Ottos that put the pieces in place for such a philosophy of rulership to develop.

This brings us back to the manipulation of symbols in the service of this evolving idea of sacral kingship, and the use of relics as a part of this program. The Ottonians, of course, were not the first rulers to consciously create a connection between kingship and relics. In the seventh century, Baldechildis, with her husband Clovis II and their sons, had actively begun to acquire holy relics for the royal palace, with the intent of transferring the power of these

---

[61]   Jonathan Shepard, 'Marriages towards the Millennium', in *Byzantium in the Year 1000*, ed. Paul Magdalino et al. (Leiden, 2003), 1–34 at 16. This was a distinctly different style than that previously seen in the Western Empire, consisting of a full-frontal depiction of the emperor crowned, holding a cross, orb, and scepter (Shepard, 'Marriages', 12; Keller, *Ottonische Königsherrschaft*, 132). An excellent example of this kind of seal exists on a charter from 966 (Otto I, Kaisersiegel, Magdeburg, Landeshauptarchiv Sachsen-Anhalt, Rep. U 1, Tit. I. Nr. 23 [24 August 966]). The changes over time in the seals of Otto I can be found in Markus Späth, 'Kaiserliche Repräsentation in den Siegelbildern Ottos I.' in *Otto der Große und das Römische Reich: Kaisertum von der Antike zum Mittelalter*, ed. Matthias Puhle and Gabriele Köster (Regensburg, 2012), 572–577.

[62]   The efforts of Henry to overthrow his brother Otto I are described by Liudprand, *Antapodosis* iv.17–34; and Widukind, *Rerum gestarum* ii.12–31. See also J. Laudage, 'Hausrecht und Thronfolge: Überlegungen zur Königserhebung Ottos des Großen und zu den Aufständen Thankmars, Heinrichs und Liudolfs', *Historisches Jahrbuch* 112 (1992), 55–65.

[63]   Mayr-Harting, *Church and Cosmos*, 4. Mayr-Harting points out that while in the past scholars focused on the practical gains for the Ottonians by being emperors, today 'few historians would rate such practical purposes above those of mystical allure and sacrality'.

[64]   Kantorowicz, *The King's Two Bodies*, 65. Gerd Althoff, *Family, Friends and Followers: Political and Social Bonds in Early Medieval Europe*, trans. Christopher Carroll (Cambridge, 2004), 86, 124, 129.

[65]   Bagge, *Kings, Politics*, 93.

saints from their traditional shrines and focusing it around the king.[66] The Carolingians, especially, had facilitated this connection between kings and saints' relics. Not merely content with active translation of saints from Italy and Spain to glorify and protect the Frankish church,[67] Carolingian monastic reform also looked to Roman relics as a way to achieve some degree of imperial control over the new Frankish episcopal religious foundations, which were established not in the local traditions of aristocratic control or in honor of local saints but in relationship to imported saints from Rome. This was an integral part of Carolingian reform efforts to establish uniformity of practice – following Roman tradition – and create a system of institutions that could serve as instruments of Carolingian political control.[68] There are suggestions in the sources, too, that it became the normal practice for Carolingian kings to actively participate in the translation of relics, as when in 838 Lothar I carried the bones of Januarius on his shoulders at Reichenau, or when in 841 and 859 Charles the Bald himself also physically translated the relics of saints.[69] What is significant for us to note here is the importance of relic translations to Carolingian rulership. Additionally, Charlemagne used rituals of relic transfer to cement conversion of the Saxons and Avars in the same tradition as Gregory the Great, who had ordered relics placed in Christian churches established in what had previously been pagan temples.[70]

Relic acquisition and devotion to the cult of saints were also of great importance to the ecclesiastical leaders and lords at the court of Louis the German.[71] Eric Goldberg notes that during the rule of Louis the German, 'the greatest royal treasures were relics, which made the king's court the meeting place of terrestrial and heavenly power'.[72] This makes sense with regard to the development of an idea of sacral kingship under the Ottonians, as well. But it was not a universal tendency. Henry Mayr-Harting remarked that 'while Henry I and Otto I … collected relics with avidity as a sign that they were endowed with divine favour', the contemporary rulers in France didn't seem any too intent on clinging to them.[73] And indeed Karl Leyser also suggested that while Henry I, Otto I, and Æthelstan all found that the transfer of relics to

---

66   Geary, *Before France and Germany*, 188. One important aspect of this collection was its mobility – instead of accessing intercessory power where saints lay, that power was co-opted and brought to where it was needed or wanted.

67   Geary, *Furta Sacra*, 18–19.

68   Geary, *Before France and Germany*, 216–217; Geary, *Furta Sacra*, 37–38.

69   Buc, *Dangers of Ritual*, 61. See Nithard, *Historia* iii.2, ed. Philippe Lauer (Paris, 1926), 86–88; and Heiric, *Miracula sancti Germani* ii.2.99–102, in L.-M. Duru, *Bibliothèque historique de l'Yonne , ou Collection de légendes, chroniques et documents divers pour servir à l'histoire des différentes contrées qui forment aujourd'hui ce département* (2 vols., Auxerre, 1850–1863), ii, 167–168. Discussion of these sources as evidence at 61 note 33.

70   Geary, *Furta Sacra*, 37.

71   Eric J. Goldberg, *Struggle for Empire: Kingship and Conflict under Louis the German, 817–876* (Ithaca, NY, 2006), 168–170.

72   Goldberg, *Struggle for Empire*, 193–194.

73   Mayr-Harting, *Ottonian Illumination* i, 51.

their kingdoms enhanced their own political currency, the people from whom
they were acquiring them often did not seem to mind letting them go.[74] It is
in the three major narrative sources for the Ottonians, Widukind of Corvey's
Rerum gestarum Saxonicarum libri tres, Liudprand of Cremona's *Antapodosis*,
and Thietmar of Merseburg's *Chronicon*, that we see, in addition to the role
relics played in diplomacy, gift exchange, and ecclesiastical foundations, an
effort made to connect sanctity with rightful rulership through the use of relics,
and the idea of a manipulation of symbols in service to this evolving idea of
sacral kingship.

Much has been made about the discrepancies between the versions of the
lance stories related in these narratives. This variety should not be seen as
problematic, since these men were not so much writing history as creating a
constructed historical memory. These discrepancies should perhaps be seen
instead as marking the evolution of an imperial mythology, the development of
stories – and maybe even a kind of medieval beta testing – to find serviceable
versions that 'rang true' in the sense of conveying endorsements of authority
and legitimacy, not necessarily in terms of relating factual accounts of events.

Widukind's *Rerum gestarum Saxonicarum* contains several connections
between specific relics and legitimate kingship. His description of an exchange
between an envoy of Charles the Simple and Henry I, while no doubt highly
unreliable as a record of the actual meeting, does convey in dramatic fashion the
idea that King Henry and the Saxons had been chosen by God and the saints to
supplant the Franks as the dominant power in the West:

When the king [Henry I] crossed the Rhine to extend his empire over Lotharingia, an
envoy of Charles [the Simple] met him, and greeted him with these words: 'My lord,' he
said, 'Charles, at one time possessing royal power, now a private person, sent me to you
saying, that nothing would make him happier, now that he is surrounded by his enemies,
nothing could be sweeter than to be able to hear something about the magnificence
of your glorious advances, and to be consoled by reports of your valor. And this sign
he sent to you of fidelity and truth,' and he brought forth from a fold the hand of the
precious martyr Denis enclosed in [a reliquary covered in] gold and gems. 'Here,' he
said, 'take this pledge of perpetual loyalty and sign of [his] love. He wants to share with
you this part of the only solace of the Franks who inhabit Gaul, after the holy martyr
Vitus abandoned us, to our sorrow, and has remained in Saxony, to your perpetual peace.
For now, after his body was translated from us, there is unceasing internal and external
war; in fact, in the same year the Danes and the Northmen invaded our lands.' The king,
receiving this divine tribute with all gratitude, prostrated himself before the holy relics,
and venerated them with the highest devotion, kissing them.[75]

74 Leyser, *Rule and Conflict*, 88.
75 Widukind, *Rerum gestarum* i, 33: 'Quando vero rex Renum transierat ad dilatandum super
Lotharios imperium suum, occurrit ei legatus Karoli, et salutato eo verbis humillimis: "Dominus
meus", inquit, "Karolus, regia quondam potestate preditus, modo privatus, misit me ad te
demandans, quia nichil ei ab inimicis circumvento iocundius, nichil dulcius esse possit quam de
tui magnifici profectus gloria aliquid audire, fama virtutum tuarum consolari. Et hoc tibi signum
fidei et veritatis transmisit"; protulitque de sinu manum preciosi martyris Dionisii auro gemmisque

Widukind highlights a number of interesting things here. First, we see the use of relics as precious diplomatic gifts, indicated here by the presentation of the hand of St Denis to Henry. The attribution of volition to relics is not unusual, but here it is used to support Widukind's message of Henry's authority and legitimacy: because St Vitus was translated into Saxony, the Western Franks are no longer protected from internal strife and foreign wars, and the Eastern Franks now enjoy his protection.[76] That the entire dialogue takes place in the context of Charles the Simple – stripped of royal power, paying homage to Henry – emphasizes Widukind's message of legitimacy. In case the reader is not clear about the point he is making, Widukind follows this passage with a description of the life of the martyr St Vitus and the various translations of his relics, culminating with their arrival in Saxony during the reign of Louis the Pious. Widukind states again that

as the envoy of Charles related, from that time [that St Vitus was brought to Saxony] the deeds of the Franks began to wane while those of Saxony increased … Therefore you should venerate such a great patron, by whose coming Saxony was freed from servitude, and from a tributary state made the mistress of many peoples.[77]

This emphasis, again, on the connection between the relics of St Vitus and the success of the Saxon people marks them as the rightful successors to the weakening West Frankish kings.

The story of the hand of St Denis is repeated in Thietmar's *Chronicon*, and his telling again emphasizes the gift as a legitimizing gesture. The most notable difference between the two versions is that Thietmar's makes no reference to St Vitus. For Widukind, the translation of St Vitus's relics was essential to the story of the *translatio imperii* and was a key legitimizing feature of the rise of Saxon power, reiterated by the formal recognition by Charles the Simple of

---

inclusam. "Hoc", inquit, "habeto pignus foederis perpetui et amoris vicarii. Hanc partem unici solatii Francorum Galliam inhabitantium, postquam nos deseruit insignis martyr Vitus ad nostram perniciem vestramque perpetuam pacem Saxoniam visitavit, communicare tecum maluit. Neque enim, postquam translatum est corpus eius a nobis, civilia vel externa cessavere bella; eodem quippe anno Dani et Northmanni regionem nostram invaserunt". Rex autem munus divinum cum omni gratiarum actione suscipiens prosternitur reliquiis sanctis et deosculans eas summa veneratione veneratus est.' See also Karl-Heinrich Krüger, 'Dionysius und Vitus als frühottonische Königsheilige. Zu Widukind I,33', *Frühmittelalterliche Studien* 8 (1974), 131–54; Matthias Becher, 'Vitus von Corvey und Mauritius von Magdeburg: Zwei sächsische Heilige in Konkurrenz', *Westfälische Zeitschrift* 147 (1997), 235–49.

[76] Regarding the volition of relics, see Geary, *Furta Sacra*, 125.

[77] Widukind, *Rerum Gestarum* i.34: 'Inde regnante Hluthowico imperatore translatae sunt in Saxoniam, et ut legatus Karoli confessus est, ex hoc res Francorum coeperunt minui, Saxonum vero crescere, donec dilatatae, ipsa sua iam magnitudine laborant, ut videmus in amore mundi et totius orbis capite, patre tuo, cuius potentiae maiestatem non solem Germania, Italia atque Gallia, sed tota fere Europa non sustinet. Colito itaque tantum patronum, quo adveniente Saxonia ex serva facta est libera et ex tributaria multarum gentium domina. Neque enim talis ac tantus summi Dei amicus tui gratia indiget, nos vero famuli ipsius indigemus. Unde ut eum possis habere intercessorem apud caelestem imperatorem, habeamus te advocatum apud terrenum regem, tuum scilicet patrem atque fratrem.' See also Bagge, *Kings, Politics*, 32 note 37.

Henry's superiority through the gift of the hand of St Denis. Thietmar's story, written a generation after Widukind's, relates that when Charles the Simple was captured by one of his own dukes and imprisoned, he appealed to Henry I for help. If Henry was successful in freeing him, Charles promised in exchange the whole of Lotharingia and the right hand of Denis the Martyr.[78] Thietmar's version of the story becomes, in essence, a legitimation of Ottonian domination of Lotharingia, a hotly contested area that was an ongoing source of disruptions and rebellions against the Ottonian kings.

While there are other stories regarding relics that appear in these accounts that are clearly intended to enhance the legitimacy of the Ottonian kings, only one relic occurs in this context in all three texts: the Holy Lance. Not surprisingly, as with the hand of St Denis, the symbolic nature of the lance in each of these texts is slightly different. The versions related by Widukind and Liudprand, despite some discrepancies, emphasize the lance's thaumaturgic and protective qualities, as well as its ability to confer legitimacy upon the owner. Widukind's first mention of the Holy Lance is as part of the coronation regalia conferred by Conrad, in a deathbed speech in which he asks his brother to 'take these insignia, this sacred lance, these golden bracelets, this chlamys, and the sword and diadem of our regal ancestors, and go to Henry, and make peace with him ...'[79] The Holy Lance was not yet part of the royal regalia at the time of Henry I's coronation, and Widukind's mention of it has puzzled historians. It is possible that he is referring to a different lance altogether.[80] It is also possible that by the time he was writing the lance was a well-known component of the imperial regalia such that its exclusion would have been more problematic than its anachronistic inclusion, especially with regard to the legitimation of Henry I. This brings us to the heart of the issue, which is not whether or not Widukind got his facts wrong, but rather what Widukind meant: by including a reference to the lance here, he clearly suggested that it was a legitimizing relic, part of the royal regalia that is held by the rightful king. The Holy Lance shows up one more time in Widukind's narrative, in his description of the Battle of Lech, a key battle in Saxon history at which Otto successfully kept the Magyars at bay, where he reports that Otto I gave an impassioned speech to his troops before leading them into battle, wielding his shield and the sacred lance.[81]

Liudprand gives a much different account of how Henry I received the Holy Lance, relating that Henry received it from King Rudolph of Burgundy, who

---

[78]   Thietmar, *Chronicon* i.23: 'Fuit in occiduis partibus quidam rex, ab incolis Karl Sot, id est stolidus, ironice dictus, qui ab uno suimet ducum captus, tenebris includitur carceralibus. Hic Heinrici regis nostri, nepotis autem sui, inplorans auxilium, dexteram Christi martiris Dionisii et cum ea omne regnum Luthariorum, si ab eo liberaretur, sibi traditurum sacramentis promisit.'

[79]   Widukind, *Rerum Gestarum* i.25 'Sumptis igitur his insigniis, lancea sacra, armillis aureis cum clamide, et veterum gladio regum ac diademate, ito ad Heinricum, facito pacem cum eo ...'

[80]   For example, Gunther G. Wolf suggests that the first lance mentioned by Widukind, with regard to the coronation of Henry I, was a different lance than his second mention of the holy lance at the Battle of Lech, which Wolf associates with the Vienna lance. ('Nochmals zur Geschichte', 30).

[81]   Widukind, *Rerum Gestarum*, iii 44–49.

had in turn received it as a gift from a certain count. Liudprand notes that the provenance of the lance is purported to derive from Constantine the Great. In this narrative, Henry learned of the lance and sent messengers to enquire whether Rudolph might give it to him. Rudolph's immediate response was to reject Henry's request to surrender the lance, but after Henry persisted, threatening to ravage and depopulate Rudolph's lands if necessary to acquire it, 'the heart of King Rudolph softened, and he personally handed over what was right to the righteous king who was rightly seeking it'.[82] Liudprand's emphatic endorsement of Henry's acquisition of the lance clearly suggests it as a legitimizing relic.[83]

Liudprand's account of the Battle of Birten, a key battle early in Otto I's reign, reflects an elaboration of Widukind's version of events. The Battle of Birten was fought in 939 when Otto's brother, Henry of Bavaria, attempted a revolt. While Widukind reports that Otto, separated from his troops by the Rhine river, prayed for their victory by extending his arms to heaven in conscious imitation of Moses and the Amalekites, Liudprand adds the lance to the vignette, recounting that Otto got off his horse and began to pray,

shedding tears before the victory-giving nails that pierced the hands of our Lord and Savior Jesus Christ, and which had been placed on his lance; and the outcome of the whole affair proved how much the prayer of a just man can be worth ... For as he prayed, while none from the ranks of his army fell, the enemy all turned to flight, and not a few of them hardly knew why they were running ...[84]

Now, this is clearly a tale that has grown with the telling, especially as Widukind asserts that the Saxons did indeed suffer losses.[85] But what is important here is not the information about the battle, or even whether any of the story is factual – what is important is the insertion of the Holy Lance into the story of a battle that was fought to determine the legitimacy of Otto as the rightful king and heir to Henry I. The story, whether crafted strategically by Liudprand to impress his royal patrons or included as a creative embellishment that captured the royal imagination, deliberately connected the Holy Lance with the royal and imperial legitimacy of the Ottonians.

As mentioned above, Widukind does report that the Holy Lance was carried into battle by Otto I at the Battle of Lech. Liudprand's narrative, unfortunately for us, leaves off about five years before this battle. And Thietmar, remarkably, does not

---

[82] Liudprand, *Antapodosis*, iv.25,: in *Liudprandi Cremonensis Opera Omnia*, ed. P. Chiesa, CCCM 156 (Turnhout, 1998) 'Quia vero quod petebatur munus erat quo caelestibus terrea Deus coniunxerat, lapis scilicet angularis faciens utraque unum, Rodulfi regis cor emollivit iustoque regi iusta iuste petenti cominus tradidit.' (Trans. Squatriti, *Complete Works*, 158).

[83] Philippe Buc argues that the main purpose of Liudprand of Cremona's writings was to legitimize Otto I's rule over Italy, 'the systematic destruction of the dynastic legitimacy of potential contenders for the Italian throne', as well as legitimization of the Ottonian dynasty. See 'Italian Hussies and German Matrons: Liutprand of Cremona on Dynastic Legitimacy', *Frühmittelalterliche Studien* 29 (1995), 207–25 at 211, 224.

[84] Liudprand, *Antapodosis*, iv.24.

[85] Widukind, *Rerum Gestarum*, iii.46.

mention either battle in his *Chronicon*. But Thietmar does report that lances were used as a way to confer a benefice, confirming that this was a traditional Germanic symbolic sign of succession among nobility.[86] Most importantly, in his report of the events following the death of Otto III, Thietmar emphasizes the importance of the Holy Lance as a key part of the royal regalia conferring legitimacy.

When Otto III died without an heir in 1002, there was clearly concern that there would be a fight for the succession. Thietmar reports that his death was kept secret until the army could be recalled and assembled, and his body was then escorted with this guard. The procession made its way to Polling, an estate owned by Bishop Siegfried of Augsburg and, according to Thietmar,

Duke Henry [the future Henry II] received them and revived their sorrow with his tears. Henry urged each of them, individually, to choose him as their lord and king, and made many promises. He took custody of the emperor's corpse, and also of the imperial insignia, except for the holy lance, which Archbishop Heribert had secretly sent ahead.[87]

Heribert was first taken into custody by Henry, and then sent to retrieve the lance while Henry held his brother hostage.[88] The fear of unrest in the brief interregnum was not misplaced, and Henry was forced to outmaneuver domestic challengers at the same time that the Slavs were opportunistically renewing pressure on the eastern borders. But even after an assembly of great nobles at Werla had determined his hereditary right to the throne, and after he was crowned by Archbishop Willigis of Mainz, Henry still had to make his way around the kingdom to secure support from the magnates.[89] When he was received in Saxony, after acclamation by the assembled men, their representative, Duke Bernhard 'grasped the lance and faithfully committed the care of the kingdom to him'.[90]

The lance, in Widukind's and Liudprand's narratives, is an important symbol. It is a protective relic and battle standard assuring the king's troops of divine oversight and a reminder, especially in their wars against the pagans, that they

---

[86] Thietmar, *Chronicon*, v.21: 'E quibus unus, calliditate eque et velocitate persepe probatus, propius accessit signiferamque lanceam, qua beneficium ducis comes isdem acceperat a rege ...' Regarding rulership symbolism and lances, see Schramm, 'Heilige Lanze', 492–537 at 501–512 for the Holy Lance in the Ottonian period. The lance as an important symbol of legitimacy and succession is evidenced by the replica of the Holy Lance that Otto III gave as a gift to the future King Stephen I of Hungary. During his reign, Stephen featured the lance in his own iconography. He had a coin struck that featured the lance, and an image of him in the embroidery of a royal robe shows him crowned, holding the lance and orb (Wolf, 'Nochmals zur Geschichte', 30; and Plates 10 and 12, 34–35).

[87] Thietmar, *Chronicon*, iv.50: 'Exin cum ad Pollingun, curtem Sigifridi presulis Augustanae, venirent, ab Heinrico duce suscepti, lacrimis eiusdem vehementer iterum commoti sunt. Quos singulatim, ut se in dominum sibi et regem eligere voluissent, multis promissionibus hortatur; et corpus imperatoris cum apparatu imperiali, lancea dumtaxat excepta, quam Heribertus archipresul clam premittens, suam sumpsit in potestatem.' (Thietmar, *Ottonian Germany*, trans. Warner, 187)

[88] Thietmar, *Chronicon*, iv.50.

[89] Thietmar, *Chronicon*, v.3, v.11.

[90] Thietmar, *Chronicon*, v.17: 'Bernhardus igitur dux, accepta in manibus sacra lancea, ex parte omnium regni curam illi fideliter committit.' (Thietmar, *Ottonian Germany*, trans. Warner, 216). See also Oberste, 'Heilige und ihre Reliquien', 77.

fight for both the king and Christ. That the Ottonians adopted St Maurice as their particular patron, and that his iconography often depicts him carrying the Holy Lance, would have made even clearer the connection that the kings were warriors for Christ.[91] But in these narratives, a royal ideology and the idea of sacral kingship was still developing. The lance, in Thietmar's *Chronicon* a generation later, had been transformed. No longer merely symbolizing divine protection for the king and the kingdom, the Holy Lance, in Thietmar's telling belonged to the rightful king, just like other relics that had been translated via human intervention but according to the saints' wishes. Possession of the lance conferred legitimacy on a claim to the throne. Henry II was aware of this symbolic connection, which explains his eagerness to acquire that particular piece of the royal regalia. Archbishop Heribert was aware of this, too, and did his best to prevent Henry, who was not his preferred candidate for king, from gaining possession of it. Merely seizing the relic, of course, did not confer kingship. But it clearly provided an advantage for a person in putting forth a claim. And, following the peculiar logic of relics, if that person were not the *right* person, he would not be in possession of it for long.

The Holy Lance is also mentioned in other kinds of writings in the eleventh century, suggesting that the effort to connect it to the Ottonian dynasty had been successful. Brun of Querfurt, writing in 1008 about Henry II, spoke of the 'sacra lancea' known to have belonged to 'dux sanctorum vester et noster Mauritius'.[92] And Thangmar of Hildesheim, in his *Vita Bernwardi* which was completed around 1022, writes both of its ability to turn the tide of battle, this time carried by Bishop Bernward of Hildesheim who brought the lance to Otto III when he was besieged at Rome in 1001, as well as its critical role in the election of Henry II.[93] While Thietmar reported that the lance was an essential symbol in securing the support of the Saxon nobles but did not mention it in connection with the actual coronation ceremony, Thangmar's description of Henry's coronation specified that Archbishop Willigis presented him with the Holy Lance.[94] This version further emphasizes the importance of the lance as a symbol of imperial legitimacy.

---

[91]   Maurice is depicted with a lance on the mid-ninth-century Flabellum of Tournus, and a mid-eleventh-century relief on the church of St Mauritz in Münster shows Maurice holding a lance and shield (Warner, 'Cult of Saint Maurice', 87). A mid-eleventh-century back cover from an evangelary also depicts St Maurice holding a lance and shield (Wolf, 'Nochmals zur Geschichte', 40, Plate 17; Stadtbibliothek Mainz, Hs II 3). Later medieval examples of specifically black St Maurice images, most of which bear lances, are catalogued in Suckale-Redlefsen, 'Mauritius', 158ff.

[92]   Wolf, 'Nochmals zur Geschichte', 38.

[93]   Thangmar of Hildesheim, *Vita Bernwardi Episcopi Hildesheimensis* c.24, c.38, trans. G. Pertz in MGH *SS* 4 (Hannover, 1841), 770, 775. Thietmar reports that Bishop Bernward had initially supported one of Henry's competitors for the throne, a detail that Thangmar tactfully omitted (Thietmar, *Chronicon*, v.4). See also Wolf, 'Nochmals zur Geschichte', 30; and Stefan Weinfurter, *Heinrich II: Herscherr am Ende der Zeiten* (Regensburg, 1999), 52.

[94]   Thangmar, *Vita Bernwardi* c.38, 775. 'Omnibus ergo pari voto in electione illius concordantibus, Willegisus archiepiscopus et Bernwardus praesul cum caeteris regni principibus domnum Heinricum Mogontiam cum summo honore ducentes, dominica octava pentecostes regimen et regiam potestatem cum dominica hasta illi tradiderunt.'

Perhaps these other references should not surprise us, especially that of
Thangmar. Mention of the lance in a *vita* written for a politically active bishop
by a Saxon monk at an important Ottonian royal center might be expected. But
the lance appears as well in a contemporary text that originated further afield.
Ademar of Chabannes (989–1034), in his *Historia*, relates how Otto III gave
the gift of a replica Holy Lance to the future King Stephen I of Hungary (r.
1000/1001–1038), and Ademar's description of the imperial lance notes the holy
nail it holds and its connection to St Maurice.[95] When, later in his narrative, he
describes the regalia conveyed to Henry II that designated him as the rightful
successor of Otto III, Ademar lists the scepter, crown, and lance.[96] For Ademar,
the lance was a key detail legitimizing these Roman emperors.

While these sources demonstrate the transformation of the lance as a political
symbol over the course of the Ottonian dynasty, references to the Holy Lance
do not just appear in texts. The Ottonians also incorporated the lance into visual
representations of their authority, further emphasizing the symbolic connection
between Holy Lance and legitimate ruler. While earlier images incorporating the
lance include seals of Henry I and Otto I, the apogee of these depictions parallels
the increasing importance attributed to the lance in the textual sources here –
the Regensburg Sacramentary coronation portrait of Henry II being crowned by
Christ while an angel places the Holy Lance in his hand.[97]

It is worth mentioning at this point that the Anglo-Saxons also had a Holy
Lance. When Duke Hugh of France (898–956) was seeking the hand of one
of Æthelstan's sisters, the gifts he sent included the Holy Lance and the

---

95   Ademar of Chabannes, *Ademari Historiarum Libri III* iii.31, in MGH *SS* 4, 129–130: 'dans ei
licentiam ferre lanceam sacram ubique, sicut ipsi imperatori mos est, et reliquias ex clavis Domini
et lancea sancti Mauricii ei concessit in propria lancea.' Wolf notes that this was a replica of the
Holy Lance, see note 86 above ('Nochmals zur Geschichte', 30).

96   Ademar, iii.33, 131: 'sceptrum et coronam cum lancea sacra'; Richard Landes, *Relics, Apocalypse,
and the Deceits of History: Ademar of Chabannes, 989–1034* (Cambridge, MA, 1995), 150.

97   There were not many ruler images during the Ottonian era that incorporated the lance
(Schramm, *Herrschaftszeichen*, 506–507), but there are seal images of Henry I and Otto I holding
the lance (Wolf, 'Nochmals zur Geschichte', 27, Plates 5–6). In the Regensburg Sacramentary (*c.*
1002–1012), also known as the 'Sacramentary of Henry II', the coronation portrait of Henry II
depicts Christ placing a crown on his head while angels place the Holy Lance and royal sword in
his hands (München, Bayerische Staatsbibliothek, MS Clm 4456, fol. 11r). This image is discussed
at length in Garrison, *Ottonian Imperial Art*, 141–142 and Mayr-Harting, *Ottonian Illumination* i,
66–67. Mayr-Harting connects this visual representation of the Holy Lance with Henry's efforts
to recover that key piece of regalia, and remarks that 'Art … was a continuation of the ritual
by which [Henry II] had struggled for the kingship' (*Ottonian Illumination* i, 195). As another
example connecting the lance to the reign of Henry II, Garrison suggests that the reference to the
Holy Lance on the cover of the 'Golden Gospels', *c.* 1003, which portrays the Crucifixion with
Longinus piercing Christ's side, would have been associated by those who saw it with Henry II:
'The choice of a Crucifixion scene that concentrates on the moment that Longinus pierced Christ's
side certainly makes reference to the Holy Lance, that last and most sacred of the royal insignia
that Henry II attained in 1002. Although this cover does not include a portrait of Henry II, such
a scene would have nevertheless established an additional commemorative connection between
Christ and the ruler' (Garrison, *Ottonian Imperial Art*, 102).

vexillum of St Maurice, relics that had previously belonged to Charlemagne.[98] An additional item sent to Æthelstan by Hugh was a sword of Constantine, which had a nail of the cross mounted on it. Æthelstan was an enthusiastic collector of relics, a fact of which Hugh was no doubt aware when he sent his embassy. And receiving both the lance and the vexillum of St Maurice as a set, as well as Hugh's recognition of Æthelstan as a potential imperial ruler by the conferment of Carolingian relics, would have been a kind of coup.[99] But other than a tenth-century poem preserved by William of Malmsbury in his twelfth-century *De Gestis Regum Anglorum*, their only other mention occurs in the relic lists at Exeter Cathedral.[100]

It is of passing interest to note the various elements of Hugh's gifts and the Ottonian lance stories that are in common – associations with Constantine and St Maurice, for example. But what is more interesting is that the lance clearly was employed differently by rulers in the various realms. The kings in both England and Germany were avid relic collectors, and they were essentially warrior-kings. In the acquisition of their Holy Lance, the Ottonians seized upon its potential for symbolism, incorporated it visibly into their royal regalia and insignia, and made it a part of their royal and martial identity. Æthelstan treasured his Holy Lance, but he did not attempt to make it, or others of his relics, part of the English royal identity or representative of his sacral and legitimate claim to the throne.

The lance as a crucial symbol of regnal and imperial legitimacy for German kings and emperors persisted into the dynasties that succeeded the Ottonians. When Henry II, the last Ottonian king, died childless in 1024, Wipo reports that his widow, Empress Cunegund, personally conveyed the imperial regalia to Conrad II as a necessary *corroboratio* to confirm his traditional election.[101] Conrad further elevated the lance as a visible part of the imperial regalia and symbol of legitimacy through its incorporation into a magnificent gold processional cross dating from about 1030. This Imperial Cross incorporated the Holy Lance and a fragment of the True Cross, as well as other relics. Measuring thirty inches tall, it would have been a commanding symbol in imperial processions.[102] Even as late as the twelfth century, the imperial insignia comprising the scepter, orb, crown, and Holy Lance 'were essential for the coronation and legitimate rule of a future king' after the death of Henry V of the Holy Roman Empire.[103] In a parallel to the events occurring after the death of Otto III, Archbishop Adalbert

---

[98] Laura H. Loomis, 'Holy Relics of Charlemagne and King Athelstan', *Speculum* 25 (1950), 437–56 at 440. This gift, which we mainly know about from William of Malmesbury, also is mentioned in a tenth-century panegyric to Æthelstan.

[99] Leyser, *Rule and Conflict*, 88.

[100] Loomis, 'Holy Relics', 437.

[101] Wipo, *Gesta Chuonradi II* c.2, ed. H. Bresslau, in MGH *SRG* 61 (Hannover, 1915), 19: 'Supra dicta imperatrix Chunegunda regalia insignia, quae sibi imperator Heinricus reliquerat, gratanter obtulit et ad regnandum, quantum huius sexus auctoritatis est, illum corroboravit'.

[102] Herwig Wolfram, *Conrad II, 990–1039: Emperor of Three Kingdoms* (University Park, PA, 2006), 144–146.

[103] Leyser, 'Frederick Barbarossa, Henry II', 224.

of Mainz, an enemy of the Hohenstaufen, seized the regalia. Imperial legitimacy was still conferred by possession of the regalia, of which the Holy Lance was a key component.[104]

At the beginning of this essay, it was noted that this investigation was driven by questions about the relationships between relics and authority, relics and texts, and text and audience. That the meaning of the Holy Lance with regard to its bearers, the Ottonian kings and emperors, came to be transformed, is evidenced by the chroniclers who incorporated stories about the lance into their histories. Whether the stories about the lance helped to create this new meaning, or whether they recorded or reflected efforts at myth-making by the Ottonian court is an endogeneic question that, in the end, is less important than the development of meaning of the lance itself. Ultimately the lance, indisputably a priceless relic, came to symbolize more than its inherent value as a relic of Christ, a relic with martial significance, and a relic with thaumaturgic and protective powers. While maintaining all of those qualities, the lance also came to symbolize legitimate kingship and imperial claims to power. The treatment of the Holy Lance in these Ottonian narratives provides a starting point for investigating these relationships between relics and power. It by no means represents the end. But it does suggest that further investigation into the conjunctions of relics and rulership may provide us with additional insights into the making of legitimacy and kingship in the early Middle Ages.

---

[104] Leyser, 'Frederick Barbarossa, Henry II', 224.

Beyond the Obvious: Ælfric and the Authority of Bede

Joyce Hill

In 989, two years after he had transferred from the cathedral monastery of Old Minster Winchester, that great powerhouse of the Anglo-Saxon Benedictine Reform, to the much more modest monastery of Cerne Abbas in Dorset, Ælfric, then only a monk and masspriest, wrote a letter to Sigeric, Archbishop of Canterbury.[1] As was appropriate for a letter from one ecclesiastic to another, this was in Latin, and the tone was suitably deferential and humble.[2] But the contents of the manuscript which the covering Latin letter sought to explain and justify departed from normal practice. What Ælfric was sending to Sigeric and in effect commending to him was a collection of forty homilies, mostly on the gospel lections for the day, organized according to the cycle of the church's year, and written in Old English. On the face of it, this might not seem to be innovative since preachers had to use the vernacular, after all, when addressing lay congregations. But what Ælfric had done was to produce a systematic collection of texts in the vernacular which embodied the patristically-based traditions that were characteristic of the Benedictine Reform as he had known it at Winchester. The reformers' adoption of these traditions, following the example of the Carolingian Reform which inspired the Anglo-Saxon one, had the same aim as did the Carolingians: to improve the standards of scholarship within the monasteries as the educational centres of the day; to eliminate error by going back to the great authorities; and thus in the long run to raise the standards of teaching and preaching within the church as a whole.

---

[1] *Ælfric's Catholic Homilies. The First Series: Text*, ed. Peter Clemoes, Early English Text Society, suppl. ser. 17 (Oxford, 1997), 175–175. For further detail about Ælfric's intellectual and ecclesiastical context, see Joyce Hill, 'Ælfric: His Life and Works', in *A Companion to Ælfric*, ed. Hugh Magennis and Mary Swan (Leiden, 2009), 35–65.

[2] The letter's rhetorical manoeuvring is analysed by Joyce Hill, 'Translating the Tradition: Manuscripts, Models and Methodologies in the Composition of Ælfric's *Catholic Homilies*', in *Textual and Material Culture in Anglo-Saxon England: Thomas Northcote Toller and the Toller Memorial Lectures*, ed. Donald Scragg (Cambridge, 2003), 241–59 at 241–246 [The Toller Memorial Lecture for 1996, originally published in the *Bulletin of the John Rylands University Library of Manchester* 79 (1997), 43–65].

Sets of Latin homilies within this tradition had come into England with the Reform, and it is clear that they had been central to Ælfric's own formation as a monk while at Winchester. But, as far as we know, before Ælfric no one in England had worked with these materials to produce new sets of homilies. Now Ælfric was doing so, not in Latin, as the Carolingians had done in their successive homily compilations within this tradition, but in the vernacular. Here was the innovation: an organized collection of homilies, in effect a small selective homiliary, firmly within the Reform tradition as defined within the Latin-dominated world of Anglo-Saxon Benedictine monasticism; composed using precisely the same techniques as Ælfric's Latin models; but with the striking difference that they were in the vernacular.[3] His objectives, nevertheless, were those that the Carolingians would have recognized: the provision of models for the secular clergy, with the aim of eliminating the 'error', *gedwyld* Ælfric called it, which was present in the preaching that was not informed by the interpretations of the Church Fathers.[4] Ælfric told Sigeric that he was preparing a further set of forty homilies, which he would send to him in due course. He did so a few years later, with another covering letter in Latin.[5] These two sets are known to us now as the First and Second Series of *Catholic Homilies* (hereafter *CH I* and *CH II*). Ælfric worked on his homily collection throughout his career, modifying and adapting existing texts and adding some others.[6] In this paper, however, I focus on the two series of *Catholic Homilies* as sent to Sigeric.

In the letter accompanying the First Series, Ælfric named the authorities on whom he had relied:

For, indeed, we have followed these authors in this exposition: namely, Augustine of Hippo, Jerome, Bede, Gregory, Smaragdus, and sometimes Haymo, for the authority of these is most willingly acknowledged by all the orthodox.[7]

So far, so obvious: in establishing one's patristic credentials, in defining one's own position as faithful to their tradition of interpretation, one cannot do better than name Augustine, Jerome, and Gregory. But why did he also name Bede,

---

3   The nature of Ælfric's participation in this tradition is exemplified by Joyce Hill, 'Weaving and Interweaving: The Textual Traditions of Two of Ælfric's *Supplementary Homilies*', in *Textiles, Text, Intertext: Essays in Honour of Gale R. Owen Crocker*, ed. Maren Clegg Hyer and Jill Frederick (Woodbridge, 2016), 211–23..

4   *Ælfric's Catholic Homilies. The First Series*, 174.

5   *Ælfric's Catholic Homilies. The Second Series: Text*, ed. Malcolm Godden, Early English Text Society, suppl. ser. 5 (London, 1979), 1–2.

6   The extent of Ælfric's continuing work on his sets of *temporale* homilies was demonstrated by P.A.M.Clemoes, 'The Chronology of Ælfric's Works', in *The Anglo-Saxons: Studies in some Aspects of their History and Culture presented to Bruce Dickins*, ed. Peter Clemoes (London, 1959), 212–47. Most of this later textual material is available in *The Homilies of Ælfric: A Supplementary Collection*, ed. John C. Pope, Early English Text Society, orig. ser. 259, 260 (2 vols., London, 1967–1968).

7   *Ælfric's Catholic Homilies. The First Series*, 173: Hos namque auctores in hac explanatio sumus secuti. uidelicet Augustinum. ypponiensem. Hieronimum. Bedam. Gregorium. Smaragdum, et aliquando Hægmonem; Horum denique auctoritas ab omnibus catholicis. libentissime suscipitur.

Smaragdus, and Haymo? The reason was that he wanted to make clear to Sigeric not only that he was perpetuating the patristic tradition – his ultimate ground of authority – but that he was doing so within the Carolingian line of transmission. In other words, he was defining himself simultaneously in terms of his intellectual tradition (the patristic) and in terms of his position within the reform tradition of the here and now, which was modelled on the Carolingians and used their texts. Here we move beyond the obvious and so open up the possibility that we can identify more precisely not simply what intellectual resources Ælfric used, but how he accessed them, how he interacted with them, and why. As a first step towards this analysis, the inclusion of these post-patristic authors in Ælfric's list of authorities requires further scrutiny.

In Ælfric's first letter to Sigeric, Bede is referred to as if he is on a par with Augustine, Jerome, and Gregory; in fact it is as if he is one of the Church Fathers himself. We can be confident that Bede would not have accepted this. At the end of his *Historia Ecclesiastica*, when reviewing his life's work, he acknowledged his utter reliance on the Church Fathers and explained that he was doing no more in his exegetical works than making brief extracts from the works of the Fathers, to which he simply added notes of his own for clarification.[8] Elsewhere he described himself as 'following the footsteps of the fathers', *patrum vestigia sequens*.[9] This is entirely just. From a modern scholarly perspective, Bede's biblical interpretations are highly derivative, even though intelligently developed and expressed with stylistic flair. Indeed, in his commentaries on Mark and Luke, Bede even paraded his patristic indebtedness, using marginal letters to indicate whose words he was using at any given point.[10] But, as I have shown elsewhere, the Carolingians did not let this hold them back from elevating Bede to the status of a 'doctor' on a par with Augustine, Jerome, and Gregory.[11] They deemed him to be the teacher of their age, they imitated his methods of composition by making extensive use of verbatim passages from the Fathers, and they often followed his practice of signalling the orthodoxy and authority of the words they were using by indicating in the margin whose words they were: for example, *A* for Augustinus, *G* for Gregorius, *H* for Hieronimus – and *B* for Beda. The complication was that sometimes when they named Bede it was because Bede was what was conveniently to hand ('Bede's' words might, after

---

8   *Bede's Ecclesiastical History of the English People* V.24, ed. Bertram Colgrave and R.A.B. Mynors (Oxford, rev. ed. 1991), 566.

9   Paul Meyvaert, 'Bede the Scholar', in *Famulus Christi: Essays in Commemoration of the Thirteenth Centenary of the Birth of the Venerable Bede*, ed. Gerald Bonner (London, 1976), 40–69 at 62–63, note 7.

10   E.J. Sutcliffe, 'Quotations in the Ven. Bede's Commentary on S. Mark', *Biblica* 7 (1926), 428–39, and M.L.W. Laistner, 'Source-Marks in Bede Manuscripts', *Journal of Theological Studies* 34 (1933), 350–54.

11   Joyce Hill, 'Carolingian Perspectives on the Authority of Bede', in *Innovation and Tradition in the Writings of The Venerable Bede*, ed. Scott DeGregorio (Morgantown WV, 2006), 227–49. For Anglo-Saxon England's acceptance of Bede's exegetical authority, see Joyce Hill, *Bede and the Benedictine Reform* (Jarrow, 1998) [The Jarrow Lecture for 1998].

all, at any point have been his own, or someone else's), and sometimes when they named Gregory, or Augustine, for example, they were actually working with a Bedan manuscript, but were using a passage that was labelled in the Bedan manuscript with *G* or *A*, and chose to preserve this ultimate authority in their own attribution. Such is medieval intertextuality, and it has considerable importance for source study in this period, particularly when we are concerned with working out whether a medieval author used a given source directly as a discrete work (that is, as we know it on our library shelves), or took the words from an intermediate transmitter, some kind of *compilatio* of verbatim or near verbatim passages, part texts, or short whole texts.[12] I shall return to this issue later in examining Ælfric's use of the authority of Bede. But in relation to the letter to Sigeric the significance of Ælfric's reference to Bede is that is indicative of a Carolingian-influenced mindset: Bede embedded amongst the great names of the patristic tradition, equal to them and just as important as a touchstone of that tradition. Beyond the obvious, once again.

The naming of Smaragdus and Haymo in the letter to Sigeric is simpler to explain since both were major figures in the Carolingian tradition of patristically-based scholarship, and so reference to them positioned Ælfric unambiguously in the contemporary reformist scene. Smaragdus, abbot of the monastery of Saint Mihiel near Verdun, was an associate of Benedict of Aniane and was thus in the inner circle of the Carolingian reformers. What Ælfric was specifically referring to in citing Smaragdus was his collection of lection-based exegetical homilies arranged for the cycle of the church's year.[13] Some homilies in Smaragdus's collection were extracted from one source, with Bede's Commentary on Mark or his Commentary on Luke being the texts most commonly used in this way for the homilies on the gospels; others were composed by creating a chain or *catena* of patristic material variously accessed, including via Bede as an intermediate transmitter, in the true Carolingian tradition.[14] But, as already noted, the two Bedan gospel Commentaries indicated in the margin whose words Bede was using at a given point, and Smaragdus often repeated these attributions in the margins of his manuscript, although he was not entirely consistent in this practice, since he sometimes attributed the words to Bede, who was his immediate source. In other cases, where he created the *catena* himself, he followed Bede's example

---

[12] I have examined these complexities from various perspectives in 'Authority and Intertextuality in the Works of Ælfric', *Proceedings of the British Academy* 131 (2005), 157–81 [The Sir Israel Gollancz Memorial Lecture for 2004]; 'Ælfric and Heiric of Auxerre', *Poetica* 75 (2011), 103–23; 'Augustine's Tractates on John and the Homilies of Ælfric', *Filologia Germanica* 5 (2013), 159–94; 'Mapping the Anglo-Saxon Intellectual Landscape: the Risks and Rewards of Source-Study', in *Aspects of Anglo-Saxon and Medieval England*, ed. Michiko Ogura (Frankfurt am Main, 2014), 49–68. On the fundamental importance of intertextuality to the scholarship of the early Middle Ages, see Martin Irvine, *The Making of Textual Culture: 'Grammatica' and Literary Theory, 350–1100* (Cambridge, 1994).
[13] The only edition of Smaragdus's homiliary is that edited in *PL* 102, cols. 13–552.
[14] The sources of Smaragdus's homilies have been identified by Fidel Rädle, *Studien zu Smaragd von Saint-Mihiel*, Medium Ævum: Philologische Studien 29 (Munich, 1974), 144–194.

of indicating the authority by marginal letter identifications, although here, too, there are times when, given the intense intertextuality of the tradition within which Smaragdus was working, the identified authority is not the ultimate (i.e., original) authority as we would understand it, and there are yet other times where the marginal identification of an apparently ultimate authority was most probably taken from an intermediate transmitter who was Smaragdus's direct source at the particular point. As a result of Smaragdus's method of proceeding, when the manuscripts of his homiliary began their circulation they had over five hundred marginal authority indicators. I have previously shown that this tradition of annotated manuscripts reached England, and that Ælfric's copy must have preserved a good many, if not all, of these marginal annotations.[15] This provided confirmation for him of the patristic validity, and it allowed him to cite these authorities by name directly within his homilies without naming Smaragdus at all. This is why there is no reference to Smaragdus within the vernacular texts, since it was not Smaragdus's name that carried weight in that interpretative context, but the names of Augustine, Jerome, Bede, and Gregory. It is thus all the more revealing that, in the different and distinctive context of the letter to an ecclesiastical superior, where he was not validating specific interpretations, as he was in the homilies, but was carefully establishing his own credentials as a bearer of reform, Ælfric took care to name Smaragdus directly.

The reason for naming Haymo in the letter was similar. He, too, was a name to conjure with in the reform tradition, being one of the homilists of the school of Auxerre.[16] He was active in the mid-ninth century, a little later than Smaragdus, although his exegetical, lection-based homiliary for the cycle of the church's year, which is what Ælfric was referring to here, was just as steeped in the patristic tradition. It was not, however, composed in quite the same way: Haymo had a rather freer mode of writing, which, while it often echoed the words of the Fathers quite closely, did not use Smaragdus's *catena* method. As a result, his homiliary had no authority attributions, and there are two instances

---

[15]   Joyce Hill, 'Ælfric and Smaragdus', *ASE* 21 (1992), 203–37. For further examples of Ælfric's interaction with a manuscript of Smaragdus's homiliary, see also Joyce Hill, 'Ælfric's Sources Reconsidered: Some Case-Studies from the *Catholic Homilies*', in *Studies in English Language and Literature. 'Doubt Wisely': Papers in Honour of E.G. Stanley*, ed. M.J. Toswell and E.M. Tyler (London and New York, 1996), 362–86; Joyce Hill, 'Ælfric's Authorities', in *Early Medieval English Texts and Interpretations: Studies Presented to Donald G. Scragg*, ed. Elaine Treharne and Susan Rosser (Tempe AZ, 2002), 51–65; and the references in note 12 above.

[16]   The only edition of Haymo's homiliary, wrongly attributed to Haymo of Halberstadt, is that edited in *PL* 118, cols. 9–804 (inclusive of the *Homiliae de Sanctis*). However, this version of Haymo's homiliary collection includes some later augmentations. Henri Barré, *Les homéliaires carolingiens de l'école d'Auxerre*, Studi e Testi 225 (Vatican City, 1962), lists these (pp. 50–51), and sets out the contents of the authentic homiliary (pp. 147–179). The *Homiliae de sanctis*, which appear separately in the *Patrologia Latina* edition, are integrated into the whole by Barré since he assumes that this was how they originally appeared. Ælfric's use of Haymo was demonstrated by Cyril L. Smetana, 'Aelfric and the Homiliary of Haymo of Halberstadt', *Traditio* 17 (1961), 457–69. The fact that Smetana followed *PL* in ascribing the authorship to Haymo of Halberstadt does not invalidate his textual analysis.

within the *Catholic Homilies* where, when working closely with Haymo's text, Ælfric was consequently obliged to name him directly.[17] For the most part, however – mainly I suspect because Ælfric found him less easy to dovetail with his other sources – Haymo tended to be used for specific details, and it is for this reason, as I have argued elsewhere, that he is set apart from the others listed in the Sigeric letter through the qualifying adverb *aliquando*, 'sometimes'.[18]

Before leaving this letter, I want to return to the first four names: Augustine, Jerome, Bede, and Gregory. Might we infer from their listing in this way that Ælfric had access to a library of relevant work by them? Almost certainly not. He was working away from the great centre of scholarship at Winchester, with its rich manuscript resources, and even if we imagine that he conceived of the *Catholic Homilies* while he was there, and began to work on them then, he must have done most of his detailed work at Cerne Abbas. In fact, I think it is more than likely that it was the move to Cerne in 987, away from the privileged context of Winchester, that prompted him to embark on this kind of work at all: comments in several of his works indicate that he was anxious about the wisdom of producing material in English, but he clearly saw a need and repeatedly steeled himself to meet it. At Cerne we can be confident that he had the useful homiliaries of Smaragdus and Haymo, to which his letter refers directly and, thanks to the investigations of Cyril Smetana in the 1950s, we can also be sure that he had a copy of the homiliary of Paul the Deacon since Smetana was able to show that many of the patristic homilies on which Ælfric drew were conveniently gathered together in Paul the Deacon's great homiletic florilegium.[19] This was commissioned by Charlemagne himself and became one of the most influential (and in the long run most augmented) of the medieval Latin homiliaries. Paul brought together a compilation of mostly whole texts; that is, whole homilies by Augustine, Gregory, Bede, and others, though some items within the collection are in fact appropriate extracts from other works by such authors, presented as if they are homilies on the prescribed lection for the day. It is a rich resource, even in its unaugmented form: the homilies are arranged (as are those of Smaragdus and Haymo) according to the liturgical year, and the rubric of each identifies the author. In the case of Smaragdus and Haymo, each individual item within the homiliary was a composition unique to them (despite their derivative nature). In the case of Paul the Deacon, by contrast, each item was as the named author in the rubric had written it. Paul's position vis-à-vis his

---

17   *Ælfric's Catholic Homilies. The First Series*, 241 (homily 8) and 470 (homily 34).
18   Joyce Hill, 'Ælfric and Haymo Revisited', in *Intertexts: Studies in Anglo-Saxon Culture Presented to Paul E. Szarmach*, ed. Virginia Blanton and Helene Scheck, Arizona Studies in the Middle Ages and the Renaissance 24 (Tempe AZ, 2008), 331–47.
19   Cyril L. Smetana, 'Aelfric and the Early Medieval Homiliary', *Traditio* 15 (1959), 163–204. There are no extant copies of the complete homiliary of Paul the Deacon as originally issued, and Smetana's summary of its contents was therefore dependent on a nineteenth-century reconstruction. This has now been superseded by that of Réginald Grégoire, *Homéliaires liturgiques médiévaux: analyse des manuscrits*, Biblioteca degli Studi Medievali 12 (Spoleto, 1980), 423–479. All references to the contents of Paul's homiliary in this paper are based on Grégoire's research.

compilatio was thus different from that of Smaragdus and Haymo with respect to their homiliaries, and this was reflected in what happened to the manuscript transmission. In the case of Paul the Deacon, the preliminary material which showed that he was responsible for the compilation was quickly dropped and the collection, as an anthology of discrete items, soon began to be freely augmented. In the case of the homiliaries Smaragdus and Haymo by contrast, their names continued to be preserved within the manuscript tradition because the items were uniquely theirs. Ælfric's copies of these two homiliaries evidently followed the usual manuscript tradition in each case, identifying them as the authors, since he could otherwise not have named them in the letter to Sigeric, but it is more than likely that his manuscript of Paul the Deacon's homiliary did not name that collection's compiler.[20] In any case, even if it did name Paul, as an anthology what mattered was not who had put it together but what was in it; hence, the names of Augustine, Jerome, Bede, and Gregory in the letter to Sigeric. So, to repeat, but with greater confidence because we now understand what lies beyond the obvious: what Ælfric was setting out to do in this letter was to identify his authoritative orthodoxy with reference to the patristic tradition but also to signal his place within the contemporary reform. We may furthermore deduce, on the basis of what Smetana revealed, that the *Catholic Homilies*, which are themselves a *compilatio* and at the level of the individual homily sometimes also a *catena* in the Carolingian tradition, are thus built upon the foundation of three homiliary manuscripts: those of Paul the Deacon (probably what Ælfric primarily had in mind in the initial listing of Augustine, Jerome, Bede, and Gregory in the letter to Sigeric), Smaragdus, and Haymo. This was by no means the only occasion when Ælfric made use of intermediary compilations as his immediate sources. That he did so several times throughout his career tells us something about the practical impetus to his work and about his relatively modest library resources. For us, as modern scholars, this intermediate transmission complicates source study. But by working with these intermediate texts, and only by working with these, we are enabled to appreciate Ælfric's mode of composition and his unique place within a long and honourable intertextual tradition, which was otherwise wholly in Latin.

Ælfric's use of the authority of Bede can be exploited as a means of exploring some of the issues that arise when we consider Ælfric's source texts. As we have seen from the letter to Sigeric, Bede counts as a patristic authority, and this is indeed how he is used within the homilies themselves. Bede is frequently named as the validating interpreter within Ælfric's homiletic exegeses, in just the same way as the Church Fathers themselves: he clearly carries the same weight, and no explanation is required. In addition, there are several other homilies where Bede is actually used without being named – if, that is, we identify sources primarily

---

[20] On the nature of Ælfric's copy of this homiliary, see Joyce Hill, 'Ælfric's Manuscript of Paul the Deacon's Homiliary: A Provisional Analysis', in *The Old English Homily: Precedent, Practice, and Appropriation*, ed. Aaron J. Kleist, Studies in the Early Middle Ages 17 (Turnhout, 2007), 67–96.

in relation to the discrete authorial texts. This is what modern scholarship tends to do when quoting textual parallels, even though it might be noted in passing elsewhere that the material could have been accessed by other means. This is in fact how Godden proceeds in his *Introduction, Commentary and Glossary* to Ælfric's *Catholic Homilies*, and it results in a summary of his analyses in the introduction which includes a list of those *Catholic Homilies* that make use of Bede's Commentaries on Mark and Luke and the Acts of the Apostles, and Bede's Homilies.[21] Similar information is presented in Michael Lapidge's study of *The Anglo-Saxon Library*, seemingly supported by the apparent specificity of Ælfric's homily numbers and line references within the homilies.[22]

The unwary, or those searching for accessible information about books available in Anglo-Saxon England, perhaps coming at the material from an allied discipline and seeking out identified facts, might well take this information at face-value. After all, what they say is correct: Ælfric does draw upon Bede's Commentaries on Mark and Luke and Acts and on Bede's Homilies. But there is a problem if one is interested in knowing what Ælfric's actual library was like (as opposed to the identification of his ultimate sources); if one is interested in thinking about the practical circumstances under which he worked; if one is interested in analysing how he worked; and if one wants to understand why he might have made the choices that he did. These, of course, are all fundamental and legitimate questions. So we should want to be able to come to terms with them, if we are fortunate enough to have the materials that allow us to do so. In Ælfric's case, we do. But in order to travel down these paths of exploration and analysis, we have to move beyond the obvious, beyond information drawn from the identification of Ælfric's ultimate sources.

Godden list of Ælfric's use of Bede's *temporale* homilies is as follows:[23]

> Hom. I.3: I.13
> Hom. I.4: I.13
> Hom. I.6: I.2
> Hom. I.7: I.2
> Hom. I.9: I.4 and 37.245–9
> Hom. I.10: I.5

---

[21]   Malcolm Godden, *Ælfric's Catholic Homilies: Introduction, Commentary and Glossary*. Early English Text Society, suppl. ser. 18 (Oxford, 2000), l–li, for the summary of Ælfric's use of works by Bede. The same reliance on the evidence of ultimate sources informs Godden's article, 'Ælfric's Library', in *The Cambridge History of the Book in Britain: Volume I c. 400–1100*, ed. Richard Gameson, (Cambridge, 2012), 679–84.

[22]   Michael Lapidge, *The Anglo-Saxon Library* (Oxford, 2006), 255–256.

[23]   In Godden's list, *Ælfric's Catholic Homilies: Introduction, Commentary and Glossary*, li, Bede's homilies are identified on the left by their numbers in *Bedae Venerabilis Opera: Pars III Opera Homiletica: Homeliarum Evangelii Libri II*, ed. D. Hurst, *CCSL* 122 (Turnhout, 1955), 1–378. Godden's reference to PDM at one point in the list is to the heavily augmented homiliary of Paul the Deacon edited by Migne in *PL* 95 cols. 1159–1566. This reproduces an edition published in Cologne in 1539 and presents a much later development of the homiliary than is appropriate as a reference point for the later Anglo-Saxon period: see 'Ælfric's Manuscript of Paul the Deacon's Homiliary', 68.

Hom. I.11: I.6
Hom. I.12: II.3
Hom. I.13: I.27 (?)
Hom. I.14: II.4
Hom. I.18: I.9
Hom. I.20: I.26
Hom. I.21: II.32
Hom. II.2: I.12
Hom. II.3: I.14
Hom. II.5: II.15 faint and doubtful
Hom. II.7: I.15
Hom. II.9: I.21
Hom. II.16: I .22 (?)
Hom. II.17: I .22 (very doubtful)
Hom. II.18: II.24
Hom. II.19: I.25 faint but possible
Hom. II.20: I.25 probable
Hom. II.21: II.27 and II.37 (possible detail; in PDM)
Hom. II.23: I.32
Hom. II.24: II.40

Here, it is important to notice that the only Bedan homilies listed which are not in Paul the Deacon's original homiliary are homilies I.6, I.13, II.7 and II.21, and if one turns to Godden's actual analyses of the *Catholic Homilies* with which they are paired in the list, it is immediately apparent that none of these is identified as providing Ælfric with a major source for the homily in question. It is thus the case that all the Bedan homilies which are shown by Godden in his detailed analyses to be major sources for particular Ælfrician items are in Paul the Deacon's collection, and so are nearly all of the other Bedan homilies listed as sources. Of the four Bedan homilies listed by Godden which are not in the original homiliary of Paul the Deacon as reconstructed by Grégoire,[24] Bede Homily I.13 and Bede Homily II.21 are not given as sources by Godden with any confidence. For Bede Homily I.13 this is signalled in the summary list by a question mark, as evident above, and it is borne out in the detailed analysis of *CH I.*27, where the only Bedan citation is in reference to Ælfric's brief statement at lines 176–177 that 'ða apostoli 7 ealle þa gecorenan. þe him geefenlæhton beoð deman. on þam micclum dæge mide criste', ' the Apostles and all the chosen who were equal with them will be judges with Christ on the Great Day [i.e. the Day of Judgement]'.[25] However, the sentence from Bede's Homily I.13 is offered by Godden simply as a parallel ('Cf.'). Furthermore, it is not especially close to Ælfric's wording, and Ælfric's brief statement, if indeed it needs a specific source at all, could have been prompted by the source-text that he immediately goes on to use, as the following source quotation in Godden's

24 *Homéliaires liturgiques médiévaux*, 423–479.
25 *Ælfric's Catholic Homilies. The First Series*, 406. For Godden's comment on the possible use of Bede, see *Ælfric's Catholic Homilies: Introduction, Commentary and Glossary*, 221–229 at 227.

analysis indicates. Ælfric's use of Bede's Homily II.21 in *CH II*.27 is given in Godden's summary without qualification (the bracketed qualification being in respect of *CH II*.37 only). But in fact the detailed analysis presents an entirely different picture. The only reference to Bede's homily is in connection with Ælfric's passing reference to Christ's special connection with James, John, and Peter at the opening of his homily. Godden notes 'A source for the idea of Christ's special concern with James, John and Peter is scarcely needed, but there is a close parallel in the Bede homily on Mt 20.20–23 (Hom. II.21, 48–51)'.[26] In a highly intertextual tradition, such a 'parallel', which Godden notes is in any case 'scarcely needed', does not demonstrate that Bede II.21 was used at this point: Ælfric would inevitably have been familiar with this well established idea and so could easily have referred to it on his own account. The other two Bedan homilies not in Paul's original *compilatio*, homilies I.6 and II.7, are included in Godden's summary list without qualification, and both homilies are quoted in his detailed analyses as significant sources for *CH I*.2 and *CH I*.15 respectively.[27] But in fact Ælfric had no need to use either of them. The details from Bede's homily I.6 which are cited in Godden's analysis are also to be found in Bede's Commentary on Luke, and this was available to Ælfric as a convenient and liturgically rubricated extract in the homiliary of Smaragdus, so that Bede's homily was not in fact required, nor even recourse to Bede's Commentary on Luke as a discrete work.[28] Likewise, Ælfric did not need to turn to Bede's homily II.7 either, because for all the Bede homily material that Godden cites as Ælfric's source, there is an equally close or closer source in Smaragdus's homiliary, where Smaragdus had used the appropriate extract of Bede's Commentary on Mark, suitably liturgically rubricated, making it easy for Ælfric to cross refer.[29]

Thus, despite the convenience of an apparently definitive list provided by Godden, there is no firm evidence from the *Catholic Homilies* as originally issued that Ælfric actually drew on anything outside his homiliaries of Paul the Deacon and Smaragdus when it came to using what Godden identifies here as the homilies of Bede. That does not in any way diminish the status of Bede as an authority within

---

[26] *Ælfric's Catholic Homilies: Introduction, Commentary and Glossary*, 575–582 at 577.
[27] *Ælfric's Catholic Homilies: Introduction, Commentary and Glossary*, 13–21 and 119–127.
[28] *PL* 102, cols. 23–27. As Rädle points out, *Studien zu Smaragd*, 215, Smaragdus supplemented Bede with etymologies drawn from Jerome. Bede is several times identified by Smaragdus as his authority by means of marginal annotations (expanded and inserted into the body of the text in *PL*), but two passages are attributed to Gregory. However, this does not indicate that there is a change of source text: they simply repeat marginal attributions present in the Bedan text: see *PL* 102, col. 24B compared with *Bedae Venerabilis Opera: Pars II. 3: In Lucae Evangelium Expositio*, ed. D. Hurst, CCSL 120, 48, line 1153, and *PL* 102, col. 25C compared with *In Lucae Evangelium Expositio*, 50, line 1242. Godden's analysis of Ælfric's homily includes citations from Gregory's homily as well as that of Bede, creating the impression that Ælfric may have drawn upon Gregory directly. But in fact Bede, in his Commentary, drew on Gregory, Smaragdus drew on Bede, and Ælfric drew on Smaragdus.
[29] *PL* 102, cols. 225–227. For Smaragdus's use of Bede's Commentary, see Rädle *Studien zu Smaragd*, 214.

the Benedictine Reform tradition, nor the particular importance and usefulness of his homilies for Ælfric. But it does tell us something very valuable about the practicalities of Ælfric's working methods, and it is significant in alerting us to the fact that his library was not as large as we might suppose, if we simply make deductions from source studies which prioritize the ultimate, discrete texts.

Yet the unwary or uninitiated, to whom I have already referred, could easily be misled by Godden's apparently helpful list, and even more by Lapidge's catalogue for Ælfric in *The Anglo-Saxon Library*. Lapidge does not list Bede's Homily II.17, which Godden's summary list notes as being 'very doubtful' as a source. But all of the other Bedan homily items in Godden's list are in Lapidge, without any indication that Ælfric had access to any of these homilies by means other than direct access.[30] Paul the Deacon appears in Lapidge's catalogue for Ælfric only in connection with Ælfric's homily on Gregory the Great, but the work in question here is Paul's *Vita Gregorii*, not his homiliary.[31] Yet we know Ælfric had access to the narrative on Gregory through a *compilatio* of saints' lives, known to modern scholars as the Cotton-Corpus Legendary, so it is inherently unlikely that he consulted Paul's *Vita Gregorii* as a discrete work.[32] This means that anyone relying on Lapidge's book for a sense of Ælfric's library – and thus by implication of his working methods – will not find in it any reference to one of his most heavily used items (i.e. the homiliary of Paul the Deacon, which gave him access to the homilies by Bede that he can be shown to have drawn upon), but will find in it a reference to a work that he almost certainly did not use independently (i.e. Paul the Deacon's *Vita Gregorii*). It is a salutary reminder of the risks that one runs in taking lists at face-value.

The situation is similar when we consider Ælfric's use of Bede's influential Commentaries on Luke and Mark, and his Commentary on Acts. Godden lists eight homilies in the First Series and six in the Second Series where source analysis indicates use of Bede's Commentary on Luke: *CH I*. 2, 9, 11, 13, 14, 21, 33, 40 and *CH II*. 5.140–142, 6, 14, 16, 28, 31.[33] But he notes that for *CH I*.33, *CH II*.28 and *CH II*.31 the relevant excerpts from the commentary were in Paul the Deacon's homiliary, and that the other parallels are slight or are in Smaragdus or Haymo 'in similar form'. There is consequently no sound evidence from the *Catholic Homilies* that Ælfric, at this point in his career, had access to this Commentary independently of its extracts in his source homiliaries, and indeed it would have been easier for Ælfric to draw this material from his homiliaries,

30 *The Anglo-Saxon Library*, 255–256.
31 *The Anglo-Saxon Library*, 263.
32 Peter Jackson and Michael Lapidge, 'The Contents of the Cotton-Corpus Legendary', in *Holy Men and Holy Women: Old English Prose Saints' Lives and their Contexts*, ed. Paul E. Szarmach (Albany NY, 1996), 131–46. Paul's *Vita Gregorii* is item 39. Ælfric's extensive use of the Cotton Corpus legendary was demonstrated by Patrick H. Zettel, 'Ælfric's Hagiographic Sources and the Latin Legendary Preserved in B.L. MS Cotton Nero E. i. + CCCC MS 9 and other Manuscripts', unpublished D. Phil. diss. (Oxford University, 1979), and 'Saints' Lives in Old English: Latin Manuscripts and Vernacular Accounts: Ælfric', *Peritia* 1 (1982), 17–37.
33 *Ælfric's Catholic Homilies: Introduction, Commentary and Glossary*, l.

where the relevant passages for the explication of the lection were appropriately selected and rubricated, than to consult the commentary directly, even if it were available. Godden himself expresses uncertainty about whether Ælfric used Bede's work directly, even while offering the summary list. Yet these references are all in Lapidge's catalogue of Ælfric's library, which thus gives the impression that he did have independent access to Bede's Commentary on Luke.[34]

For Bede's Commentary on Mark, Godden has five Ælfrician homilies which seem to show some usage: *CH I*. 34 and *CH II*. 14, 23, 24, 25. But he notes that the material used in *CH II*. 24 and *CH II*. 25 was available in extracted form in Paul the Deacon's homiliary and that the material used in *CH I*. 34 was available in Smaragdus. He is doubtful about the usage in *CH II*. 14, describing it as 'slight', which is a problem in an intertextual tradition. But he states that *CH II*. 23 'seems to show direct use of the commentary'.[35] This is not so, however, because in this homily, where Ælfric acknowledges Gregory as his main source,[36] the Bedan influence that Godden identifies can readily be accounted for by reference to Smaragdus's homiliary, where the homily for the day (the Third Sunday after Pentecost, the same day for which Ælfric's was writing his homily) is in fact an extract from Bede's Commentary on Luke (not Mark), which is reasonable enough since the day's lection is Luke 14.16–24.[37] The close analysis needed to demonstrate the complex intertextual relationships between Gregory's homily, Bede's Commentary on Luke, and Smaragdus's homily (drawn from Bede, not Gregory, *pace* Godden)[38] has been carried out elsewhere and led me to the conclusion that Ælfric's immediate source text for this homily was Smaragdus, who extracted the relevant passage from Bede's Commentary on Luke, who in turn depended at this point entirely on Gregory's homily, which he abbreviated.[39] That Ælfric was able to name Gregory as his authority for the interpretation is because this was the attribution in the margins of his copy of Smaragdus. Again, then, there is no evidence from the *Catholic Homilies* that Ælfric needed to look beyond his source homiliaries. By now, it will come as no surprise that, despite this, Bede's Commentary on Mark figures in Lapidge's catalogue of Ælfric's library, where he gives as evidence all the instances listed by Godden.[40]

---

34   *The Anglo-Saxon Library*, 256.
35   *Ælfric's Catholic Homilies: Introduction, Commentary and Glossary*, l.
36   *Ælfric's Catholic Homilies. The Second Series*, 213, line 21.
37   *PL* 102 cols. 355–358.
38   In his full analysis of this homily, *Ælfric's Catholic Homilies: Introduction, Commentary and Glossary*, 549–555, Godden states that Smaragdus's homily 'is primarily a condensation of Gregory's' (549), not recognizing that Smaragdus was in fact drawing upon Bede's Commentary on Luke, as noted by Rädle, *Studien zu Smaragd*, 214, and that it was Bede who adapted Gregory's homily, as Hurst's edition of *In Lucae Evangelium Expositio* shows, 278, source note to lines 1902–2023. Godden's confusion about Smaragdus's source is further compounded by the later assertion (550) that 'Bede's commentary on Mark is used by Smaragdus in his homily'.
39   'Ælfric's sources reconsidered', 372–377.
40   *The Anglo-Saxon Library*, 256.

I turn now to an apparent instance of Ælfric's use of Bede's Commentary on the Acts of the Apostles in order to demonstrate how Ælfric might have worked in this kind of textual arena. Godden is confident that Ælfric used Bede's Commentary on Acts in *Catholic Homily* I.21.[41] But this was not the only source that Ælfric used. According to Godden he also used Bede's Commentary on Luke and, as his major source, a homily of Gregory the Great.[42] Gregory's homily was available to Ælfric in the homiliary of Paul the Deacon, where the rubric gave Ælfric Gregory's name, and so allowed him to cite Gregory within the homily as his authority.[43] But in this homily, which is a complex *catena*, Ælfric appears to have supplemented the Gregorian material with material drawn from Bede on Luke and Bede on Acts (there are other possible sources authorities within this homiletic *catena*, but I am here focusing on the Bedan material). This supplementation from Bede on Luke and on Acts seems reasonable because the day in question is Ascension Day, for which the New Testament has more than one account. Ælfric first deals with the fullest account, that in Acts (the epistle for the day), but when paraphrasing this in the homily, he draws in supplementary detail from Luke, probably from memory; and he then moves on to the alternative account in Mark, which is the gospel for the day. It is the Mark account on which Gregory's homily is based, and so Ælfric's use of Gregory is concentrated in the second part of his homily. Now, Ælfric was working to the liturgical cycle. He would have known what the gospel and epistle lections were and he would, one imagines, have looked up what his homiliaries had to offer for Ascension Day. In Paul the Deacon's homiliary he would have found Gregory's homily on the day's gospel (the Mark account). So far so good. But he would have known that there is a parallel account of the ascension in Luke and a far more detailed account in Acts. So, in composing a homily for Ascension Day, Ælfric might well have thought it worthwhile to start with the account in Acts (the day's epistle). But since, for the Feast of the Ascension, the homiliary of Paul the Deacon offered only Gregory on Mark (the day's gospel), it would have been natural for Ælfric to see what his other homiliaries had to offer. It was Smaragdus who supplied something useful: an extract from Bede's Commentary on Acts serving as a homily on the fullest account of the Ascension.[44] The homiliaries of Paul and Deacon and Smaragdus thus provided authoritative sources for the explication of the gospel and the epistle respectively. Furthermore, if – as Godden shows was the case – Ælfric decided to deal with what preceded the ascension, as narrated in Luke 24. 36–47, he would have found that in Smaragdus's homiliary

---

[41] *Ælfric's Catholic Homilies: Introduction, Commentary and Glossary*, 1. This is the only use of Bede's Commentary on Acts about which Godden is confident. He is very tentative about the others homilies: 'possibly details in I.20, II.14 and II.24'.

[42] For Godden's detailed analysis of the sources for this complex homily, see *Ælfric's Catholic Homilies: Introduction, Commentary and Glossary*, 166–175.

[43] *Ælfric's Catholic Homilies. The First Series*, 345–353. Gregory is named at line 110.

[44] *PL* 102, cols. 308–310. Smaragdus's source is identified by Rädle, *Studien zu Smaragd*, 219.

also, where the treatment of this gospel reading was yet another an extract from Bede's Commentary on Luke.[45] It was the reading for the Tuesday of Easter Week, but Ælfric would of course have known that; and since he had not at that stage written – and did not ever write – a homily for the Tuesday of Easter Week, it was available for him to exploit. What, then, do we suppose that Ælfric did? Did he draw upon Gregory's homily from the homiliary of Paul the Deacon and then, notwithstanding the wonderful convenience of what he had in Smaragdus, search in other books for passages from Bede's Commentaries on Acts and Luke for supplementation, always supposing that they were available in his monastery at Cerne Abbas? In considering the likelihood of this option, it is important to bear in mind that the material in discrete copies of the commentaries is not preselected and not liturgically rubricated, so is not amenable to rapid cross-reference. Or did Ælfric work with two of his three readily accessible homiliaries within a liturgical framework of prescribed and familiar lections? I think I know which one is the more likely scenario. But that recognition of how Ælfric worked is not open to us unless we move beyond the obvious and consider how he had access to his material.

It was particularly easy to read across between the two homiliaries of Smaragdus and Paul the Deacon, as I have here suggested he did for his Ascension Day homily, because he was using the same lectionary as they were, and because both of these homiliaries signal their patristic authorities: Paul's homiliary in the rubrics, and Smaragdus's in marginal letter abbreviations. But it is possible to take a further step beyond the obvious, and think about what, in practical terms, drove the borrowing. As we can see from Grégoire's reconstruction, most of the Bedan material in Paul's homiliary is from Bede's homily collection.[46] These homilies overlap in content and often in phraseology with his Commentaries on Mark and Luke, but whereas the Commentaries move systematically through the New Testament sentences, the homilies range more freely. The differences are comparable to those between Augustine's sweeping homilies, and his more methodical commentary, his Tractates on John's Gospel. In composing his homiliary, Smaragdus made heavy use of Bede's Commentaries for his homilies on Mark, Luke, and Acts and Augustine's systematic Tractates for his Johannine lections.[47] For Matthew, where commentary material of this systematic kind was not so readily available, Smaragdus created complex *catenae*, but with a heavy input from Bede's commentaries, taking full advantage of the overlap between the three synoptic gospels, which often allowed the commentary on Mark or Luke to be exploited to elucidate a lection from Matthew. Rädle's source analysis of Smaragdus's homilies on Matthean lections show that occasional details from the homilies seem to be present, but these instances are rare, and they

---

45   *PL* 102, cols. 237–241. Smaragdus's source is identified by Rädle, *Studien zu Smaragd*, 215.
46   Grégoire, *Homéliaires liturgiques médiévaux*, 430–478.
47   Smaragdus's sources for homilies on lections from these books are analysed by Rädle, *Studien zu Smaragd*, 213–220.

represent the only use of Bede's homilies by Smaragdus.[48] In terms of the Bedan material, then, the homiliaries of Paul the Deacon and Smaragdus offered Ælfric complementary material, a complementarity that is likewise evident in their different balances of choice as between Augustine's homilies (favoured by Paul) and Augustine's Tractates (favoured by Smaragdus). So this was a useful bonus for Ælfric when reading across from one to the other, presumably as he had them both open in front of him. But it is notable that, whereas Ælfric uses Bedan homilies many times as his major source, the commentary material (through Smaragdus or Paul the Deacon, as we have seen) most usually functions as supplementation; and there are no instances where a Bedan Commentary (via Smaragdus or Paul the Deacon) forms the main source and is supplemented by elements from a Bedan homily. This is an observation that has not been made before. Having considered its implications carefully, my conclusion is that it was easier to pick out supplementary information from the systematic commentary material than from the more wide-ranging and rhetorically ambitious homilies. It was much easier to spot, extract, and so incorporate details from the commentary structure than from the homiletic. I admit that this notion of the practicalities of borrowing to create a *catena* is conjectural, but I think it is worth considering as a further insight into the way Ælfric worked. Beyond the obvious yet again.

Source study is a vital tool in coming to terms with the intellectual context of the early Middle Ages. But there are, as I hope I have shown, hidden dangers and serious limitations in the way we prioritize ultimate sources in presenting our evidence. The challenge now is to look beyond the obvious – by which I mean beyond the identification of what the sources are in terms that make sense to us with our modern libraries – and to think about how our medieval author had access to this material, how he worked with it, and why. In Ælfric's case we can develop a clearer understanding of his impetus, which was practical rather than scholarly; we can understand how he coped with the limitation of his library in Cerne Abbas (although he might well have proceeded in the same way, had he still been at Winchester, given what he was trying to achieve); and there are clues to his manner of composition. But none of this is apparent unless we look beyond the obvious. My example of Ælfric's interaction with the authority of Bede in his First and Second Series of *Catholic Homilies* is a means of uncovering and exploring some of these issues.

---

[48] Smaragdus's sources for homilies on lections from Matthew are analysed by Rädle, *Studien zu Smaragd*, 203–213.

4

Byrhtferth's *Historia regum* and the Transformation of the Alfredian Past[*]

Katherine Cross

In his comparison of Alfred the Great and Æthelred the Unready, Simon Keynes argued that the contrast in the two kings' reputations developed primarily from the different types of narrative sources for their reigns.[1] He raised the question of whether such comparisons were ever made during Æthelred's reign, especially since interest in Alfred seems to have been growing during this period. Keynes suggested in a footnote that an investigation of the use of Asser's *Life of Alfred* in Byrhtferth of Ramsey's *Historia regum* would give us some idea of Alfred's reputation during Æthelred's reign.[2] This article takes up Keynes's suggestion, and argues that Byrhtferth's history of Alfred's reign was shaped by just such a comparison with the contemporary situation and the actions of the current king.

The *Historia regum* thus provides us with another example of political opinion during Æthelred's reign, to place alongside the homiletic writings of Ælfric and Wulfstan, a substantial body of royal diplomas, and vernacular literature such as the *Battle of Maldon*. Since the Anglo-Saxon Chronicle for this period was written after Cnut's conquest, its criticisms of Æthelred's actions against the Danes are coloured by the knowledge of their ultimate failure.[3] These texts written during Æthelred's reign provide a contemporary perspective on his actions and reveal the wider range of opinion which Æthelred encountered.

Byrhtferth's *Historia regum* now forms the first part of Symeon of Durham's *Historia de regibus Anglorum et Dacorum* – itself often called the *Historia regum* – which covers folios 52r–129v of Cambridge, Corpus Christi College

[*]   I would like to thank Antonio Sennis and Susan Irvine for their comments on an earlier version of this paper.
[1]   S. Keynes, 'A Tale of Two Kings: Alfred the Great and Æthelred the Unready', *Transactions of the Royal Historical Society* 5th ser., 36 (1986), 195–217.
[2]   Keynes, 'A Tale of Two Kings', 217, note 78.
[3]   S. Keynes, 'The Declining Reputation of King Æthelred the Unready', in *Anglo-Saxon History: Basic Readings*, ed. D.A.E. Pelteret (London, 2000), 157–90, at 157–166.

MS 139.[4] The manuscript, dating from the 1160s, is a historical collection of primarily (but not exclusively) northern English interest.[5] Since Symeon's *Historia de regibus* was edited by Thomas Arnold in the nineteenth century, folios 52r–75r of the manuscript have been recognized as forming a separate, probably tenth-century, composition.[6] These folios contain a history covering the years 616 to 887, which Symeon copied, augmented, and used as the beginning of his own history, which extends to 1129.[7] Hunter Blair's detailed analysis firmly established that the beginning of the *Historia de regibus* to 887 was the work of one author.[8] It has now been over thirty years since Michael Lapidge and Cyril Hart both demonstrated, independently and conclusively, that this tenth-century core was the work of Byrhtferth of Ramsey, through various features found also in his other writings.[9] Michael Lapidge and David Rollason's forthcoming edition of Symeon's *Historia de regibus* will further illuminate the relationship between Byrhtferth's and Symeon's histories.[10] Following the conventions of this edition, this article calls Byrhtferth's original text '*Historia regum*', and Symeon of Durham's compilation '*Historia de regibus Anglorum et Dacorum*', the title in CCCC 139's rubric.

We know of Byrhtferth's text only through Symeon's *Historia de regibus* in CCCC 139. The origin of the manuscript has been debated, but the most recent investigations seem to settle its Durham origins. An *ex libris* of Sawley abbey

---

4   The manuscript can be viewed online at http://parkerweb.stanford.edu. The *incipit* is at the bottom of fol. 51v. The foliation given here is that used in the online facsimile and catalogue (it should be noted that this differs from that given by D. Baker, note 11 below).

5   See S. MacLean, 'Recycling the Franks in Twelfth-Century England: Regino of Prüm, the Monks of Durham, and the Alexandrine Schism', *Speculum* 87 (2012), 649–81, and note 11 below.

6   M. Lapidge, 'Byrhtferth of Ramsey and the early sections of the *Historia Regum* attributed to Symeon of Durham', *ASE* 10 (1981), 97–122, at 97; *Symeonis Monachis Opera Omnia*, ed. T. Arnold, RS 75, 2 vols. (London, 1885), II, xvii–xxv.

7   1129 is considered to be the date of Symeon's death, one of several arguments linking him to the composition of the *Historia de regibus*. Symeon's authorship of the work has often been questioned, but further investigations have led back to this attribution: D. Rollason, 'Symeon's Contribution to Historical Writing in Northern England', in *Symeon of Durham. Historian of Durham and the North*, ed. D. Rollason (Stamford, 1998), 1–13, at 5–6, 10; and J. Story, 'Symeon as Annalist', in *Symeon of Durham*, ed. Rollason, 202–15, at 212–213.

8   P. Hunter Blair, 'Some Observations on the "Historia Regum" Attributed to Symeon of Durham', in *Celt and Saxon: Studies in the Early British Border*, ed. N.K. Chadwick (Cambridge, 1963), 63–118. The five sections he identified as comprising this beginning correspond to the four outlined below (see note 22; the second item, below, appears as two separate items in his article). In giving four sections, I follow *Byrhtferth of Ramsey. The Lives of St Oswald and St Ecgwine*, ed. M. Lapidge (Oxford, 2009), xli.

9   Lapidge, 'Byrhtferth of Ramsey'; C. Hart, 'Byrhtferth's Northumbrian Chronicle', *EHR* 97 (1982), 558–82.

10   *Symeon of Durham: Historia de regibus Anglorum et Dacorum, incorporating Byrhtferth of Ramsey, Historia regum, with John of Hexham, Historia xxv annorum, and Anonymous, De obsessione Dunelmi et de probitate Uhtredi comitis, et de comitibus qui ei successerunt, and De primo Saxonum aduentu siue de eorundem regibus*, ed. M. Lapidge and D. Rollason, Oxford Medieval Texts (Oxford, forthcoming).

indicates that the manuscript was later passed to the library there.[11] It is unclear how and at what point Byrhtferth's text travelled from Ramsey to Durham, although it is noteworthy that Byrhtferth did have access to northern source materials: the *Historia regum* includes a list of Northumbrian kings, and much of it is based on a series of Northern Annals.[12] While his use of these sources hints at a northern connection, the circumstances of the *Historia*'s intermediate transmission between Byrhtferth and Symeon remain obscure.[13]

For Lapidge and Hart, the significance of the authorial attribution was to establish Byrhtferth as a prolific and 'major figure in Anglo-Saxon literary culture'.[14] A monk of Ramsey abbey in Huntingdonshire near Ely, Byrhtferth wrote between *c.* 986 and 1020.[15] It is now clear that he produced a substantial corpus of works during that time, including his own Latin computistical work, and later a bilingual handbook, the *Enchiridion,* which identify him as author in the texts and manuscript rubrics. This scientific interest was matched by Byrhtferth's production of hagiographical narrative texts, the *Vita Sancti Oswaldi* and the *Vita Sancti Ecgwini.*[16] Read alongside these works, the *Historia regum* increases our knowledge of Byrhtferth as a scholar and of the state of learning in this period. But the *Historia regum* is also an intriguing historical document that reveals much about late Anglo-Saxon political culture, especially through its view of the viking past.

[11]   The Durham origin of CCCC MS 139 is demonstrated by C. Norton, 'History, Wisdom and Illumination', in *Symeon of Durham,* ed. Rollason, 61–105 (esp. 87, 101); Story, 'Symeon as Annalist', 211–215; and B. Meehan, 'Durham Twelfth-Century Manuscripts in Cistercian Houses', in *Anglo-Norman Durham: 1093–1193,* ed. D. Rollason et al. (Woodbridge, 1994), 439–49; MacLean, 'Recycling the Franks', 652. Previously, Blair, 'Some Observations', proposed Sawley as the origin of the manuscript, an identification upheld in D.N. Dumville, 'The Sixteenth-Century History of Two Cambridge Books from Sawley', *Transactions of the Cambridge Bibliographical Society* 7 (1977–80), 427–44, repr. in D.N. Dumville, *Histories and Pseudo-Histories of the Insular Middle Ages* (Aldershot, 1990); M.R. James, *Catalogue of the Manuscripts of Corpus Christi College* (Cambridge, 1912), 323, ascribed the manuscript to Hexham, an attribution investigated further by H.S. Offler, 'Hexham and the *Historia Regum*', *Transactions of the Architectural and Archaeological Society of Durham and Northumberland* n.s., 2 (1970), 51–62; D. Baker, 'Scissors and Paste: Corpus Christi, Cambridge, MS 139 Again', in *The Materials, Sources and Methods of Ecclesiastical History,* ed. D. Baker, Studies in Church History 11 (Oxford, 1975), 83–123, claimed an origin at Fountains Abbey.

[12]   D. Rollason, 'Northern Annals', in *The Blackwell Encyclopaedia of Anglo-Saxon England,* ed. M. Lapidge, J. Blair, S. Keynes and D. Scragg (Oxford, 1999), 333–34, discusses the source of these annals.

[13]   D. Rollason, 'Symeon of Durham's *Historia de Regibus Anglorum et Dacorum* as a Product of Twelfth-Century Historical Workshops', in *The Long Twelfth-Century View of the Anglo-Saxon Past,* ed. M. Brett and D.A. Woodman (Aldershot, 2015), 95–111, at 110, suggests possible opportunities for the text's transmission.

[14]   Lapidge, 'Byrhtferth of Ramsey', 122.

[15]   M. Lapidge, 'Byrhtferth of Ramsey *(fl. c.*986–*c.*1016)', *Oxford Dictionary of National Biography,* Oxford University Press, 2004 [http://www.oxforddnb.com/view/article/4268, accessed 15 Dec 2014].

[16]   *Byrhtferth's Enchiridion,* ed. P. Baker and M. Lapidge (Oxford, 1995); *Byrhtferth of Ramsey,* ed. Lapidge.

A close focus on the text and its process of composition reveals a new take on the ninth-century viking wars that seems to respond to the political context in which it was written. At present we cannot confirm the date of the *Historia regum* any more precisely than the period in which Byrhtferth was active (*c.* 986–1020).[17] However, the *passio* of two seventh-century Kentish princes, St Æthelberht and St Æthelred, which forms the opening to the work, allows us to suggest a narrower time span for the *Historia regum*'s composition. Byrhtferth seems to have written the *passio* on the occasion of the saints' translation to Ramsey abbey, which took place sometime between 978 and 992, probably in 991, and later used it in his history. It is therefore likely that Byrhtferth completed the *Historia regum* sometime after the 991 translation.[18] Given the materials available for Byrhtferth to use, it is likely that he worked on it while still at Ramsey, which he probably left for Evesham after 1016.[19] Thus Byrhtferth composed his history during precisely the period in which England suffered a new wave of viking activity which led to the eventual conquest by Cnut in 1016. To a certain extent, therefore, Byrhtferth's account of Alfred's viking wars may be interpreted as a response to the renewed viking threat.

In this context, Byrhtferth's authorial decisions created a politicized historical narrative. Among his contemporary writers, the rhetoric of English opposition to the Danes intensified as pressure from Scandinavian armies mounted.[20] Byrhtferth's history displays a similar rhetoric, but in this case projected back onto the Alfredian past. A close reading of his *Historia regum* reveals an English identity expressed in historical terms, and a demonstration of the themes deemed key to that identity's preservation. As such, it indicates the kind of opinion that may well have influenced Æthelred's actions in the final years of his reign.

Byrhtferth compiled the *Historia regum* from a diverse range of sources of a variety of genres, which were not integrated in a seamless narrative. Due to the varied nature of its constituent parts, the resulting text is not a standard history or chronicle. The sources used by Byrhtferth can be briefly summarized as follows: first, a *passio* of the murdered Kentish princes Æthelberht and Æthelred, apparently composed by Byrhtferth himself; second, a list of Northumbrian kings,[21] and a selection of material derived from Bede (extracts

---

[17]   Lapidge, 'Byrhtferth of Ramsey (*fl. c.*986–*c.*1016)', *ODNB*; *Byrhtferth of Ramsey*, ed. Lapidge, xxix.

[18]   *Chronicon Abbatiae Rameseiensis*, ed. W. Dunn Macray, RS 83 (London, 1886), 55; D. Rollason, *The Mildrith Legend. A Study in Early Medieval Hagiography in England* (Leicester, 1982), 17; *Byrhtferth of Ramsey*, ed. Lapidge, xli.

[19]   *Byrhtferth of Ramsey*, ed. Lapidge, xxix.

[20]   S. Keynes, 'An Abbot, an Archbishop, and the Viking Raids of 1006–7 and 1009–12', *ASE* 36 (2007), 151–220 (esp. 158–159).

[21]   Byrhtferth may have derived this list from a regnal list such as that found in the Moore manuscript of Bede's *Historia ecclesiastica*. However, the reign lengths he gives do not agree with any of the extant regnal lists that circulated independently, either the Moore Memoranda or those associated with the Anglian Collection of genealogies (see D.N. Dumville, 'The Anglian Collection of Royal Genealogies and Regnal Lists', *ASE* 5 (1976), 23–50, esp. 29–30, 32, 35–36).

from Bede's *Historia ecclesiastica* and *Historia abbatum*, and verses attributed to Bede, including the *Versus de dei iudicii)*; third, a series of northern annals covering the years 732 to 802, prefaced by a prayer particularly associated with Byrhtferth;[22] and fourth, Asser's *Life of Alfred.*

In this article, I focus on the fourth item, Byrhtferth's use of Asser's *Life of Alfred*. As suggested above, this section reveals a re-imagination of the First Viking Age in the context of the Second. Indeed, the ways in which Byrhtferth rewrote his source text reveal a changed perspective on the viking wars. Byrhtferth adapted the *Life of Alfred* to emphasize English unity, royal military leadership, and supernatural assistance in war.

Asser's *Life of Alfred* transformed

Asser's *Life of Alfred* constituted Byrhtferth's main, if not exclusive, source for the ninth-century conflicts with the Danes. The *Historia regum* follows the *Life of Alfred* very closely, but few passages were left unaltered. The extensive revisions made by Byrhtferth produced a text concentrated on the conflicts between Danes and English, retold in overtly religious and nationalist terms. A close comparison between Asser's *Life of Alfred* and the section of the *Historia regum* based on it reveal Byrhtferth's editorial interventions in this direction. However, the comparison is not straightforward, especially because no complete manuscript of either text survives.

Firstly, our knowledge of Byrhtferth's original *Historia regum* is imperfect. Because the tenth-century text of the *Historia regum* has only survived within Symeon's twelfth-century history, we cannot know the exact stages of transformation it underwent between its original composition and the production of the manuscript we now possess. However, the identification of the *Historia regum* as a tenth-century text and its attribution to Byrhtferth of Ramsey are based upon recurring stylistic features, 'habits of mind', and literary allusions.[23] The passages which contain these distinctive characteristics are abundant, consistent, and significant enough for a full analysis of the sections of the *Historia regum* derived from Asser's *Life*.

Secondly, Asser's *Life* now only survives in early modern editions and transcriptions of the sole known manuscript (London, British Library, Cotton MS Otho A xii), which was destroyed by fire in 1731. This manuscript apparently dated from

---

[22]   The annals in Byrhtferth's *Historia regum* are an important witness to a series of eighth-century annals kept contemporaneously in northern England: J. Story, *Carolingian Connections: Anglo-Saxon England and Carolingian Francia, c. 750–870* (Aldershot, 2003), 93–133. These annals survive in various recensions, including in the Ramsey annals: see Rollason, 'Northern Annals'. The two-line prayer at the opening of this section, taken from Arator's *De actibus apostolorum*, was also used by Byrhtferth in his *Vita Sancti Egwini* and *Enchiridion*: Lapidge, 'Byrhtferth of Ramsey', 118; Hart, 'Byrhtferth's Northumbrian Chronicle', 573.

[23]   Lapidge, 'Byrhtferth of Ramsey', 99.

around the year 1000.[24] It is therefore possible that the Cotton manuscript was available to Byrhtferth.[25] However, other variants seem to have been in circulation. In the twelfth century, Asser's *Life* was used both by John of Worcester and by the compiler of the *Annals of St Neots*, and it seems that this latter text derived from a version which differed from the Cotton manuscript in a number of places. Whitelock has shown that the manuscript used by the *Annals of St Neots* compiler was closer to Byrhtferth's source, if not the same manuscript.[26] However, the compiler of these annals edited and abbreviated the text he was using, and so they do not provide a straightforward witness to their source. Therefore, the comparison here has used Stevenson's edition of Asser's *Life*, which was based primarily on the transcripts of the Cotton manuscript. In fact, Byrhtferth's edits frequently took the form of paraphrase, and so depart substantially from the text of all witnesses to the *Life*: divergences between the *Annals of St Neots* and Stevenson's edition affect none of the examples given below.

Previous discussion of the relationship between the two texts has focused on the textual history of Asser's *Life*. Alfred Smyth made the most recent, and most assertive, case that the *Life of Alfred* was a tenth-century forgery.[27] He went on to suggest that the *Life of Alfred* itself was composed originally by Byrhtferth, who then revised it for the *Historia regum*.[28] However, Smyth's arguments did not meet with general acceptance. The most detailed refutation may be found in Simon Keynes's review of Smyth's *King Alfred the Great*.[29] Of the points made

---

[24] D. Whitelock, *The Genuine Asser. The Stenton Lecture 1967* (Reading, 1968), 17 summarizes the palaeographical reasons for this dating of the Cotton manuscript. They are based on Wanley's examinations before the manuscript's destruction, and on the 'facsimile' plate made by Wise, reproduced in *Asser's Life of King Alfred*, ed. W.H. Stevenson (Oxford, 1904; repr. 1959; hereafter Asser), opposite xxxii.

[25] Stevenson thought it likely that the *Historia regum* used this Cottonian manuscript: Asser, lix. However, Whitelock has argued that the *Historia regum* derives from a better version of the *Life*, though one which shared some errors with the Cotton manuscript: *Genuine Asser*, 18. For further details on the transcriptions and other possible witnesses to the *Life*, see Asser, xi–lxv; A. Smyth, *The Medieval Life of King Alfred the Great: A Translation and Commentary on the Text Attributed to Asser* (Basingstoke, 2002), 64–81.

[26] Whitelock, *Genuine Asser*, 18–20.

[27] A. Smyth, *King Alfred the Great* (Oxford, 1995) and Smyth, *Medieval Life of King Alfred*. Smyth was not the first to suggest that the *Life* was a later forgery. V.H. Galbraith did so in *An Introduction to the Study of History* (London, 1964), 85–128, but his argument was answered in full and shown to be untenable by Whitelock (*Genuine Asser*).

[28] Smyth, *Medieval Life of King Alfred*, esp. 206.

[29] Simon Keynes, 'On the Authenticity of Asser's *Life of King Alfred*', *Journal of Ecclesiastical History* 47 (1996), 529–51. See also Lapidge, 'A King of Monkish Fable?' *The Times Higher Education Supplement*, 8 March 1996, 20; J. Nelson, 'Waiting for Alfred', *EME* 7 (1998), 115–24. Some responses were particularly critical: D.R. Howlett, review of Smyth, *King Alfred the Great*, *EHR* 112 (1997), 942–44. Smyth did receive some positive reviews, but even these tended not to accept his conclusions about the *Life*: M. Altshul, review of Smyth, *King Alfred the Great*, *American Historical Review* 102 (1997), 1463–64; J. Campbell, 'Alfred's Lives', *Times Literary Supplement*, 26 July 1996, 30. On the composition of the *Life of Alfred* by Asser, see A. Scharer, 'The Writing of History at King Alfred's Court', *EME* 5 (1996), 177–206, at 185–206.

by Keynes, we may emphasize further that it is not possible to accept that the *Life of Alfred* and the *Historia regum* were written by the same person. The stylistic differences between Asser's text and Byrhtferth's redaction of it in the *Historia regum* have been detailed by Lapidge, who demonstrated that the qualities which identified the *Historia regum* as Byrhtferth's work are generally lacking in the *Life of Alfred*.[30] Furthermore, as Keynes indicated, the works demonstrate different views of the English past, responding to different political situations.[31] The following section of this article elucidates these differences.

We can safely attribute the majority of these changes to Byrhtferth himself, rather than an earlier or later editor. There is a clear pattern and logic to these editorial decisions throughout the work, suggesting that they were made by the same adapter. It is difficult to be certain in the case of omitted sections, since it is possible that Byrhtferth's manuscript of the *Life* did not contain all of the text found in the Cotton manuscript. However, there is no evidence that an abridgement was in circulation. The *Annals of St Neots* also contain only excerpts from the *Life*, but the omitted passages are infrequently the same as those Byrhtferth omitted; and John of Worcester omitted a different set of passages.[32] It is most likely that these omissions were made independently by Byrhtferth, by the compiler of the *Annals of St Neots*, and by John of Worcester, as Dumville suggests: all three users of Asser's *Life* had a similar aim, 'to excerpt what related directly to the narrative of English political history'.[33] Frequently, the hallmarks of Byrhtferth's style indicate that he was responsible for a certain passage. Indeed, many adaptations are primarily stylistic, as discussed in detail by Lapidge,[34] but here I shall consider more substantive changes, which generally take the form of additions and paraphrases.

These substantive changes have implications for our understanding of the development of both Alfred's and Æthelred's reputations. Byrhtferth's adaptation represents one of the earliest employments of Alfred's memory in the promotion of a contemporary political agenda. Asser's presentation of an ideal king underlies numerous subsequent characterizations of Alfred as 'the most perfect character in history';[35] that Byrhtferth, writing a hundred years after Asser, should have felt

---

30   Lapidge, 'A King of Monkish Fable?', 20.

31   Keynes, 'The Authenticity', 538, highlights a couple of Byrhtferth's additions, and notes that, if Asser's text is genuine, as he believes it to be, then Byrhtferth's editorial decisions 'would be of special interest not least because they would represent a response to King Alfred formulated during the reign of King Æthelred the Unready'.

32   They are listed in *The Anglo-Saxon Chronicle. A Collaborative Edition. Vol 17: The Annals of St Neots with Vita Prima Sancti Neoti*, ed. D. Dumville and M. Lapidge (Cambridge, 1985), xlii; Asser, lv–lvii.

33   *Annals of St Neots*, ed. Dumville and Lapidge, xlii.

34   Lapidge, 'Byrhtferth of Ramsey'; *Byrhtferth of Ramsey*, ed. Lapidge, xliv–lxv.

35   Richard Abels, 'Alfred and his Biographers: Images and Imagination', in *Writing Medieval Biography, 750–1250: Essays in Honour of Professor Frank Barlow*, ed. D. Bates, J. Crick and S. Hamilton (Woodbridge, 2006), 61–75, at 74–75; the quotation is from E.A. Freeman, *The History of the Norman Conquest of England, Its Causes and Its Results*, 6 vols. (Oxford, 1867–79), I, 51.

moved to adapt the king's qualities to suit a new, more focused ideal is noteworthy, and suggests the different pressures of the historical moment in which he was writing. Æthelred has suffered – posthumously – from a bad press, sometimes explicitly in comparison to Alfred, seen as an ineffective ruler incapable of resisting the viking threat. However, recent scholarship emphasizes disagreements between Æthelred's various advisors, and the importance of considering a diversity of actors and points of view, and in this regard the evidence of Byrhtferth's *Historia regum* is highly significant in understanding the politics of Æthelred's reign.[36] In particular, Byrhtferth's *Historia regum* provides us with a view of kingship and conflict that did not emanate from the political centre and so, when considered in combination with other contemporary sources, highlights points of specific interest and political tension.

An English history

Byrhtferth's *Historia regum* as a whole seems to have been conceived as a national history of the English. The diversity of Byrhtferth's source material demonstrates that he had attempted to gather information on all the former Anglo-Saxon kingdoms. Moreover, he suggested that he was filling a gap left after the death of Bede.[37] Nevertheless, the materials used were uneven. Asser's *Life of Alfred* is a case in point: it dealt with the history of one particular dynasty and kingdom, yet it was Byrhtferth's only source for the period concerned. In using this text, Byrhtferth applied the history of the West Saxon kings to the entire kingdom as it stood under Æthelred. Since Æthelred was a direct descendant of Alfred, this approach may well have seemed logical. On the other hand, the English kingdom had significantly expanded since Alfred's time. Many of Byrhtferth's adaptations, therefore, may have originated in the attempt to make Asser's biography of Alfred more appropriate for a history of the English kingdom as a coherent unit.

Firstly, Byrhtferth removed the biographical structure and viewpoint of Asser's *Life of Alfred* from the *Historia regum*; in doing so, he reformulated Asser's text to suit its new role as one component of a national history, rather than a biography. In chapter 21 of the *Life*, Asser had explained his inspiration in writing, as a preface to his 'small account … of the infancy and boyhood of

---

[36]   J.E. Damon, 'Advisors for Peace in the Reign of Æthelred Unræd', in *Peace and Negotiation: Strategies for Coexistence in the Middle Ages and the Renaissance*, ed. D. Wolfthal (Turnhout, 2000), 57–78; S. Keynes, 'Re-Reading King Æthelred the Unready', in *Writing Medieval Biography*, ed. Bates, Crick and Hamilton, 77–97, at 85–87.

[37]   Symeon, *Opera*, II, 13: '… nunc Northanhymbrorum libet demonstrare, ut ad eorum tempora valeamus pervenire, de quibus non est narratum post obitum reverentissimi sacerdoti Bedae'; 27: 'His peractis gaudiis ex sanctissimi doctoris Anglorum rivalis, libet ex ipsius historia fundamentum assumere hujus operis …'

my esteemed lord Alfred'. This section does not appear in Byrhtferth's text.[38] At every subsequent point where we hear Asser's voice in the *Life*, the text has been curtailed, and chapters 79 and 81, giving Asser's personal history, have also been omitted. Byrhtferth removed every signpost which Asser gave to the direction of his biography, instead fitting the text into a new framework.

Secondly, Byrhtferth changed Asser's terms for peoples and places, making them more inclusive. Alfred and his family were, of course, the royal dynasty of the kingdom of Wessex, but Byrhtferth rarely called them kings of the West Saxons. Throughout his narrative, but especially regarding Alfred, Byrhtferth changed the titles that Asser employed – 'Angul-Saxonum rex' and 'Occidentalium Saxonum rex' – to less specific titles that implied a wider authority over all the English. Byrhtferth usually called Alfred 'rex Anglorum' or 'rex Saxonum'.[39] Not only were they more generalized, but these titles were also more up to date than the archaic 'Angulsaxonum rex'. 'Rex Anglorum' was the title most often used by Æthelred II in his charters and on his coinage.[40] In this way, Byrhtferth created a direct parallel between the historical Alfred and the contemporary king, Æthelred.

In general, Byrhtferth ignored the geographical and regional labels which Asser had employed. He often omitted the origins of people and armies, and almost always excised information relating to the locations of encampments and battles. The removal of geographical information was the most consistent change he made throughout Asser's text: on at least twenty-three occasions, Byrhtferth cut out Asser's geographical descriptions and even sometimes the names of the sites of battles, strongholds, and places where the viking armies overwintered. Byrhtferth's original impetus for making these changes may have been a simple lack of interest – the one occasion when he actually added geographical information concerned Thanet, about which he had personal knowledge (taking the evidence of the opening *passio*).[41] However, the effect of these changes was to give the various episodes a much wider relevance. The battles, removed from the specific topography of the landscape, now became generalized for the overall struggle of the English against the Danes, rather than the defence of a particular area. Moreover, the excision of labels referring to political divisions of the ninth century meant that battles which had taken place across Northumbria, Mercia, East Anglia, and Wessex all appeared as part of the

---

[38] Asser, 19 (trans. in *Alfred the Great*, ed. S. Keynes and M. Lapidge (Harmondsworth, 1983), 74): 'aliquantulum ... de infantilibus et puerilibus domini mei venerabilis Ælfredi'.

[39] Asser: 'Angulsaxonum rex' for Alfred at 1, 14, 19, 49, 50, 53, 69, 73: none were retained by Byrhtferth. Symeon, *Opera*, II: 'rex Anglorum' for Alfred at 69, 81 (twice), 88; 'rex Saxonum' at 82, 84, 86, 89. Byrhtferth usually retained Asser's 'Saxonum rex' or 'Occidentalium Saxonum rex' for Æthelwulf, but did call him 'rex Anglorum' at 72; and he used the same title for Æthelred I at 79.

[40] M. Dolley, 'An Introduction to the Coinage of Æthelraed II', in *Ethelred the Unready: Papers from the Millenary Conference*, ed. D. Hill (Oxford, 1978), 115–33; K. Cross, 'Enemy and Ancestor: Viking Identities and Ethnic Boundaries in England and Normandy, c.950–1015' (unpub. doctoral thesis, University College London, 2014), 255–257.

[41] Symeon, *Opera*, II, 73.

same campaign. 'The English' in the text thus reflected the expanded English kingdom of Byrhtferth's time.

Yet Byrhtferth's *Historia regum* focuses much more narrowly than Asser's *Life of Alfred* on the English people and kingdom, even if these categories themselves had expanded. Particularly striking is the exclusion of information relating to peoples other than the English. Several significant omissions are chapters concerned with Frankish history (chapters 68, 70 and 85). The one section relating to Frankish history which Byrhtferth included was elaborated into a battle account of his own composition.[42] This passage generalized the struggle between Franks and vikings in religious terms: the Christian forces of the Franks were raised by 'seeing the impious powers of the ungodly break forth'. Characterized as a 'brave and warlike people', they came from all sides, 'from their castles, towns, cities and towers'. The Franks were described as lions, just as the English kings were elsewhere in the text, which suggested that the Christian forces of the Franks and the English were fighting the same war.[43] Of all the information relating to Frankish history which Asser provided, only the section devoted to viking war was retained: it seems to have acted primarily as a background for the conflict occurring in England.

Other omitted chapters detailed Alfred's relationship with Rome, Wales and the foreign scholars and monks whom he imported (chapters 78–80, 86, 93 and 94).[44] Byrhtferth included only the section which referred to scholars of English origin. These excluded sections contained some criticism of the English, claiming that foreigners were brought in through necessity, since there were no willing monastic candidates among the English. Moreover, Asser stated in chapter 94 that he himself saw 'unum paganicae gentis' – presumably a Dane – living as a monk at Athelney, and that others of this background followed suit.[45] This was certainly not the image of the Danes cultivated by Byrhtferth in the *Historia regum* despite the fact that he knew through personal acquaintance the truth of Asser's statement.[46] Thus, while Asser had presented Alfred as a

---

[42] Symeon, *Opera*, II, 85; cf. Asser, 48.

[43] Symeon, *Opera*, II, 85: '… quod mirabile videri potest, quod visibiles hostes contra tam fortem bellicosumque populum auderent insurgere. At tunc feroces Franci, invicta fortitudine, a castellis, et oppidis, et civitatibus atque turribus viriliter progredientes, more leonum succensi sunt ira, videntes nefarias sceleratorum potestates emergere …'; 75: Alfred and Æthelred, 'quasi intrepidi leones'; 78: Ealdorman Æthelwulf, 'qui prius ut leo fremuit in bello'.

[44] The only omitted chapters not mentioned here are 95–97 (Asser, 81–85), a self-contained story about a crime at Alfred's monastery at Athelney, which has probably been excluded for the simple reason that it is a long digression. It may be worth noting, however, that the story concerns foreigners: an Old Saxon abbot and two Gallic monks.

[45] Asser, 81: 'In quo etiam monasterio unum paganicae gentis edoctum in monachico habitu degentem, iuvenem admodum, vidimus, non ultimum scilicet eorum'. An individual *paganicae gentis* almost certainly relates to one of Danish descent, as Asser does not refer to any other type of pagan in the *Life of Alfred*.

[46] He recorded the Danish descent of Archbishop Oda, Oswald's relative, in his own *Vita Sancti Oswaldi*: see *Alfred the Great*, ed. Keynes and Lapidge, 272 (note 233) and Asser, 334–335; *Byrhtferth of Ramsey*, ed. Lapidge, 16–17.

king who attracted men from all countries to his court and kingdom, Byrhtferth focused more narrowly on specifically English achievement. This narrower focus may be attributed to Byrhtferth's own perspective, rather than a wholly changed political culture, since Æthelred, too, seems to have had some imperial ambitions: his charters frequently style him 'emperor of Britain' and ruler of 'the English and all the peoples living around them';[47] and these aspirations were backed up by action in the year 1000, when he raided Cumbria in a campaign that appears to have been a show of dominance over the kingdoms of Strathclyde and Man.[48]

Instead, Byrhtferth's text cultivated an English national identity, of which Alfred was the main figurehead, in opposition to the Danish enemy, who were sometimes simply named 'inimici Anglorum'.[49] The qualities Byrhtferth ascribed to the English, such as bravery, were highlighted by their opposites in the Danes, whom he presented as cowards.[50] Byrhtferth's descriptions emphasized the unholy and evil nature of the attackers, calling them 'perverse robbers' ('perversi raptores') and 'a most unworthy army' ('indignissimus exercitus'), while explaining their actions 'because they are a depraved people' ('quod pravorum est').[51] Although he changed the '*pagani*' of Asser's original to '*Dani*', the image of the Danes is of stereotypical pagans. The terms have become equivalent in the *Historia regum*, making the paganism of the enemy an inescapable ethnic attribute. Even when describing the establishment of peace, Byrhtferth emphasized the religious and moral difference between English and Dane. Taking Asser's brief reference to Æthelred's and Alfred's return home, he stated that 'peace was established between the kings and the pagans, and they departed from one another, being separated as are sheep from goats'.[52] The gospel allusion (Matthew 25:32) hints at the point made more explicitly elsewhere, that the Christian English would all go to heaven, while the pagan Danes were destined for hell. These religious distinctions solidified the opposition constructed between English and Danes.

In addition, the motives Byrhtferth gave for English warriors fighting the Danes were frequently national in character. They were said to fight 'for their people's freedom' ('pro gentis suae liberatione'), and to die 'for their homeland and their ancestral laws' ('pro patriis legibus et patria ceciderunt').[53] In these statements, the *Historia regum* is reminiscent of other texts written in Æthelred's reign, which also emphasized the importance of protecting national unity. Most

---

47   Cross, 'Enemy and Ancestor', 257–258, 260–261; G. Molyneaux, 'Why Were Some Tenth-Century English Kings Presented as Rulers of Britain?', *TRHS* 21 (2011), 59–91, at 63.

48   R. Lavelle, *Aethelred II: King of the English 978–1016* (Stroud, 2002), 101–102.

49   Symeon, *Opera*, II, 77.

50   Symeon, *Opera*, II, 86, Byrhtferth added 'concussi terrore'; at 70 'terrore perculsi'; at 80 'timorque inmensus apprehendit eos'.

51   Symeon, *Opera*, II, 78, 86, 85.

52   Symeon, *Opera*, II, 76: 'Facta est inter reges et paganos pax, et segregati ab invicem, sicut oves ab hoedis sequestrantur.' Cf. Asser, 25.

53   Symeon, *Opera*, II, 71, 80.

significantly, the *Battle of Maldon* depicts a force of Englishmen composed of representatives of all regions, battling on behalf of 'Æthelred's kingdom, my lord's people and country'.[54] In specifying that the English fought for their laws, in particular, Byrhtferth's text tied national sentiment to governance in a similar way. However, his *Historia regum* is unusual in its dramatization of nationalism through accounts of past conflict, rather than allusions to the contemporary situation. Given the similarity of language and sentiment, it is difficult to avoid the conclusion that Byrhtferth intended direct parallels between Alfred's viking wars and those of his own time.[55]

Consciousness of such parallels may explain the *Historia regum*'s presentation of Danes and English in a purely conflictual relationship, with no reference to a history of settlement and coexistence. This was achieved through a combination of omissions and amendments. While Byrhtferth took the Danish wars as his main theme, he did remove or abridge several incidents concerning vikings: only those which referred to agreements and treaties made between viking armies and English kings or subjects.[56] Most significantly, the adapted text gives very little indication that Danes settled in England. Chapter 50 of Asser's *Life of Alfred*, translated from the Anglo-Saxon Chronicle, records that Halfdene divided out Northumbria amongst his followers, where they settled. In the *Historia regum*, this passage was completely omitted.[57] Likewise, in Chapter 33, Asser recorded the dominance of a viking army over East Anglia, a detail which Byrhtferth removed (though he did retain a similar statement from Chapter 60 – the only hint of settlement in the whole text).[58] Moreover, Byrhtferth took Asser's claim that Alfred was king over all the English 'who were not in captivity with the Vikings', and transformed it into another English victory: instead, Alfred ruled over all the English, *including* 'those whom he had freed from captivity'.[59] Thus, the text nowhere implied that Danes had maintained a presence in England, but instead emphasized the success of the English and the foreignness of the vikings. The corollary of this settlement, the flight of the English from occupied areas, was also removed; again, this small amendment reinforced the picture of a people unified in resistance.[60] The text presented the Danes as ultimately unsuccessful in their attacks on an increasingly unified – and clearly distinguished – English kingdom.

---

54 *The Battle of Maldon*, ed. D.G. Scragg (Manchester, 1981), lines 53–54: 'Æþelredes eard, ealdres mines folc and foldan'.
55 Byrhtferth discussed the contemporary viking attacks in his *Vita Oswaldi*: *Byrhtferth of Ramsey*, ed. Lapidge, 154–159.
56 Asser, 35 (cf. Symeon, *Opera*, II, 82), 37 (cf. 82), 41 (cf. 83), 54 (omitted completely).
57 Asser, 38.
58 Asser, 26, 48; Symeon, *Opera*, II, 76–77, 85.
59 Asser, 69 (trans. Keynes and Lapidge, 98): 'qui … cum paganis sub captivitate erant', where Stevenson has substituted '*sub*' for the Cotton manuscript's original '*sine*': *Alfred the Great*, ed. Keynes and Lapidge, 266, note 199 argue that this emendation is 'nonsensical'; Symeon, *Opera*, II, 88: 'qui … a captivitate liberati [erant]'.
60 Asser, 40, 45 ; cf. Symeon, *Opera*, II, 82–83.

Military action between English and Danes dominates Byrhtferth's narrative. Virtually every encounter with viking armies which Asser included also appears in the *Historia regum*, always completely rewritten and often at much greater length, though no new information has been added. Nor was Byrhtferth especially knowledgeable about warfare – Asser's references to *testudines* (shield walls) seem to have been barely understood.[61] Battles offered the opportunity for dramatic passages, which Byrhtferth certainly relished, but this does not provide a complete explanation; on a few occasions, he either toned down Asser's language or even omitted a dramatic battle scene.[62] Those passages he toned down showed the Danes in a heroic or successful light, or suggested English cowardice: for a defeat, Byrhtferth excluded Asser's remark that the English had 'turned their backs', and emphasized that Ealdorman Æthelwulf, who was killed in the battle, 'roared like a lion from the beginning of the conflict'.[63] His additions frequently emphasize the size and threat of the Danish forces, such as in the description of 'an enormous multitude of Danes and, I may say, crowds of armies had gathered, to the extent that many thousands seemed to be present, as if, from one thousand, twenty myriads had sprung up'.[64] These embellishments heightened the brilliance of English victories against the vast Danish armies.

In fact, the *Historia regum* presents an overwhelming narrative of English military success. In sections of Asser's text which clearly describe Danish victories, Byrhtferth either maintained ambiguity over the result of the battle, or decisively rewrote the episode to give the English victory.[65] In 867, for example, Asser stated that virtually the entire force of the Northumbrians at York was wiped out ('maxima ex parte omnes Northanhymbrensium coetus ... deleti occubuerunt') whereas Byrhtferth made it appear that the Northumbrians were stronger ('fortiores') and won.[66] In the following year, at Nottingham, Asser reported that the English were unable to breach the Danish defences: Byrhtferth had the Danes coming to Alfred for peace.[67] In this respect, he used just those methods that Lapidge has identified in Byrhtferth's composition of the *Vita Sancti Oswaldi*, by which he revealed himself less concerned with trying to be accurate in every detail than with the validity of his overarching narrative.[68]

---

[61] Asser, 28, 45; cf. Symeon, *Opera*, II, 79, where Byrhtferth interprets *testudines* as 'machinas et machinatorum propugnacula', whereas at 83 he simply uses 'multitudine'.

[62] Asser, 28, 43, 23; Symeon, *Opera*, II, 78, 83, 75.

[63] Asser, 28 (trans. Keynes and Lapidge, 78): 'terga vertentibus'; Symeon, *Opera*, II, 78: 'qui prius ut leo fremuit in bello'.

[64] Symeon, *Opera*, II, 76: 'Danorum vero enormis multitudo, et, ut ita dicam, legionum catervae congregatae sunt, ita ut multa viderentur milia affore, et sicut de mille in ... xx. myriadas excrevissent'.

[65] Cf. Page's discussion of the adaptations made to the Chronicle account by Æthelweard, Byrhtferth's contemporary: R. Page, *A Most Vile People* (London, 1987), 11–12.

[66] Asser, 23; Symeon, *Opera*, II, 75.

[67] Asser, 25; Symeon, *Opera*, II, 76.

[68] M. Lapidge, 'Byrhtferth and Oswald', in *St Oswald of Worcester: Life and Influence*, ed. N. Brooks and C. Cubitt (Leicester, 1996), 64–83, at 68: 'My impression is that Byrhtferth was sublimely unconcerned about the details of mere chronology, because he had his eye on a higher goal'.

Through Byrhtferth's revisions, the broad narrative of the *Historia regum* prevails against matters of historical detail, such as the outcomes of individual battles, in a general account of English triumph.

Military leadership

Military conflict constituted a central aspect of the late tenth-century discourse of English unity. Uniting against a common enemy cohered the English peoples; it was also, perhaps, a necessary response to attack. In the verses quoted earlier from the *Battle of Maldon*, loyal nationalism was coupled with incitement to military action – even in the face of defeat. Likewise, Wulfstan and Ælfric both coupled English national loyalty with armed hostility to contemporary Danish invaders. In a homily of 1009, Ælfric criticized 'those English people who turn to the Danes, and mark themselves with the devil, in allegiance to him, and do his works, to their own destruction, and betray their own nation to death'.[69] Here, Ælfric called for loyalty to the English nation, expressed through military action, as a matter of Christian duty. Byrhtferth's *Historia regum*, though describing past conflict, reflects this wider theme.

The military passages emphasize English, but specifically royal, leadership. When referring to Alfred, Byrhtferth inserted glorifying superlatives, usually focused on military virtues. Thus, while Asser consistently identified Alfred with the title 'Angulsaxonum rex', Byrhtferth praised the king as 'ipse armipotens rex', 'rex Saxonum audacissimus ducum', and 'principum princeps'.[70] Of course, his source text provided Byrhtferth with many opportunities for the glorification of Alfred: he retained Asser's use of the years of Alfred's life as a means of dating, and at every mention he endowed Alfred with further honours. Yet Byrhtferth gave the same treatment to other kings who acted as war leaders. Æthelwulf was 'bellipotens rex Saxonum' and 'rex gloriosae potestatis' rather than merely 'Occidentalium Saxonum rex', as Asser had it.[71] Asser identified these historical figures clearly, but Byrhtferth presented them as English heroes of the highest order and models of secular leadership.

In his descriptions of battles, Byrhtferth focused on the role of kings in leading their forces into war and inspiring them to fight boldly. He held up Æthelwulf as a source of inspiration, whose forces were 'fighting more strongly,

---

[69] M. Godden, 'Apocalypse and Invasion in Late Anglo-Saxon England', in *From Anglo-Saxon to Early Middle English: Studies Presented to E.G. Stanley*, ed. M. Godden et al. (Oxford, 1994), 139; *Homilies of Ælfric: A Supplementary Collection*, ed. J.C. Pope, 2 vols., Early English Text Society 259–60 (London, 1967–68), II, 521: 'swa swa þa Engliscan men doð þe to ðam Deniscum gebugað, and mearciað hy deofle to his mannrædene, and his weorc wyrcað, hym sylfum to forwyrde, and heora agene leode be(læwað) to deaðe'.

[70] Symeon, *Opera*, II, 87, 86.

[71] Symeon, *Opera*, II, 70, 71. These markers of admiration were not restricted to kings: we also meet Æthelwulf as 'comes *insignis*' (Symeon, *Opera*, II, 72), while Alfred's 'mater' becomes 'ejus dignissima genitrix' (74).

because they saw their king battling so bravely', and he similarly praised the examples given by Burhred of Mercia, Æthelred, and Alfred.[72] Such passages asserted that the English people needed their king to provide an example and an inspiration through his own valour. A similar sentiment, in the negative, is invoked in the Anglo-Saxon Chronicle for 1003, which remarks on a defeat that 'As the saying goes: "When the commander weakens then the whole raiding army is greatly hindered".'[73] Among the qualities of a good king, Byrhtferth explicitly emphasized military action: 'The kings not only exhorted the people to be steadfast with words, but truly overcame their enemies by warlike force of arms'.[74] This insistence on words being reinforced with military action closely recalls certain statements of Ælfric, such as in his *Letter to Sigeweard*, in which he emphasized that the Maccabees 'did not wish to fight only with fair words, speaking well but going back on that afterwards'.[75] As Mary Clayton has commented, in the context of contemporary events, this interjection appears somewhat pointed on the part of Ælfric.[76] Byrhtferth's similar statement takes the implication further: it should be the king himself who followed up his words with military action.

In fact, King Alfred's qualities, extolled in such great detail by Asser, now appeared as primarily military. Byrhtferth showed little interest in Alfred's personality or distinctive features. Sections containing personal and biographical information were decisively abridged, or more often entirely omitted.[77] Many of these chapters described Alfred's spiritual and intellectual life. Notably, Byrhtferth silently excised Asser's account of Alfred being struck with illness at his wedding in order that he might remain chaste (found in chapter 74). These chapters also included details of various aspects of Alfred's kingship, such as his international court and administration. Chapters 100 to 106, of which Byrhtferth retained only one short chapter, described Alfred's division of revenue, his invention of a clock, and his exercise of justice. But Byrhtferth

---

[72] Symeon, *Opera*, II, 70: '... fortiter repugnantes, quia viderunt atrociter regem bellare ipsorum ...'; 75–76.

[73] *The Anglo-Saxon Chronicle: A Collaborative Edition 7: MS E*, ed. S. Irvine (Cambridge, 2004), s.a. 1003: '... swa hit gecweðen is: ðonne se heretoga wacað, þonne bið eall se here swiðe gehindred' (trans. M. Swanton, *The Anglo-Saxon Chronicles* (London, 1996).

[74] Symeon, *Opera*, II, 80: 'Reges autem non solum verbis populum constantem hortabantur, verumetiam armis hostes bellica virtute prosternebant'.

[75] H. Magennis, 'Ælfric of Eynsham's *Letter to Sigeweard* (*Treatise on the Old and New Testaments*)', in *Metaphrastes, or, Gained in Translation: Essays and Translations in Honour of Robert H. Jordan*, ed. M. Mullett, Belfast Byzantine Texts and Translations 9 (Belfast, 2004), 210–35, at 224; *The Old English Version of the Heptateuch, Aelfric's Treatise on the Old and New Testament, and his Preface to Genesis*, ed. S.J. Crawford, Early English Text Society 160 (Oxford, 1922), 49: 'Heo noldon na geahton mid fegere wordum ane, swa þet heo wel spæcon, ⁊ awendon þet eft ...'

[76] M. Clayton, 'Ælfric and Æthelred', in *Essays on Anglo-Saxon and Related Themes in Memory of Lynne Grundy*, ed. J. Roberts and J. Nelson (London, 2000), 65–88, at 75, note 36.

[77] The following chapters containing such information were entirely omitted: 25, 73, 74, 76, 88, 89, 90, 100, 102, 103, 104, 105, and 106.

discarded these details, creating a text in which the actions and duties of the king were concentrated primarily on warfare.

Byrhtferth's emphasis on royal military action, written while the English kingdom was plagued by viking assault, reveals a controversial political opinion. This opinion differs markedly from the attitude displayed by Byrhtferth's teacher, Abbo of Fleury, in the *Passio Sancti Eadmundi*, in which King Edmund surrenders, casting aside his weapons, as a willing martyr of the vikings.[78] Abbo used the example of St Edmund to demonstrate his 'political theology' of kingship, which emphasized the priestly role of the king, and rejected the military.[79] Byrhtferth, in contrast, glorified military action against the vikings, and emphasized especially the role of the king on the battlefield. Indeed, although referring directly to Abbo's *Passio*, Byrhtferth retained Asser's statement that Edmund fought against the vikings, adding that he did so 'viriliter cum suis'.[80] This difference in attitude surely resulted from the increasing severity of viking assaults experienced in the years intervening between the composition of the two texts. In the context of Æthelred's struggle to resist viking attack, Abbo's idealization of passive resistance must have appeared problematic. Contemporaries required a more practical, active solution to their afflictions, and they looked to the king to provide it. The Chronicle lays out his ultimate failure, bewailing Æthelred's inability to defend the kingdom convincingly.

In fact, Æthelred seems to have received criticism not only for his general lack of military resistance to viking armies, but for personally avoiding the battlefield. A now incomplete text by Ælfric known as *Wyrdwriteras*, written after 1005, responds directly to this issue. *Wyrdwriteras* argues that the king should delegate military authority to generals, and provides examples from history to indicate successful precedents.[81] We may read this text, which appears to be a letter directed to high ranking ealdormen or even the king himself, as a defence of the king's policy of delegation.[82] Yet several scholars have noted hints of criticism in Ælfric's words, leading them to query the purpose of the text.[83] The evidence of Byrhtferth's *Historia regum* adds strength to the idea that the king's military role was a point of heated debate: Byrhtferth, in direct contrast to Ælfric's *Wyrdwriteras*, asserted that the leadership of a royal military commander in battle was crucial to success, and he, too, furnished examples from history – in this case providing more recent and obvious parallels. Moreover, Ælfric argued in *Wyrdwriteras* that the king should not fight because

[78]   Abbo of Fleury, *Life of St Edmund*, in *Three Lives of English Saints*, ed. M. Winterbottom (Toronto, 1972), 65–87.

[79]   M. Mostert, *The Political Theology of Abbo of Fleury* (Hilversum, 1987), 157, 165–167, 170–171, 173.

[80]   Symeon, *Opera*, II, 77.

[81]   *Homilies of Ælfric*, ed. Pope, II, 725–733.

[82]   First proposed in W. Braekman, '*Wyrdwriteras*: An Unpublished Ælfrician text in Manuscript Hatton 115', *Revue belge de philologie et d'histoire* 44 (1966), 959–70, at 963–964.

[83]   Clayton, 'Ælfric and Æthelred', 82–85; *Old English Homilies from MS Bodley 343*, ed. S. Irvine (Oxford, 1993), 12; Keynes, 'An Abbot, an Archbishop, and Viking Raids', 165.

he must concentrate on his other duties; Byrhtferth excised Asser's accounts of Alfred's other such duties and qualities from his source text. This insistence on the military leadership of the king reveals another viewpoint in a political controversy that may well have influenced Æthelred's later actions.

Holy war

But why should the king take such a central role in military action? Byrhtferth provides a few answers in the *Historia regum* as he demonstrates, through the example of Alfred, the responsibilities of an English king. When recounting Alfred's election as king, Byrhtferth (quoting Psalm 149) asserted that his duty was 'to execute vengeance upon the nations, chastisements among the people'.[84] These two themes emerge from his accounts of the viking wars. Firstly, the conflict between English and Danes took on a religious, as well as national, significance, because of the Danes' paganism. Secondly, victory was only assured when the English people demonstrated their spiritual righteousness.

The *Historia regum*'s sharp distinction between Christian English and pagan Danes, as described above, meant that their conflicts represented battles between good and evil. For example, Byrhtferth inserted the following passage, explaining the divergent fates of Danes and English killed in battle:

Those who fell for their land and for their ancestral laws were led, as we may believe, to the land of eternal happiness; the others were led to him of whom it is said: 'He is the author of all injustice'.[85]

Thus he presented the conflict as a righteous war for the English nation against the forces of evil: the slaughter of the Danes returned them to the devil, while English casualties were assured of a place in heaven. At another point, Byrhtferth asserted a parallel with Biblical warfare. Rewriting a passage describing the 871 battle at Ashdown, he heaped praise on King Æthelred I, describing him as 'a warlike Judas' (Maccabeus), a Biblical hero distinguished by his defeat of pagan forces. This parallel is especially significant, since Ælfric also applied the story of the Maccabees to state that war against the vikings was just.[86] Byrhtferth's text, therefore, appears to reflect a more widely held view that justified military action against viking attackers on account of their paganism.

---

[84] Symeon, *Opera*, II, 81: 'ut eis praeesset ad faciendam vindictam in nationibus, increpationes in populis'.
[85] Symeon, *Opera*, II, 80: 'Qui pro patriis legibus et patria ceciderunt, perducti sunt, ut credi libet, ad patriam aeternae felicitatis. Alii vero ad eum perducti sunt, de quo dictum est: "Ipse est caput omnis injustitiae".' Cf. Asser, 30.
[86] Symeon, *Opera*, II, 79: 'quasi Judas bellicosus'. *Aelfric's Lives of Saints*, ed. W. Skeat, 2 vols. (London, 1881–1900), II, 114: '*Iustum bellum* is rihtlic gefeoht wið ða reðan flot-menn'. Byrhtferth used the same analogy in a different context in the *Vita Sancti Oswaldi* (*Byrhtferth of Ramsey*, ed. Lapidge, 128).

Fighting for the English, in these contexts, was synonymous with fighting for the Christian cause.

The second duty of the king, to chastise his people, indicates the requirement for spiritual righteousness in order for God to grant victory. Viking attack had long been seen as a punishment for wicked behaviour among the assailed; this kind of rhetoric increased in England during Æthelred's reign. Most notably, in his *Sermo Lupi* of 1014, delivered 'when the Danes were persecuting [the English] most greatly', Archbishop Wulfstan II matched military defence to moral restoration, both of which Wulfstan saw as essential for withstanding the evil enemies of the Christian English.[87] Byrhtferth rarely picked up on this penitential angle in his *Historia regum*, however, which retains a triumphalist narrative. Instead, he emphasized godly preparation before battle and appropriate thanksgiving after victory. Prayer thus became a weapon: for instance, he stated that, because King Æthelred I heard mass before fighting, he arrived at the battlefield 'girded with arms and prayers'.[88] Victories were similarly celebrated: Byrhtferth added to Asser's account of the battle of Aclea that as the Christians left the battlefield they 'gave thanks to God with hymns and prayers'.[89] Contemporary practice matched the text's emphasis on liturgical preparation for war, reaching its zenith in the measures of VII Æthelred (1009).[90] This law code enjoined the singing of masses 'contra paganos', three days of fasting, and barefoot procession, in order to solicit God's help against the vikings. Byrhtferth's *Historia regum* suggested that such measures were necessary and brought results.

In Byrhtferth's account, therefore, military victory was only assured because God supported the English. A just cause and a godly people were necessary because God required them, and it was only through his intervention that the English would prevail. Asser alluded to this idea only in the most general terms, but Byrhtferth made various additions that highlighted the role of divine assistance in battle. Before two of the battles found in Asser's text, Byrhtferth inserted speeches exhorting the English not to fear the enemy because God was on their side.[91] When faced with an overwhelming viking army, Byrhtferth reported that Æthelwulf called his people together and reminded them that, '"however more strongly they attack, arranged in battle lines against us, indeed our leader, who is Christ, is stronger than them". The Christians then faced the Danes, trusting in the protection of Christ's name'.[92] He also emphasized the military protection afforded by Christian faith. Twice he referred to 'the triple

87 *Sermo Lupi Ad Anglos,* ed. D. Whitelock (Exeter, 1939, repr. 1976), 47: 'Sermo Lupi ad Anglos quando Dani maxime persecuti sunt eos.'
88 Symeon, *Opera,* II, 79: 'praecinctus armis et orationibus'.
89 Symeon, *Opera,* II, 70: 'grates reddentes Domino in hymnis et confessionibus'.
90 See the full discussion in Keynes, 'An Abbot, an Archbishop, and Viking Raids', 179–189.
91 Symeon, *Opera,* II, 75–76, 78.
92 Symeon, *Opera,* II, 78: '"Qui si aliquando contra nos aciem struens valentior incubuerit, noster quidem dux, qui Christus est, fortior illis est." Obviant denique Christiani Danis, confidentes in tuitione Christi nominis'.

breastplate of faith, hope, and the love of God' alongside physical armour.[93] But it was not merely a matter of defence. Every victory was explicitly attributed to the will of God.[94]

Divine assistance arrived in several forms. Most unusually, Byrhtferth several times claimed that the English enjoyed the aid of angels. The first mention of angelic assistance came in a phrase that appears to refer to Gregory the Great's 'non Angli, sed angeli', which was of course well known in England through Bede's account. Byrhtferth asserted that the Danes were attacked 'by the English, supported by the spirits of angels'.[95] The use of Gregory's wordplay alluded to the divine guardianship which led to the conversion of the English as a people; in the immediate context, however, the pun further asserted the religious motivation of English warfare against the Danes. Later on in the narrative, Byrhtferth referred more explicitly to angelic aid in battle, again playing on the name of the English. He stated that the English people 'sought aid from the angels, that they would deem it worthy to supply the support of divine help to them'.[96] The association between the English and angels, expressed through punning wordplay, suggested that they were a nation who enjoyed special divine protection and assistance. Byrhtferth's third invocation of angelic help combined this idea with the central role of the king, who, he implied, had angelic qualities:

Rising up, they boldly called forth their forces to battle, trusting in the kindness of the Creator, safe and fortified by the wall of the king's presence, whose countenance shone brightly like that of a gleaming angel... The Overseer therefore, perceiving the desire of the earthly king from his sanctuary above, conceded to him the support of angelic power.[97]

In this passage, Alfred's central role in battle provided protection in the manner of an angel. Moreover, God's intervention related directly to the king's own action and desire. Royal military leadership thus appears in this passage to be the key to divine assistance. The form that this assistance took is unclear: either the literal presence of angels on the battlefield or, in an intriguing alternative reading, the delegation of angelic power to the English king.

Byrhtferth may also have claimed that King Alfred received saintly assistance in battle. The *Historia regum* refers to a story which is also recorded in the *Historia de Sancto Cuthberto*, a text compiled by the community of St Cuthbert

---

[93] Symeon, *Opera*, II, 84: '[induerunt] ... fidei, spei, charitatisque Dei'; and 78: 'trilicis toracis circumdatus'.

[94] E.g. Symeon, *Opera*, II, 76: 'Tandem per gratiam omnipotentis Domini cessavit ventus turbinis'.

[95] Symeon, *Opera*, II, 73: 'ab anglis, suffultis a spiritibus angelicis'.

[96] Symeon, *Opera*, II, 78: 'Anglorum populus ... auxilium implorabant angelorum, ut eis dignarentur impendere adminiculum divini adjutorii'.

[97] Symeon, *Opera*, II, 84: 'Hi exsurgentes a solo audacter provocabant in celebres ad bellum, de clementia Conditoris sperantes, securi ac vallo muniti astantis regis, cujus vultus ut angeli splendentis refulsit ... Cernens igitur Speculator insignis desuper penetral Sui terreni regis desiderium, concessit ei angelicae potestatis suffragium'.

in the tenth and eleventh centuries.[98] In this episode, Cuthbert appeared to Alfred the night before the Battle of Edington and promised that he would aid the king to victory. The *Historia regum* states:

King Alfred, comforted by the fitting speech by St Cuthbert, fought against the Danes, and achieved victory at the time and place that the saint had ordered. And always afterwards he was terrible and invincible to his enemies, and he held St Cuthbert in particular honour. How he triumphed over his enemies is read a little after this.[99]

It has been argued that the above passage was a later Durham insertion into the *Historia regum*, rather than original to Byrhtferth's text.[100] It should be acknowledged that the *Historia regum* passage is brief, and seems to assume prior knowledge of the vision narrative; moreover, it is repeated almost verbatim later in Symeon's *Historia de regibus*.[101] Another view holds that the episode was itself an eleventh-century interpolation into the *Historia de Sancto Cuthberto*, and for this reason the passage must have been added to the *Historia regum* at a later date. However, a number of compelling arguments have demonstrated that the episode is original to the *Historia de Sancto Cuthberto*.[102] At present, therefore, it should remain an open question whether this passage is original to Byrhtferth or an insertion made at Durham.

The problem of the passage's originality is compounded by the fact that it was precisely at this point in Asser's *Life of Alfred* that Archbishop Parker added material relating to St Neot.[103] This addition only adds to the confusion, for the *Vita Prima Sancti Neoti*, the ultimate source of Parker's material, also contains a remarkably similar episode, in which St Neot appeared to Alfred the night before the battle.[104] So, in both the *Historia de Sancto Cuthberto* and the *Vita Prima Sancti Neoti*, it is stated that the saint in question (Cuthbert or Neot) appeared to Alfred before the Battle of Edington in 878, and predicted his victory. The saints' words, in both versions, constituted more than a prophecy: they promised to assist Alfred against the enemy. Given the similarities of the

---

98   *Historia de Sancto Cuthberto*, ed. T. Johnson South (Cambridge, 2002), 25–36 proposes an eleventh-century composition, but an earlier date is argued for by Sally Crumplin, 'Rewriting History in the Cult of St Cuthbert from the Ninth to the Twelfth Centuries' (unpub. doctoral thesis, Univ. of St Andrews, 2005), 34–41, 61–70.

99   Symeon, *Opera*, II, 83: 'Rex Elfredus apto confortatus oraculo per sanctum Cuthbertum, contra Danos pugnavit, et, quo ipse sanctus jusserat tempore et loco, victoria potitus est, semperque deinceps hostibus terribilis et invincibilis erat, sanctumque Cuthbertum praecipue honori habuerat. Qualiter hostes vicerit paulo post hic legitur.'

100   *Historia de Sancto Cuthberto*, ed. Johnson South, 10–11, 27–32.

101   Symeon, *Opera*, II, 111. Note that Arnold considered this passage to have been revised by Symeon.

102   Crumplin, 'Rewriting History', 40; Luisella Simpson, 'The King Alfred/St Cuthbert Episode in the *Historia de Sancto Cuthberto*: Its Significance for Mid-Tenth-Century English History', in *St Cuthbert, His Cult and His Community to AD 1200*, ed. G. Bonner, D. Rollason and C. Stancliffe (Woodbridge, 1989), 397–411.

103   Asser, 41–43.

104   *Annals of St Neots*, ed. Dumville and Lapidge, 127–133.

two stories, but lack of any textual connection, it seems most likely that some form of this narrative circulated orally, and was then adapted to the different saints. If this were the case, then Byrhtferth could well have encountered the story in oral form, rather than in either of these texts. Suggestive of this idea is the likelihood that the *Vita Prima Sancti Neoti* was probably written in the first half of the eleventh century (and perhaps slightly earlier), at Eynesbury near Ramsey.[105] Although their connection is not clear, the *Vita Prima Sancti Neoti* and Byrhtferth's *Historia regum* may both suggest that narratives of Alfred's saintly assistance in battle circulated in the fenland monasteries in the early eleventh century.

Byrhtferth's various expressions of supernatural help in battle might also be linked to ideas from the continent. He may have been influenced by traditions from Fleury, which maintained close contacts with Ramsey. For example, Byrhtferth knew at least some of the *Miracula Sancti Benedicti* composed at Fleury, and applied it to his own description of contemporary viking attacks.[106] In another section, the *Miracula* described the presence of St Benedict on the battlefield, fighting on the side of the Frankish forces.[107] Against the background of these traditions, we may read Byrhtferth's statements more literally as evidence of a belief in supernatural assistance in battle.

The origins of the concept of Holy War that eventually became the idea of Crusade have long been located in the Viking Age.[108] Carolingian pre-battle liturgies and masses *contra paganos* suggested the initial connection – a theme which has been investigated more fully by Simon Coupland (though more research into the Anglo-Saxon context, especially the promulgations of VII Æthelred, would illuminate the issue still further).[109] However, this accumulating evidence for belief in tangible military assistance from God, the saints and – in the case of Byrhtferth's *Historia regum* – angels provides another element to the Viking Age origins of Holy War. Indeed, it seems that the perceived contrast between Alfred's success and Æthelred's impending failure may have stimulated a consideration of the need for divine help and the forms which this might take.

---

[105] *Annals of St Neots*, ed. Dumville and Lapidge, lxxxv–xcvi, ci; Malcolm Godden, 'The Old English Life of St Neot and the Legends of King Alfred', *ASE* 39 (2010), 193–225, at 194–202, 206–207.

[106] *Les Miracles de Saint Benôit*, ed. E. de Certain (Paris, 1868), 74; used by Byrhtferth in his *Vita Oswaldi*: *Byrhtferth of Ramsey*, ed. Lapidge, 158. See further J. Nightingale, 'Oswald, Fleury and Continental Reform', in *St Oswald of Worcester: Life and Influence*, ed. N. Brooks and C. Cubitt (Leicester, 1996), 23–45.

[107] *Miracles de Saint Benôit*, ed. Certain, 88–89.

[108] C. Erdmann, *The Origin of the Idea of Crusade* (Princeton, 1977), 25–29, 95–96.

[109] S. Coupland, 'The Rod of God's Wrath or the People of God's Wrath?', *Journal of Ecclesiastical History*, 42 (1991), 535–54; the Frankish precursors of the measures in VII Æthelred are explored in Keynes, 'An Abbot, an Archbishop, and Viking Raids', 184–186.

Conclusion

Byrhtferth's methods of compilation and rewriting, inserting glorifying epithets and elaborating battle scenes, created a history of united English success against their Danish enemies, led by their kings. In doing so, he encouraged his readers to identify with the English leaders he described by asserting the unity of the English past. His history, infused with the rhetoric of holy war, implied that such an identification was a religious obligation.

While Byrhtferth's text fits into a wider tradition of literature asserting English unity, his account of the viking wars in particular seems to relate to contemporary events. In two recent articles, Leonard Neidorf has discussed the *Battle of Maldon* and the *Beowulf* manuscript as cultural products created in response to agreements and conflicts with viking forces.[110] The *Battle of Maldon*, he argued, was written in the context of recent tribute payment and (a treaty like) II Æthelred, whereas the *Beowulf* manuscript was produced during the dire times of conflict in 1009–1012. According to his method, we should attribute Byrhtferth's *Historia regum* to the latter part of Æthelred's reign, as a text intended to provoke loyalty among the English and resistance to the Danes. However, we might alternatively see it as an expression of political opinions which, if they were shared by others, may have been brought to bear on Æthelred and actually influenced his actions in the years 1009–1012.

The insistence on the king's personal role in battle seems to have related to a point of political tension during Æthelred's reign. The Chronicle records his personal leadership of the army on only three occasions, in 1000, 1009, and 1014.[111] If Æthelred did indeed suffer criticism for avoiding the battlefield – as the combination of Byrhtferth's *Historia regum* and Ælfric's *Wyrdwriteras* suggests – then perhaps his actions in these years were a response to such pressure. Moreover, the earliest of his laws compiled by Wulfstan (V and VI Æthelred, 1008) distinguished between penalties for a deserter from the army depending on whether the king was present, suggesting that this was an issue of new significance in the later part of his reign.[112]

Byrhtferth's insertion of claims to supernatural assistance in warfare may also have reflected wider feeling. In addition to Byrhtferth's *Historia regum*, a number of texts composed around this period allude to supernatural assistance in battle with viking armies; that this was more than a hagiographic trope is demonstrated by the injunctions found in VII Æthelred. The three days of fasting, masses, and alms giving that VII Æthelred enjoined were specifically

---

[110] L. Neidorf, 'II Æthelred and the Politics of the Battle of Maldon', *Journal of English and Germanic Philology* 111 (2012), 451–73; L. Neidorf, 'VII Æthelred and the Genesis of the *Beowulf* Manuscript', *Philological Quarterly* 89 (2010), 119–39.

[111] Clayton, 'Ælfric and Æthelred', 84.

[112] V Æthelred 28; VI Æthelred 35 (*The Laws of the Kings of England from Edmund to Henry I*, ed. and trans. A.J. Robertson (Cambridge, 1925), 86–87, 102–103).

designed to entreat 'that God Almighty may have mercy upon us and grant us victory over our enemies'.[113] In employing this strategy, Æthelred prioritized seeking divine help against the viking threat. Moreover, the text describes the three-day fast as 'a national penalty' ('gemænelicre dædbote'), and the measures are to be carried out by 'the whole people' ('eal folc'), reflecting the belief that God granted military victory not merely to the king himself, but to the nation as a whole.[114] Consequently, the English nation had to demonstrate their righteousness before God. It has long been recognized how this attitude is more generally present in Wulfstan's thought – he was, after all, Æthelred's legislator. [115] Byrhtferth's text reveals that such attitudes to the moral unity of the nation, and its relationship to military victory and defence, were also held outside such influential circles. Moreover, Byrhtferth's *Historia regum* provided its readers with historical examples of supernatural assistance that demonstrated the efficacy of such an approach.

This presentation of historical precedent suggests why Byrhtferth might have chosen to present his political viewpoints in the format of an extended historical narrative. When Ælfric and Wulfstan discussed similar issues, they did so in homilies, which were designed to be delivered to an audience, and in letters, also with specific recipients. However, they did employ historical precedent to make their points: Ælfric discussed a series of Roman emperors and Old Testament rulers, and both he and Wulfstan on occasion referred to Æthelred's West Saxon royal predecessors.[116] Byrhtferth's decision to write a national history similarly allowed him to express his political opinion more freely, precisely because it read as exhortation rather than criticism. Indeed, far from appearing critical, the history would have been more likely to inspire national feeling and loyalty to the king. After all, Alfred and the other kings whose exploits Byrhtferth celebrated were the ancestors of King Æthelred, and established his right to rule over the English.

However, the social role of a national history such as Byrhtferth's *Historia regum* is still somewhat unclear. Moreover, it seems to have had a very limited circulation in the pre-Conquest period, given that our only knowledge of the text is through Symeon of Durham's *Historia de regibus*. We may conclude, therefore, that the contemporary impact of Byrhtferth's text remained minimal. The value of Byrhtferth's *Historia regum* for the historian lies in the evidence it provides of political opinions in Æthelred's reign. Byrhtferth's *Historia regum*

---

[113] VII Æthelred 8 (*Laws of the Kings of England*, ed. Robertson (Cambridge, 1925), 116–117: 'wið ðam þe us God ælmihtig gemiltsige ⁊ us geunne þæt we ure fynd ofercuman motan').

[114] VII Æthelred 1 (*Laws of the Kings of England*, ed. Robertson (Cambridge, 1925), 114–115).

[115] J. Wilcox, 'Wulfstan's *Sermo Lupi ad Anglos* as Political Performance: 16 February 1014 and Beyond', in *Wulfstan, Archbishop of York*, ed. M. Townend (Turnhout, 2004), 375–96; A. Cowen, '*Byrstas* and *bysmeras*: The Wounds of Sin in the *Sermo Lupi ad Anglos*', in *Wulfstan*, ed. Townend, 397–411; Godden, 'Apocalypse and Invasion', 142–156.

[116] E.g. Ælfric's epilogue to his version of the Book of Judges: *Old English Heptateuch*, ed. Crawford, 416–417.

thus adds an understudied voice to the contemporary view of Æthelred and late Anglo-Saxon political culture.

Here only Byrhtferth's use of Asser has been considered. The forthcoming edition should open up the text for more readers, who may, by investigating earlier sections of the *Historia regum*, gain similar insights into other aspects of Byrhtferth's use of the past and attitudes to the present.

Geoffrey le Bel of Anjou and Political Inheritance in the Anglo-Norman Realm

Mark E. Blincoe

The coronation of Henry II as king of England on 7 December 1154 marked the formal conclusion of a nearly twenty-year conflict over the succession of Henry I. While a personal victory for the young king, the supporters of King Stephen were willing to accept his coronation because of a compromise reached the previous year that recognized Henry's right of succession without delegitimizing Stephen's kingship.[1] The parties finalized the terms for peace at Winchester in November 1153. Stephen appointed Henry as his successor and heir 'by hereditary right', promising to include Henry 'in all the affairs of the kingdom'. Henry agreed that Stephen would remain king so long as the magnates and bishops of England swore an oath to recognize his succession peacefully upon Stephen's death.[2] This compromise, which gave Henry uncontested rights to the crown, redefined the legitimacy of his succession and shaped how contemporaries remembered his parents. Edmund King observes that chroniclers began to write about the civil war as a reflection of the conflict between Stephen and Henry, diminishing or denying altogether any authority that Matilda or her husband, Count Geoffrey le Bel of Anjou, had claimed in the Anglo-Norman realm.[3] This tendency can be seen in the *Historia Gaufredi*, a biography of Count Geoffrey that was written for the court of Henry II by John of Marmoutier, a monk from Touraine. Although Geoffrey had become duke of Normandy, John clarifies that the count of Anjou invaded the duchy 'so that he could defend the inheritance for his son'.[4] This allowed him to rehabilitate Geoffrey's legacy as

---

[1]   Edmund King, 'The Accession of Henry II', in *Henry II: New Interpretations*, ed. Christopher Harper-Bill and Nicholas Vincent (Woodbridge, 2007), 24–46.
[2]   Henry of Huntingdon, *Historia*, 770–771; *The Chronicle of Robert de Torigni*, in *Chronicles of the Reigns of Stephen, Henry II and Richard I*, ed. R. Howlett, 4 vols. (Roll Series, London, 1884–1889), iv, 177. Stephen issued a charter from Winchester that confirmed Henry's rights and also made provisions for his sole surviving son, William. See *Regesta*, iii, no. 272.
[3]   Edmund King, *King Stephen* (New Haven and London, 2010), 327–330.
[4]   John of Marmoutier, *Historia Gaufredi Ducis*, in *Chroniques des Comtes d'Anjou et des Seigneurs d'Amboise*, ed. Louis Halphen and René Poupardin (Paris, 1913), 224. 'Consul vero Andegavensis Gaufredus, contractis viribus, Normanniam, ut filii sui hereditatem vindicet, ingreditur.'

the conqueror of Normandy within the context of the political compromises that existed after Henry received the duchy from his father in 1150.

The purpose of this study is to establish how Geoffrey le Bel viewed his rightful place in the Anglo-Norman realm from the beginning of his marriage. It is has been difficult for scholars to evaluate Geoffrey's expectations without viewing him as the precursor to Henry II. Charles Haskins tried to simplify the issue by focusing on the charters and writs produced by Geoffrey's chancellery in Normandy. His explanation about why Geoffrey chose to maintain Norman administrative practices centers on Geoffrey's decision in 1150 to abdicate the ducal title in favor of his son. He argues that Geoffrey never intended to conquer Normandy as an expression of his own rights to the Anglo-Norman realm. The conquest and administration of Normandy was for the benefit of Henry II's rightful place as the successor to Henry I.[5] Josèphe Chartou's treatment of Geoffrey as count of Anjou reinforces this position. While noting that some narrative sources claimed he would have inherited the crown through his wife, Chartrou ultimately agrees with Haskins that the primary motivation for the conquest of Normandy was to protect the inheritance for Henry II.[6] Subsequent research has generally accepted these conclusions.[7]

Haskins was a pioneer in the evaluation of charters as instruments of government, but subsequent research on the use of charters as a reflection of social and political culture provides a better framework for understanding how Geoffrey viewed the nature of his authority as it relates to his wife and children. This can be seen most clearly in donations to monasteries. Monks and their donors were concerned about overlapping claims to property rights and sought to include confirmations from kin who could feasibly contest the alienation of land and other moveable goods. This often included young children as a safeguard against future complaints once they reached adulthood and came into their inheritance.[8] Many of the acts completed by Geoffrey in Normandy concern property rights and tax exemptions claimed by religious houses under previous dukes. One example is an extract of a charter that Geoffrey had issued for the church of Saint Mary at Bec between 1147 and 1150. This document reflects a confirmation of the 'customs, exemptions and freedoms' (*consuetudines et quietudines et libertates*) that had been established for the monastery under Henry I. Geoffrey is the principal confirmer of these rights, but it also states

---

5   Charles Homer Haskins, 'Normandy under Geoffrey Plantagenet', *EHR* 27, no. 107 (July 1912), 423–24; Charles Homer Haskins, *Norman Institutions* (Harvard, 1918), 130–131.

6   Josèphe Chartrou, *L'Anjou de 1109 à 1151* (Paris, 1927), 47–49.

7   W.L. Warren, *Henry II* (Berkeley, CA, 1973), 32; C.W. Hollister and T.K. Keefe, 'The Making of the Angevin Empire', *Journal of British Studies*, 12 (1973), 18 and n. 79; John Le Patourel, *The Norman Empire* (Oxford, 1976), 275–276; Edmund King, *Anarchy of King Stephen's Reign* (Oxford, 1994), 24–25; Edmund King, *King Stephen* (New Haven and London, 2010), 265, 329. For a modification of this perspective, see Kathyrn Dutton, 'Geoffrey, Count of Anjou and Duke of Normandy, 1129–51', Ph.D. Thesis (University of Glasgow, 2011), discussed below.

8   Stephen D White, *Custom, Kingship, and Gifts to Saints: The* Laudatio Parentum *in Western France, 1050–1150* (Chapel Hill, NC, 1988) is a foundational study on these issues.

that he made this concession 'with the counsel of my son Henry and my barons' (*consilio H. filii mei et baronum meorum*).[9] Haskins is correct in observing this as an example of Geoffrey integrating his son into the government of Normandy.[10] It does not, however, explicitly identify young Henry as Geoffrey's heir. The charter reflects Geoffrey's status as duke, since the monks were obtaining his confirmation, and associates Henry as an advisor, whose right to participate depended on his relationship with his father. The monks were validating the legitimacy of Geoffrey's authority while also safeguarding the future stability of their rights by including his son and heir in this process.

My argument is that Geoffrey le Bel used his charters and writs to assert his right to govern the Anglo-Norman realm, and that he consciously refused to use language that would establish legitimacy for young Henry apart from his own authority. These documents represent the expression of political rights that he had claimed from early in his marriage. As such, they need to be viewed as a reflection of his struggle to achieve legitimacy rather than just a series of acts confined to the administration of Normandy. To a certain extent this parallels the way Matilda expressed her authority in England between 1139 and 1148. Marjorie Chibnall argues that Matilda pursued her own claims to the throne and that she intended to use the title *domina Anglorum* as a substitute until she received formal recognition as queen. Matilda continued to use this designation well after she began to introduce Henry as her heir, ending this practice in 1148 only after it became clear that he stood a better chance of securing the loyalty of Stephen's supporters.[11] The difference is that Geoffrey received consecration as duke, which Matilda recognized in some of her charters, allowing him to establish a line of succession that included his personal rule.[12]

Expectations of marriage

The charters that Geoffrey issued for Normandy are best understood within the context of the political rights he thought belonged to him as Matilda's husband. Research on aristocratic marriages in the Loire and other parts of France demonstrates that husbands and wives generally shared control over property and lordships. This normally involved the integration of a woman into her husband's lands while establishing rights for a man over his wife's dowry.[13]

9   *Regesta*, iii, no. 79.
10   Haskins, *Norman Institutions*, 131. Also see W.L. Warren, *Henry II*, 32 and n. 3.
11   Marjorie Chibnall, *The Empress Matilda* (Oxford, 1991), 88–117, 143–151.
12   Several of the charters issued by Matilda around 1144 recognize Geoffrey as duke of Normandy. See *Regesta*, iii, nos. 43, 370, 372.
13   Amy Livingstone, *Out of Love for my Kin: Aristocratic Family Life in the Lands of the Loire, 1000–1200* (Ithaca, NY, 2010), 120–140, 170–189; Theodore Evergates, *The Aristocracy in the County of Champagne, 1100–1300* (Philadelphia, PA, 2007), 93–115. For some observations on the dowry in Maine, see Bruno Lemesle, *La Société aristocratique dans le Haut-Maine (XI–XII siècles)* (Rennes, 1999), 124–131.

This provided aristocratic women with great power as they managed lordships for their husbands. An example of this includes Henry I's sister, Adela, who governed alongside her husband Stephen of Blois and then assumed control of Blois-Chartres on behalf of her young sons when Stephen died on the First Crusade.[14] Marriage to an heiress could often result in the transfer of a lordship to her husband upon the death of her father.[15] Henry I was able to provide the earldom of Gloucester for his eldest natural son Robert of Caen by arranging his marriage to Mabel fitz Hamon. Another son, Richard, would have inherited lands from the fitz Osbern family in Normandy if he had not died before marrying the heiress Amicia of Gael.[16] The most pertinent examples for Geoffrey were his own parents. His mother Aremburgh was the daughter and heiress to Count Helias of Maine. When her father died in 1110 his authority passed to Geoffrey's father, Count Fulk V of Anjou, who governed as count of Maine until he left for Jerusalem in 1129.[17] Fulk went to the Holy Land because he had arranged a marriage for himself to Melisende, the daughter and heiress to King Baldwin II of Jerusalem. He vacated Anjou permanently and became king of Jerusalem when Baldwin died in 1131.[18]

It would have been normal for Geoffrey to expect that his marriage would give him a right to share in the governance of the Anglo-Norman realm. His disagreements with Henry I were based on what he considered to be reasonable claims to his wife's inheritance. Scholars agree that Henry I did not intend to give Geoffrey any appreciable role in his government.[19] This may have been his preference, but he still had to navigate Geoffrey's conflicting expectations as he was integral to assuring Henry's plan for a peaceful succession. Geoffrey married Matilda in June 1128 with the understanding that she had received oaths of loyalty from the greater part of the Anglo-Norman nobility in January 1127. William of Malmesbury comments that the nobles and church officials who attended Henry's Christmas court agreed to accept her as their *domina*, but only if

---

14   Kimberly LoPrete, *Adela of Blois: Countess and Lord (c. 1067–1137)* (Dublin, 2007), 71–163; Kimberly LoPrete, 'Adela of Blois: Familial Alliances and Female Lordship', in *Aristocratic Women in Medieval France*, ed. Theodore Evergates (Philadelphia, PA, 1999), 15–29. For similar circumstances in the county of Flanders, see Karen S. Nicholas, 'Countesses as Rulers in Flanders', in *Aristocratic Women*, 111–137.
15   Evergates, *The Aristocracy in the County of Champagne*, 128–129; Lemesle, *La société aristocratique*, 122–123.
16   Kathleen Thompson, 'Affairs of State: The Illegitimate Children of Henry I', *JMH* 29 (2003), 131.
17   Robert LaTouche, *Histoire du comté du Maine pendent le Xe et le XI siècle* (Paris, 1910), 52–53; Bruno Lemesle, *La société aristocratique*, 43–45.
18   H.E. Mayer, 'The Succession to Baldwin II of Jerusalem: English Impact on the East', *Dumbarton Oaks Papers* 39 (1985), 139–47.
19   The most comprehensive assessments of Henry I's plan for the succession are Hollister and Keefe, 'The Making of the Angevin Empire', 11–18; Judith A. Green, 'Henry I and the Origins of the Civil War', in *King Stephen's Reign*, ed. Paul Dalton and Graeme J. White (Woodbridge, 2008), 11–26. Also see Chibnall, *The Empress Matilda*, 56–57; C. Warren Hollister, *Henry I* (New Haven, 2001), 313–326, 467–483; Judith A. Green, *Henry I* (Cambridge, MA, 2009), 202–203, 217–220.

the king died without a male heir. Unless Henry's second wife Adeliza produced a son, the nobility swore to recognize that legitimate succession lay in Matilda alone (*cui soli legitima debeatur succession*).[20] Symeon of Durham assumed that these terms reflected a conventional understanding that the authority vested in succession would pass to Matilda's husband. He also notes that this was contingent upon Henry I's failure to produce a legitimate son.[21] Adeliza never gave birth to an heir who would trump the oaths given to Matilda, though this realization could only have come with Henry's death. Geoffrey knew that he had married a potential heiress whose rights had been guaranteed so long as Henry's new marriage remained childless.

The first sign of tension came in the summer of 1129 when Geoffrey is said to have repudiated his wife and sent her back to Normandy.[22] Chibnall noted that two letters written by Archbishop Hildebert of Tours indicate that Geoffrey was resisting Henry I's expectations for the marriage as much as he was rejecting his wife. The first letter, directed to Geoffrey in 1131, expresses Henry I's displeasure that the count of Anjou was planning a pilgrimage to Compostela when he had pressing matters to attend to in his realm. The second letter was sent to Henry I and expresses joy that he had reconciled with his son-in-law.[23] Moreover, Hildebert mentions that the young count pledged himself to Henry's wishes regarding 'all that pertained to him and his daughter'.[24] It is in this spirit that Henry I agreed to support Geoffrey's request that his wife return. Henry convened a council at Northampton in September 1131 that resolved to send Matilda back to her husband and renewed the oaths supporting her status as the successor to the Anglo-Norman realm.[25] This was, in theory, the same oath that Matilda had received in January 1127. The difference is that this oath was given in the context of her marriage to the count of Anjou.

Henry I presumed that the marriage could be repaired without directly addressing Geoffrey's grievances. He had to trust that Matilda would maintain his priorities as she repaired her relationship with her husband. These plans unraveled as Henry I's relationship with his daughter deteriorated in 1134–35. Henry of Huntingdon mentions that the king directed his anger towards Matilda because she addressed various disputes that had arisen between him and the count of Anjou. It was an issue that Matilda would not abandon and caused her father to delay the regular governance of his realm.[26] William

---

20   William of Malmesbury, *HN*, 6–7.
21   Symeon, *Opera*, ii, 281–282.
22   Symeon, *Opera*, ii, 283.
23   Chibnall, *The Empress Matilda*, 57–58; Hildebert of Tours, 'Epsitolae', *PL* 171, cols. 131–133, 272.
24   Hildebert of Tours, 'Epistolae', *PL* 171, col. 272. 'Audivi autem ex relatione quorumdam quod solum in infirmitate mea mihi cessit ad gaudium, scilicet vos bene esse cum nostro comite, eumque se totum vestro commsisse consilio, ita ut in omnibus quae ad vos et ad vestram respiciunt filiam, vestram sit secuturus voluntatem'.
25   Henry of Huntingdon, *Historia*, 486–489; William of Malmesbury, *HN*, 18–21.
26   Henry of Huntingdon, *Historia*, 490–491.

of Malmesbury notes that Henry I was frustrated primarily with Geoffrey's demands. He comments that Henry, as he lay dying, 'assigned all his lands on both sides of the sea to his daughter in lawful and lasting succession, being somewhat angry with her husband because he had vexed the king by not a few threats and insults'.[27] The king still anticipated that his daughter would assume control over the Anglo-Norman realm, but maintained his displeasure with his son-in-law.

Thus Matilda became an advocate for her husband just as her father was trying to placate his nobility by maneuvering around any rights that Geoffrey could expect through marriage. William of Malmesbury implies that the leaders who came to reject Matilda were reacting to her Angevin marriage. He relates an explanation made by Roger, bishop of Salisbury, who insisted that he was released from his oath to Matilda because he had sworn his loyalty on the condition that the leading men of the realm would be consulted if she was married outside the kingdom. He claimed that the arrangements for Matilda's marriage had been made in secret, without his knowledge, thus nullifying his previous oath.[28] This suggests there was an understanding that whoever married Matilda would be able to claim authority within the Anglo-Norman realm and that there was some hesitancy in accepting a non-Norman in that role. By default, the renunciation of oaths to Matilda eliminated any potential claims that Geoffrey could make regarding England or Normandy.

A charter issued for the monks of Saint-Florent of Saumur on 1 July 1133 is an important link between the reconciliation of Henry I and Geoffrey in 1131 and the breakdown of Henry's relationship with Matilda in 1134–35. The document records Geoffrey's promise never to raise a fortification on the motte of the old *castellum* next to the monastery of Saint-Florent. He was joined by his wife Matilda, his brother Helias, and his sister Sibyl in providing their *signum* for the act.[29] In doing so, Matilda participated with her in-laws in providing *laudatio* for the concession. This was especially important since she had given birth to young Henry at Le Mans in March 1133 and was now responsible for representing her son's interests.[30] The charter also includes statements that reflect the way Geoffrey and Matilda agreed to present their public authority. The monks refer to Geoffrey as 'count of the Angevins, son of King Fulk of the Jerusalemites, and also husband of Matilda, daughter of the king of the

---

27   William of Malmesbury, *HN*, 24–25.
28   William of Malmesbury, *HN*, 10–11.
29   *Livre d'argent de Saint-Florent*, Angers, AD Maine-et-Loire, H 3714, fols. 48r–49r, printed in Chartrou, *L'Anjou*, no. 46. While similar, the version recorded in the *Livre Rouge de Saint-Florent* lacks the *signum* of the count or his family. See *Livre rouge de Saint-Florent*, Angers, AD Maine-et-Loire, H 3715 fols. 22v–23r. Chibnall, *The Empress Matilda*, 70 and n. 27 follows a poor excerpt printed in *Chroniques des comtes d'Anjou*, ed. Paul Marchegay and Andre Salmon, vol. 2, (Paris 1871), xv n. 1, which is misattributed to the *Livre blanc de Saint-Florent* and misdated to 29 June 1130.
30   Chibnall, *The Empress Matilda*, 60–61.

English and former wife of Henry, namely the Roman emperor'.[31] This shows respect to Matilda's lineage and the status she had achieved in her previous marriage.[32] It adds greater stature to Geoffrey's identity as well. He appears as a political co-equal to his wife, each being presented as the offspring of monarchs. Furthermore, the *datum* clause signals an effort to establish more directly his connection to the Anglo-Norman realm by identifying Geoffrey as the son-in-law to Henry I.[33]

The language of this charter shows that Geoffrey was using his public acts as a means of establishing his connection to the Anglo-Norman realm. Matilda signaled her support for Geoffrey's statements by placing her *signum* at the end of the charter. When she returned to Rouen in 1134, she alienated her father by seeking a more permanent position for her husband in Normandy. Orderic Vitalis attempts to remove her from the center of the dispute by presenting the situation as an argument between 'the proud-spirited monarch' and the 'proud youth'. He frames the violence committed by Geoffrey along the southern frontier of Normandy in 1135 as frustration over his inability to secure recognition of his rights to Matilda's dowry. He does not comment on whether Geoffrey's complaints were justified, noting only that the count of Anjou 'aspired to the great riches of his father-in-law and demanded castles in Normandy, asserting that the king had covenanted with him to hand them over when he married his daughter'.[34] Robert of Torigni maintains this impression, though he states that Geoffrey was demanding recognition of his claims to the whole realm.[35] In either case, Matilda had accepted that her husband should share in her inheritance against the wishes of her father.

Enforcing a joint inheritance

The coronation of Stephen of Blois as king of England in December 1135 was a direct challenge to any rights that Geoffrey could expect through marriage. Until that point he had focused on securing his authority over Matilda's inheritance. Now it was necessary for Geoffrey to assert his wife's claim as the successor to the Anglo-Norman realm. He demonstrated this by sending Bishop Ulger of Angers to the *curia* of Innocent II in 1139 in order to gain papal recognition of Matilda's right of succession and remove Stephen from the throne.[36] These

---

31 *Livre d'argent*, fol. 48r and *Livre rouge*, fol. 22v. 'Ego Goffridus Martellus, Andegavorum comes, Fulconis regis Ierosolimitanorum filius, idemque Mathildis, regis Anglorum filiae, Henrici videlicet Romani imperatoris quondam uxoris, maritus …'.

32 Chibnall, *The Empress Matilda*, 70.

33 *Livre d'argent*, fol. 49r and *Livre rouge*, fol. 23r. 'regnante … Henrico in Anglia, Goffrido ejus genero Andegavorum comite …'.

34 OV, vi, 444–445.

35 *The Chronicle of Robert de Torigni*, 128.

36 John of Salisbury, *Historia Pontificalis*, ed. M. Chibnall (Oxford, 1986), 84.

circumstances did not change the way Geoffrey introduced himself in his charters, which suggests that his political expectations remained constant despite the failure to secure a peaceful succession. It also demonstrates that he shared his wife's reluctance to claim official authority until he possessed it legally. Matilda emphasized the legitimacy of her cause by referring to her status as Henry I's daughter. She began to use the phrase *domina Anglorum* to establish her sovereignty after Stephen was captured at the battle of Lincoln on 2 February 1141.[37] Geoffrey likewise refrained from claiming the ducal title until he could receive consecration, even when it was clear by the end of 1143 that he was in control of Normandy.[38]

There were other ways that Geoffrey could express his rights. The most common was the use of language in his charters that served to broaden his identity to reflect a more regal lineage. This was a product of his father's succession as king of Jerusalem in 1131, at which point Geoffrey began to style himself as 'the son of Fulk, king of Jerusalem' or 'the Jerusalemite'. The first datable reference comes from the charter that Matilda witnessed for her husband at Saint-Florent of Saumur in July 1133 and appears again in their joint charter of 1138.[39] He used this designation frequently in the charters he issued on his own prior to 1144.[40] Geoffrey may have been motivated by Anglo-Norman concerns about his relatively low status compared to Matilda.[41] Even so, these claims could only serve as a symbolic gesture. He was not born of a king, nor was his authority in France based on royal lineage. The birth of Baldwin, the son of Fulk and Melisende, all but guaranteed that Geoffrey would never hold a practical claim to kingship in the Holy Land.[42] The association with his father

---

37   Chibnall, *The Empress Matilda*, 70–71.
38   Chartrou, *L'Anjou*, 63–65; Haskins, *Norman Institutions*, 129–130.
39   *Livre d'argent*, fol. 48r and *Livre rouge*, fol. 22v; *Recueil des Actes de Henry II*, no. 1.
40   Most of Geoffrey's surviving charters for the period between 1133 and 1144 designate that he is the son of King Fulk of Jerusalem. See *Cartulaire de l'Abbaye de Saint-Aubin d'Angers*, 3 vols., ed. Bertrand de Broussillon (Paris, 1903), nos. 9, 627, 644, 933; *Cartulaire de l'Abbaye du Ronceray d'Angers*, ed. Paul Marchegay (Paris, 1900), no. 92; *Cartulaire de Chateau-du-Loir*, ed. Eugène Vallée, in *Archives Historiques du Maine* 6 (Le Mans, 1905), no. 81; *Cartulaire du Chapitre Royal de Saint-Pierre-de-la-Cour*, ed. Menjot d'Elbenne and L.-J. Denis, in *Archives Historiques du Maine* 4 (Le Mans, 1903), no. 16; *Cartulaire du Chapitre de Saint-Laud d'Angers*, ed. Adrein Planchenault (Angers, 1903), no. 38; *Cartulaire de Cormery*, ed. J.-J. Bourassé (Tours, 1861), no. 61; *Cartulaire de Saint-Victeur au Mans*, ed. Bertrand de Broussillon (Paris, 1895), no. 17; *Cartulaire noir de la Cathedrale d'Angers*, ed. Ch. Urseau (Angers, 1908), nos. 138, 210; *Cartulaires des Abbayes Saint-Pierre de la Couture et Saint Pierre de Solesmes* (Le Mans, 1881), no. 46; *Grand Cartulaire de Fontevraud*, 2 vols., ed. Jean-Marc Bienvenu (Poitiers, 2000–2005), no. 868; Chartrou, *L'Anjou*, nos. 16, 49, 53–54, 57.
41   Robert of Torigni responded to concerns about Geoffrey's relatively low rank by devoting a section to his lineage in his interpolation of the *GND*, ed. van Houts, ii, 242–244. Matilda herself apparently had reservations about the match. See John Gillingham, 'Love, Marriage and Politics in the Twelfth Century', in *Forum for Modern Language Studies* 25 (1989), 296–97; Chibnall, *The Empress Matilda*, 55.
42   Hans E. Mayer, 'Studies in the History of Queen Melisende of Jerusalem', *Dumbarton Oaks Papers* 26 (1972), 100–102.

did, however, serve to demonstrate that he was his wife's equal. He would continue to refer to himself as the son of the king of Jerusalem regularly until he became duke of Normandy.[43]

This emphasis on Angevin kingship extended beyond reassurance that the count of Anjou was a suitable match for the Empress. Orderic Vitalis was aware that Geoffrey was using his father's authority as king of Jerusalem as a point of comparison for his own proper status in the Anglo-Norman realm. When announcing the marriage of Geoffrey and Matilda, Orderic devotes far more attention to the impact of his father's succession as king, noting that Fulk 'effortlessly acquired the kingdom of Jerusalem and principality of Antioch'. However, problems ensued as Fulk began to replace the experienced leaders of the kingdom with newcomers. Orderic claims that Fulk 'gave the chief places in the counsels of the realm and the castellanships of castles to new flatterers', causing dissension that led to civil war.[44] This portion of the *Ecclesiastical History* was completed after Geoffrey and Matilda's marriage failed to produce a peaceful succession in the Anglo-Norman realm.[45] The comparison between the two marriages is intentional and implies that unwelcome change would have come to Normandy even if they had accepted Matilda's claims to the throne. Even more to the point is the understanding that female succession would have lead to Angevin kingship, as had been the case in Jerusalem.

At times Matilda added her support to her husband's political statements. This can be seen in a charter Geoffrey issued in 1138 that records the concession of a *vinagium* to the monks of Saint-Florent of Saumur. The donation was confirmed in stages: the concession by Geoffrey at Le Mans, the confirmation of Matilda and their sons Henry and William at Carrouges, and the confirmation by their third son Geoffrey at Saumur.[46] The monks were clearly seeking *laudatio* from the family. The act itself did not require a trip to Normandy as the vineyards in question were located near Saumur in southern Anjou. Matilda's approval at Carrouges did provide the count of

---

[43] A notice for Saint-Évroul refers to Geoffrey as 'Andegavorum comes, Fulconis bone memorie Iherusalem regis filus', placing it before Geoffrey's accession as duke of Normandy. See *Regesta*, iii, no. 774; Chartrou, *L'Anjou*, 294. Geoffrey seems to have dropped the regular use of this phrase after becoming duke of Normandy. It appears in a charter for the college of Saint-Laud at Angers, but this could have been completed shortly after he became duke in 1144. See *Cartulaire du Chapitre de Saint-Laud d'Angers*, no. 2 (also *Regesta*, iii, no. 1102). The phrase continued to resonate among the Angevins, as the monks of Saint-Serge comment that a donation made by Bechet, sergeant at the *castellum* of Brissac, was completed 'tempore Goffredi Andecavorum comitis, filii videlicet Fulconis regis Jerusalem ...' This was done after the death of Abbot Herveus (31 March 1150). See *Cartulaires de l'abbaye Saint-Serge et Saint-Bach d'Angers*, ed. Yves Chauvin (Angers, 1997), no. 403.

[44] OV, vi, 390–393. Orderic is referring to the revolt of Count Hugh II of Jaffa and Romulus of Le Puy, who rose up against King Fulk in 1134. See Hans Eberhard Mayer, 'Angevins *versus* Normans: The New Men of King Fulk of Jerusalem', in *The American Philosophical Society* 133.1 (March 1989), 2–4.

[45] For the dating see OV, vi, 392 n. 2.

[46] *Recueil des Actes de Henry II*, ed. Léopold Delisle and Élie Berger (Paris, 1896), no. 1.

Anjou an opportunity to make a public statement about his authority while in Normandy.[47] The document not only identifies Geoffrey as count of Anjou, but it also adds that he is 'the son of Fulk, in good memory king of Jerusalem' (*filius Fulconis, bone memorie regis Jerusalem*). Language pertaining to Matilda's status as the daughter of Henry I appears midway through the document as she provides her initial concession. Geoffrey identifies her as 'my wife, daughter of Henry king of the English, married to me legally after the death of Henry, emperor of the Romans'.[48] Matilda and her children completed the act at Carrouges in the presence of Count Geoffrey. Thus, in front of a Norman audience, she reinforced her husband's concession and the statements contained within his charter.

Geoffrey and Matilda rarely issued joint charters, but they did recognize the need to maintain a cooperative approach in their effort to unseat Stephen. This can be seen most clearly in some of the agreements reached with nobles who were willing to negotiate with Matilda after she traveled to England in 1139. She granted the *castellum* of Briavel to Miles of Gloucester on 30 September 1139 in recognition of the homage (*homagium*) that he had given to her. This was done because Miles had recognized Matilda as the 'rightful heir of the kingdom of England'.[49] A more complete version of the agreement shows that the submission had been arranged prior to Matilda's arrival and under the guidance of her husband. It states that Matilda had made the arrangements 'by the counsel and command of lord Geoffrey, count of Anjou' (*consilio et precepto domini Galfridi comitis Andegauie*), and that they both had agreed to protect Miles' rights. This directly impacted later negotiations with Geoffrey de Mandeville and his brother-in-law Aubrey de Vere in July 1141.[50] Matilda reached a preliminary agreement with Geoffrey de Mandeville at Westminster in which she recognized his right to the earldom of Essex and the land that his grandfather had possessed in England and Normandy.[51] Additional promises were granted when they met again at Oxford with the understanding that Matilda would seek the approval of her husband and their son Henry.[52] In a separate charter she confirmed for Aubrey de Vere the office of Chamberlain and promised him an earldom, likewise agreeing to obtain security from Geoffrey and their eldest son.[53]

---

[47]   Orderic Vitalis comments that Geoffrey returned to Normandy with a large army in June 1138. See OV, vi, 514–515.

[48]   *Recueil des Actes de Henry II*, no. 1. 'Hanc concessionem facit mecum Matildis, uxor mea, Henrici regis Anglorum filia, post mortem Henrici Romanorum imperatoris michi legitimo conubio sociata'.

[49]   *Regesta*, iii, no. 391. Matilda wished to record that Miles 'recepit me ut dominam et sicut illam quam justam heredem regni Anglie recognovit'.

[50]   London, BL Sloane MS 1301, fol. 422r–v and commentary in Edmund King, 'A Week in Politics: Oxford, Late July 1141', in *King Stephen's Reign*, 67.

[51]   *Regesta*, iii, no. 274.

[52]   *Regesta*, iii, no. 275.

[53]   *Regesta*, iii, no. 634.

The *conventiones* between Matilda, Geoffrey de Mandeville and Aubrey de Vere hold great significance as a reflection of Geoffrey le Bel's status in the Anglo-Norman realm. It is clear that no one considered the agreements secure without the input of the count of Anjou. The language of the Oxford charters suggests that Matilda was doing her best to gain recognition of her husband's authority in addition to her own. She states in her charter for Geoffrey de Mandeville that both 'my lord the count of Anjou and I' (*dominus meus Comes Andegaviae et ego*) could confer the lands held by his maternal grandfather Eudo the Steward. The charter also confirmed lands and revenues for Ernulf of Mandeville, adding an additional grant for the service of ten soldiers 'to hold from my lord the count of Anjou and from myself' as an inheritance.[54] Furthermore, she emphasizes that Geoffrey and his men would be entering the service of 'my lord the count of Anjou and myself' when she promised that they could keep any land that they had added from the time they entered this agreement.[55] The charter for Aubrey de Vere repeats this last provision.[56]

By themselves these documents suggest that Matilda was working towards the recognition of her husband's rights of lordship as she was establishing her own authority in England. However, a charter was also issued in the name of 'Henry, son of the daughter of King Henry, proper heir to England and Normandy' that confirms the terms of the agreement reached by Matilda and Aubrey de Vere.[57] Scholars do not challenge the authenticity of this document, but there are some inconsistencies that raise questions as to its reliability as a reflection of Matilda's position on the succession at the time.[58] Despite its insistence that Henry represents the true heir to England and Normandy, it copies language from Matilda's charter emphasizing that Aubrey of Vere was entering the service of his parents.[59] Furthermore, the language used to introduce Henry in his charter is far different than that his mother used when introducing her son to her supporters after he arrived in England during the autumn of 1142.[60] She reserved for herself

---

54 *Regesta*, iii, no. 275. 'Et praeter hoc do et concede eidem Ernulfo e libertas terrae de terries eschaeatis, et servicium X militum ad tendendum de domino meo Comite Andegav(ie) et de me in capite haereditarie sibi et haeredibus suis de nobis et de haeredibus nostris.'

55 *Regesta*, iii, no. 275. 'Concedo etiam eidem Gaufredo quod ipse et omnes homines sui habeant et lucrentur omnia essarta sua libera et quieta de omnibus placitis facta usque ad diem qua service(io) domini mei Comitis Andegavie ac meo adhesit'.

56 *Regesta*, iii, no. 634. '... ad diem qua servitio domini mei Comitis Andevavie et meo adhererunt'.

57 *Regesta*, iii, no. 635. 'Henricus filius filae Regis Henrici rectus heres Anglie et Norman(ie)'.

58 John Horace Round, *Geoffrey de Mandeville: A Study in Anarchy* (London, 1892), 184–185 views the charter as authentic proof of young Henry's claims. More recent assessments accept it without commenting directly on its implications for Henry's parents. See Chibnall, *The Empress Matilda*, 143; King, *King Stephen*, 180–181.

59 *Regesta*, iii, nos. 634 and 635. Both charters state: 'ad diem qua servitio domini mei Comitis Andevavie et meo adhererunt'.

60 For the timing of Henry's arrival, see A.L. Poole, 'Henry Plantagenet's Early Visits to England', *EHR* 47 (1932), 447–449.

association with Henry I as his daughter and claimed the designation *domina Anglorum* as a statement of her authority.[61] Henry participated in his mother's acts only a few times towards the end of his visit. A charter issued by Matilda for Humphrey of Bohun early in 1144 refers to Henry as 'the son of the count of Anjou'.[62] Sometime later he helped his mother confirm a donation to Godstow abbey as 'her son'.[63] Before he left England Henry began to recognize his father's rights to Normandy. He introduced himself as the 'son of the duke of Normandy' when assisting his mother restore the inheritance of Geoffrey Ridel.[64]

As Edmund King observes, these charters represent moments during negotiations in which Stephen's supporters were able to partially control the terms of their submission to the Angevins.[65] I would suggest that Henry's charter represents a continuation of the *conventiones* begun in 1141. The initiative for this charter came from Geoffrey of Mandeville, who sent Hugh of Ing to Normandy to receive the boy's confirmation.[66] He returned to England with a far bolder statement on Henry's authority than Matilda had provided for her son earlier.[67] It does correspond to the way William of Malmesbury presented English expectations towards Henry. He records that the count of Anjou allowed Robert of Gloucester 'to take to England his eldest son by the empress, so that on seeing him the nobles might be inspired to fight for the cause of the lawful heir'.[68] Henry's charter offered a way forward for those who had rejected Matilda in 1135 and refused to admit guilt in their decision. It would enable them to affirm her right of succession without submitting to her authority. Perhaps more importantly, it would allow them to ignore any claims that Geoffrey made to the Anglo-Norman realm by right of marriage.

Geoffrey as rightful duke of Normandy

Young Henry's journey to England in 1142 marks his formal entry into the politics of the civil war. Matilda and her advisors had wanted her husband to join them, but Geoffrey insisted on completing the conquest of Normandy before involving himself directly in English affairs.[69] Disagreement on strategy did not mean that they were working towards different goals. Orderic Vitalis recognized that the Angevin campaigns in England and Normandy were intricately linked.

---

61   On Matilda's continued emphasis of her rights of succession, see Chibnall, *The Empress Matilda*, 102–104.
62   *Regesta*, iii, no. 111.
63   *Regesta*, iii, no. 372.
64   *Regesta*, iii, no. 43.
65   King, 'A Week in Politics', 65–70; King, *King Stephen*, 164–167.
66   Chibnall, *The Empress Matilda*, 112; King, *King Stephen*, 180–181.
67   One of her charters for the foundation of Bordesley Abbey, issued around the time of the *conventiones*, refers to Henry as her heir (*heredis mei*). See *Regesta*, iii, no. 116.
68   William of Malmesbury, *HN*, 126–127.
69   William of Malmesbury, *HN*, 122–127.

He reports that after Stephen's capture, Robert earl of Leicester obtained a truce with Geoffrey that allowed his brother Waleran of Meulan to return from England and arrange formal submission for his Norman lands.[70] He also comments that the garrisons of Verneuil and Nonancourt surrendered and 'recognized the lordship (*domitatus*) of Count Geoffrey and Matilda'.[71] This is strikingly different to an earlier passage, which depicts Geoffrey 'acting as his wife's stipendiary commander' when he led an army into Normandy during 1137.[72] The situation in 1141 seems to have compelled Orderic to revise how he presented the count of Anjou, recognizing now that he was claiming sovereignty alongside Matilda.

The charters produced for Geoffrey in Normandy offer an even bolder statement on the nature of his authority. He desired to govern as the rightful ruler of Normandy, not as its conqueror, and his charters enforce the idea that he was the heir to Henry I. An unpublished dissertation by Kathyrn Dutton provides an analysis of this issue. She argues that Geoffrey used his charters to challenge the legitimacy of Stephen's rule, asserting his status as Henry I's heir while also preparing the way for his son to take over the ducal title.[73] This offers a subtle revision to Haskins' argument. Dutton accepts that Henry was being prepared for ducal rule throughout the 1140s, but concludes that Geoffrey also 'exercised ducal authority in his own right'.[74] I suggest a more assertive reassessment of Geoffrey's expectations. Matilda and her offspring had been part of Henry I's plans for succession since 1127. When the civil war ended, the nobility received young Henry as heir to the throne, a position that many of them were willing to accept while Stephen was held in captivity in 1141. Geoffrey, however, had been rejected since at least 1134, if not from the beginning of his personal rule as count of Anjou in 1129. The administration of Normandy provided him the opportunity to place himself at the center of his family's right of succession. If the English nobility were still trying to work around his claims to the Anglo-Norman realm, as the *conventiones* of 1141 suggest, then Geoffrey used his charters as a mechanism to assert his rights and redefine the legitimacy of succession.

This process can be seen in a charter that Geoffrey issued for the monks of Saint-Évroul in the early months of 1144, before he assumed the ducal title at Rouen.[75] The charter offers his concession for all their possessions, free and

---

[70]   OV, vi, 548–549; Robert of Torigni, *Chronica*, 142. The submission of Waleran of Meulan secured central Normandy for the count of Anjou. See David Crouch, *The Beaumont Twins: The Roots & Branches of Power in the Twelfth Century* (Cambridge, 1986), 51–55.

[71]   OV, vi, 548–551.

[72]   Ibid., 482–483.

[73]   Kathyrn Dutton, 'Geoffrey, Count of Anjou and Duke of Normandy', 57–61, 197–243. I was introduced to Dr Dutton's research while revising the initial draft of this study. We come to similar conclusions about Geoffrey's use of charters as political instruments.

[74]   Dutton, 'Geoffrey, Count of Anjou and Duke of Normandy', 59–60, 103–105, 243.

[75]   Geoffrey was formally invested as duke on 23 April 1144. See *Recueil des historiens des Gaules et de la France*, 24 vols., ed. M Bouquet et al., (Paris, 1734–1904), xii, 785.

quiet (*libere et quiete*), 'just as they held them in the time of King Henry, my ancestor' (*sicut habebant in tempore regis Hainrici antecessoris mei*). The act itself is a statement on Geoffrey's right to issue such a confirmation, both on the part of the count of Anjou and on the part of the monks. He was still using the designation that appears frequently in his Angevin charters, styling himself as 'count of Anjou, son of Fulk, in good memory king of Jerusalem' (*comes Andegavorum, Fulconis bone memorie Jherusalem regis filius*). More importantly, the document establishes continuity with the reign of Henry I, who appears not as the father of Matilda, from whom Geoffrey held any claims to Normandy, but as 'my ancestor'.[76] This parallels the way Geoffrey styled himself in the charter he issued with Matilda for the monks of Saint-Florent in 1133. Both refer to his father as the king of Jerusalem and the earlier charter refers to Geoffrey as the son-in-law to Henry I.[77]

Geoffrey used similar terminology after he began to use the title 'duke of the Normans and count of the Angevins'. In two charters for the monks of Montebourg Geoffrey refers to his father-in-law as 'King Henry, my predecessor' (*H. rex predecessor meus*) and 'King Henry, my ancestor' (*rex Henricus antecessor meus*). These documents are companions, as they both provide a general confirmation for the concessions recorded in the 'charters and summaries' (*cartas et brevia*) the monks possessed from Henry I. They also record an additional donation made by Geoffrey at the time of his confirmation. He added a strip of land situated between the property belonging to the monks and a forest near their monastery.[78] Geoffrey's instructions to his officials were clear. He held 'in his personal protection the abbey of Montebourg, all the monks, the goods pertaining to them, and his personal alms, just as my ancestor King Henry held (them)'.[79]

Most of Geoffrey's charters and writs are confirmations of previous rights granted by Henry I or otherwise claimed by his supporters. Maintaining the basic structure of documentation used in the Norman chancellery reflects his effort to establish continuity between his reign and that of Henry I.[80] The goal was to stabilize the duchy by preserving the basic relationships that had been established by his predecessor. As Dutton observes, it also served to reinforce his right to act as Henry I's successor.[81] Geoffrey confirmed a monthly payment of 40 *libri* for the leper hospital of Mont-aux-Malades in response to an earlier agreement that Henry I had established with community. The monks had presented Geoffrey with the original charter, and so he explained that he was

---

76   *Regesta*, iii, no. 774.
77   *Livre d'argent*, fol. 48r and *Livre rouge*, fol. 22v, also discussed above.
78   *Regesta*, iii, nos. 595–596.
79   *Regesta*, iii, no. 596. 'Sciat quod habeo in mea propria custodia abbatiam de Monteburgo, omnes monachos, et omnes res ad eos pertinentes tamquam meam propriam elemosinam sicut habuit rex Henricus antecessor meus'.
80   On the structure and style of Geoffrey's charters and writs, see Haskins, *Norman Institutions*, 135–143.
81   Dutton, 'Geoffrey, Count of Anjou and Duke of Normandy', 215–220.

making this concession 'just as King Henry had given it to them and is attested by his charter'.[82] Similarly, the monks of Savigny Abbey received Geoffrey's confirmation for the donation of the churches of Dampierre, Saint-Avoye, and the chapel of Fresnay-la-Mère that Henry I had previously given to their monastery. Geoffrey was validating the previous act: 'I give all that Henry, the venerable king of England and duke of Normandy, gave and conceded to abbot Vitalis to found a priory and a convent of monks.'[83] In both of these acts Henry I is still the primary authority on the validity of their concessions. This gives the impression that Geoffrey is performing *laudatio* for charters that have already been issued by his father-in-law, something that was denied to him while Henry was still alive. It was the responsibility of the kin of the deceased to ensure that their ancestors' donations remained intact. Geoffrey was fulfilling this role on his own.[84]

These confirmations served to promote a sense of continuity between the reign of Henry I and Geoffrey's governance of Normandy. Dutton argues that Geoffrey purposely omitted any acts that Stephen may have completed for religious houses as a means of delegitimizing his ducal rule. She notes, in particular, that Stephen had renewed Henry I's privileges to the guild of cordwainers and cobblers of Rouen in 1137. When Geoffrey, and later his son Henry, confirmed these privileges, they referred back to the concession of Henry I without acknowledging Stephen's renewal.[85] Some of Geoffrey's charters use language that implies criticism of conditions in Normandy under Stephen. For example, when Geoffrey confirmed for the monks of Marmoutier their rights to the priory of Héanville, he promised that they should possess it 'just as they held it better and undisturbed in the time of King Henry'.[86] He used the same type of language when he confirmed for the monks of Saint-Amand their right to collect the tithe of the forests of Eu and Alihermont, stating that they should possess it 'just as they held it better in the time of King Henry'.[87] Use of the term *melius* (better) suggests that these acts were intended to represent a restoration of rights that had been abrogated after Stephen became duke of Normandy. Geoffrey certainly wanted to promote himself as the restorer of rights that had been lost since the time of King Henry, whether or not conditions had become worse for these monastic communities.

---

[82] *Regesta*, iii, no. 730. 'sicut rex H(enricus) eis dedit et carta [ejus te]statur'.
[83] *Regesta*, iii, no. 808. 'Que omnia Henric(us) venerabilis rex Anglorum et dux Normannorum pro salute anime sue et prolis sue et amicorum suorum dono Vitali abbati ejusdem ecclesie priori fundatori et conventui monachorum donavit et concessit'.
[84] White, *Custom, Kinship and Gifts to Saints*, 158.
[85] Dutton, 'Geoffrey, Count of Anjou and Duke of Normandy', 215–216 and App. I no. 82, who notes that the version printed in *Regesta*, iii, no. 728 is misattributed to Henry II. She follows the version contained in a fourteenth-century manuscript, Paris AN MSS JJ102 fol. 102v, no. 313, which describes the confirmation of Henry I's act by Geoffrey le Bel and the later confirmation by young Henry after he became duke. For Stephen's confirmation of 1137, see *Regesta*, iii, no. 727.
[86] *Regesta*, iii, no. 578. '… sicut melius et quietus tenuerunt tempore regis Henricus'.
[87] *Regesta*, iii, no. 732. '… sicut eam melius habuit tempore Henrici regis'.

In many cases Geoffrey would reissue an act by employing the same language that had been used in Henry I's chancellery. As Haskins noted, this practice functioned as a means of maintaining rights that had been granted by previous dukes of Normandy.[88] It also served as a way for Geoffrey to assert his authority in familiar terms. Haskins observed that Geoffrey made few modifications when he reissued for the monks of Vignats the exemption from tolls and customs that had been granted by Henry I for the goods produced by their monastery. He reused the original greeting, addressing the 'barons, all viscounts, and ministers of England, Normandy, and sea ports', substituting his name and status as duke of Normandy for that of his father-in-law as king of England. He was not simply recopying the previous charter. He personalized the donation, adding the phrase *sicut mee res proprie* to define his right to grant the exemption, and updated the witness list to represent his officials.[89] Geoffrey chose to use his own greeting, in the style of the Norman chancellery, when he issued instructions to 'Fulk of Alnou, Robert of Nouville, and all his justices, ministers, and custodians of the forest of Argentan' to enforce his concession of 'all customs and freedoms' that the abbess of Alemènches 'had held in the time of King Henry' in the forest of Gouffern. The only point of reference for Geoffrey's authority is his designation as duke of Normandy, by which he held the right to dispose of the property and revenues that had been granted previously by Henry I.[90]

The documents produced by Geoffrey's chancellery in Normandy make no attempt to justify his right to govern the duchy. As much as his early charters for Anjou emphasized the theoretical basis for his authority as the husband of Matilda, his Norman charters take his rights by marriage for granted. He issued instructions and made donations without reference to Matilda or her right of succession. The use of the Norman style in recording his acts reflected his right to control the chancellery, not simply copy the language that had been used by previous dukes. Geoffrey was concerned about providing a stable foundation for his governance of Normandy. His strategy for assuming control of the duchy emphasized continuity with the reign of Henry I, exercising his rights as the successor to Henry I without reference to Matilda.[91] The writs produced by

---

[88]   Haskins, *Norman Institutions*, 142–143.

[89]   *Regesta*, iii, no. 747. 'G(alfridus) dux Norm(annorum) comes And(egavorum) baronibus et omnibus vicomitibus et ministries totius Anglie et Normannie et portuum maris salute'. For the charter of Henry I, see Haskins, *Norman Institutions*, 306, no. 20.

[90]   *Regesta*, iii, no. 17. 'G(alfridus) dux Norm(annorum) comes Andeg(avorum) Fulc(oni) de Alnou et Roberto de Novavilla et omnibus justiciis suis et omnibus ministries et custodibus foreste Argentomii salutem. Sciatis quod concedo quod abbatissa Alemenescharum habeat in foresta mea de Goff(er) omnes illas consuetudines et libertates bene et in pace quas ipsa habebat in tempore regis Henrici'.

[91]   Matilda seldom asserted her authority in Normandy while Geoffrey was in control of its government. See Marjorie Chibnall, 'The Charters of Empress Matilda', in *Law and Government in Medieval England and Normandy: Essays in Honour of Sir James Holt*, ed. George Garnett and John Hudson (Cambridge, MA, 1994), 288.

his chancellery reflect his status as duke of Normandy and were written to his Norman officials with the expectation that they would carry out the directives just as the previous dukes had expected of their followers.

Henry as the son of Duke Geoffrey of Normandy

Matilda accepted Geoffrey's control of the Norman government. She made a donation at Godstow abbey towards the end of the conquest for the safety of 'Geoffrey duke of Normandy and count of Anjou'.[92] She also decided to send Henry back to his father. He would spend the next six years moving between Anjou, Normandy, and England as his presence gained greater importance in light of his parents' conflict with Stephen.[93] It was left to Geoffrey to supervise his son's transition into adulthood, and this included preparing him for the political role he would inherit in the future. He expressed this to Henry at the end of a letter he wrote in the early months of 1145 notifying his son about the resolution of a dispute in favor of the monks of La Trinité de Vendôme. Geoffrey emphasizes that Henry had the responsibility to preserve the agreement because he would 'succeed me in the governance of my land' (*ad regimen terre mee michi te successurum*) and that their family had protected the monks since the foundation of their monastery. He concludes with a final appeal based on the authority that Henry should receive one day, hoping that Henry would 'surpass me and all my predecessors in power and dignity' (*me et omnes antecessors meos potestate et dignitate ... superabis*), and thus would have an even greater capacity to protect the interests of the monks.[94]

It was around this time that Geoffrey began to include his son in some of his business in Normandy. Henry appeared with his father in a similar way as he did with his mother in England.[95] As seen in the charter mentioned earlier from Bec, Henry's role sometimes reflected that of an advisor alongside other ducal officials.[96] Geoffrey issued a charter for Saint-Wandrille 'with the counsel and concession of my son Henry' (*consilio et concessu Henrici filii mei*).[97] Like some of his other acts, Geoffrey used this moment to establish continuity with the reign of Henry I, as he was restoring to the monks 'all tithes and alms in wheat, *denarii* and in all things just as they held them in the time of king Henry'.[98] By including his son in the act Geoffrey could emphasize that this

---

92   *Regesta*, iii, no. 370. '… incolumitate domini mei G(aufredi) duci Norm(annorum) et comitis And(egavoruam)'. She expresses similar sentiment in another donation at Godstow abbey around the same time. See *Regesta*, iii, no. 372.
93   For his movements during these years, see Poole, 'Henry Plantagenet', 450–452.
94   *Chartes de Saint-Julien de Tours*, no. 87.
95   Chibnall, *The Empress Matilda*, 102–104.
96   *Regesta*, iii, no. 79.
97   *Regesta*, iii, no. 780.
98   *Regesta*, iii, no. 780. 'reddidisse monachis Sancti Wandreg(isil) omnes decimas et elemosinas in bladis et in denariis et in omnibus rebus sicut in tempore regis Henrici habebant'.

line of succession included young Henry, whose support would be necessary since it would eventually fall to him to preserve the agreement recorded in the charter. In some cases Geoffrey chose to give Henry a more authoritative role by including his son as a joint concessor. For example, Geoffrey and Henry together sent notice to their men that they had conceded to abbot Henry of Fécamp, by authority of their *sigillum*, the rights and possessions associated with their monastic church.[99] Henry also joined his father in confirming for the monks of Bec their exemption from paying tolls and other customary taxes for their possessions at Arques and Dieppe.[100]

The charters that Henry completed with his father identify him as the son of the duke of Normandy. They avoid the type of language used in the confirmation issued in his name for Aubrey de Vere, which presented him as the 'proper heir to England and Normandy'. This suggests that Geoffrey was trying to integrate Henry into his government while maintaining the associations that reflected his own authority. Henry seems to have been a willing participant in this endeavor. He reissued his father's charter when he conceded to the abbess of Alemènches the rights they held in the forest of Gouffern. This was not a joint act. It was sent by 'Henry, son of the duke of Normandy and count of Anjou' in front of a new set of witnesses. The rest of the charter repeats verbatim the earlier act completed by his father.[101] Henry may have been reissuing another of his father's charters when he conceded to the abbey of Saint-Ouen their possession of the customs (*consuetudines*) that they had held 'better and freer in the time of Henry king of England, my grandfather'.[102] It is consistent with the way Geoffrey tried to represent himself as the continuator of Henry I's good policies. If this is the case, then his son was also making subtle changes to reflect his relationship with King Henry. Geoffrey used vague terminology, identifying Henry I as his predecessor and ancestor, since he could not establish a direct personal relationship to his father-in-law. Young Henry could be more specific, as he was Henry I's direct descendent through his mother. However, the charter does not use this association as a means of establishing Henry's authority to complete the act. It grants him this right as the son of the duke of Normandy (*Henricus, ducis Normannorum et comitis Andegavorum filius*).

---

[99] *Regesta*, iii, no. 304. The charter was issued jointly by 'G(aufridus) dux Norm(annorum) et comes And(egavorum) et H(enricus) filius ejus'.

[100] *Regesta*, iii, no. 78. The notice for this act was altered by the time it was preserved in an eighteenth-century manuscript by Dom Jouvelin-Thibault, Bib. Nat. MS 13905, fol. 85v. Either Jouvelin-Thibault or an earlier copyist condensed the prologue into a brief French translation before continuing with a Latin summation of the confirmation. The notation that 'Geofroy duc de Normandie et d'Anjou, Henri 2d son fils, conferment et declarant ...' probably is accurate in reflecting a joint act, but the monks certainly did not designate Geoffrey's son as Henry II in the original charter.

[101] *Regesta*, iii, no. 18. 'H(enricus) ducis Norm(annorum) et com(itis) Andegavorum filius ...' For his father's act, see *Regesta*, iii, no. 17 discussed above in note 90.

[102] *Recueil des Actes de Henri II*, no. 5. 'Sciatis me reddidisse et concessisse abbati Sancti Audoeni omnes consuetudines ... melius et liberius tenuit tempore Henrici regis Anglorum, avi mei'.

This is more than a reflection of the way the Norman chancellery was balancing the rights of Duke Geoffrey and his son. The charters Henry issued during his last pre-ducal visit to England in 1149 demonstrate similar patterns. At this point it became clear that Henry's parents were preparing to transfer their rights of succession fully to their son. Matilda signaled this by dropping the term *domina Anglorum* from the acts she completed after returning to Normandy in 1148.[103] Henry had the opportunity to assert his authority among his mother's supporters at Devizes in April 1149. Those in attendance included the earls of Hereford, Gloucester, Cornwall and Salisbury. While there he resolved a dispute with Bishop Jocelin of Salisbury, restoring the manor of Cannings with its hundred rights, freedoms, customs, and all property pertaining to it, just as the preceding bishops held them 'in the time of my grandfather Henry and his predecessors' (*tempore avi mei regis Henrici et predecessorum ejus*), but reserving the castle of Devizes for himself. Rather than boldly assert his rights as 'the proper heir', which no doubt his supporters understood him to be, he continued in the tradition of his Norman charters and used the designation *ducis Norm(annorum) et comitis And(egavorum) filius*.[104]

The prayer that Henry offered for his family in the charter he issued for Quarr Abbey provides a glimpse at how he approached his English supporters with his political claims. He conceded Loxwell as the location for a monastery 'for the health and safety of the lord Geoffrey, duke of Normandy and count of Anjou, and for the health of the lady Empress Matilda my mother, and of my own (health), and for the public order of the kingdom of England, and for the souls of King Henry my grandfather, and Queen Matilda and all of my deceased predecessors'.[105] This statement establishes the legitimacy of Henry's claims by its reference to Henry I and his deceased 'predecessors', a term that Geoffrey had used to define his right of succession in Normandy five years earlier. It also establishes a line of succession, in reverse order, that includes both his mother and his father. Matilda is granted her preferred title of Empress and Geoffrey is recognized as the duke of Normandy and count of Anjou. Young Henry, now representing the fullest expression of his family's authority in England, appears at the head of the charter as the 'son of the duke of Normandy'. The strongest supporters of the Angevin war effort in England had turned out for Henry's arrival. They expected and received 'the proper heir' at Devizes. Henry presented his political rights in a way that recognized legitimacy through his parents rather than around them.

---

[103] Chibnall, *The Empress Matilda*, 102, 147–150.

[104] *Regesta*, iii, no. 795. Other charters from this visit introduce Henry in the same way. See *Regesta*, iii, nos. 420, 666, 704.

[105] *Regesta*, iii, 666. 'pro salute et incolumitate domini Gaufridi Normannie ducis et Andegavie comitis, necnon pro salute domine imperatricis matris mee et mea, et pro statu regni Anglorum et pro animabus Henrici regis avi mei et M(athildis) regine omniumque predecessorum meorum defunctorum'.

Conclusion

When Henry of Huntingdon wrote about Geoffrey le Bel's death, he described him as the son-in-law of Henry I and the son of the king of Jerusalem. As far as his legacy was concerned, he wrote that Geoffrey 'left Anjou and Normandy to Henry, his first born son, and passed to him the hereditary right of England, of which he was in the process of gaining possession, though as yet he did not have it'.[106] This statement reflects Henry of Huntingdon's impression of the rights that Geoffrey sought through his marriage. Quite remarkably, Matilda is absent from her husband's Norman acts. She certainly did not relinquish her claims to the Anglo-Norman realm. She had a guiding influence on some of Henry II's early acts as duke of Normandy.[107] At the same time, her absence reflects an understanding that she and Geoffrey had developed about his authority within her inheritance. In order to make their marriage work, Matilda supported Geoffrey's efforts to gain sovereignty within the Anglo-Norman realm. There was no clean succession, and the manner in which Matilda and Geoffrey were able to lay claim to the entire inheritance shifted over time. Geoffrey's charters and writs present a clear depiction of what he thought about his rightful place in the family. He viewed himself as the successor to Henry I through his wife, by whom young Henry could expect to receive his inheritance. In this way, Geoffrey was following in the footsteps of his own father, Fulk V of Anjou, who had ruled the county of Maine and the kingdom of Jerusalem by marriage as well.

Geoffrey insisted on his legitimacy in the face of English nobles who refused to accept that he should have any claim to govern the Anglo-Norman realm. The *conventiones* of 1141 set the framework for future discussions on the succession. Matilda worked to defend the rights of her family among English magnates who were willing to compromise so long as it meant acceptance of a Norman monarch. Geoffrey countered this with bold statements on his rights in the public acts he completed after becoming duke of Normandy. However, he had earned that right through conquest, and the unconquered English nobility were unmotivated to change their minds. Geoffrey's death in 1151 allowed greater room to negotiate the terms of Henry's succession. The peace agreement established at Winchester in November 1153 was the perfect compromise for those torn between their commitment to Stephen and their sympathies towards Henry. Robert of Torigni offers an interesting interpretation on the significance of this agreement. He comments that 'the king in the sight of all adopted Henry as his son and granted him the government of the kingdom. In return, Henry accepted Stephen as a father, granting him the name of king and the resources of kingship.'[108] This statement holds deep significance for a generation divided

---

[106] Henry of Huntingdon, *Historia*, 756–757.
[107] *Regesta*, iii, nos. 71–72, 80, 88.
[108] *The Chronicle of Robert de Torigni*, 177.

over pathways to legitimate rule in England. It was the final response of nobles who had rejected Geoffrey's rights of succession in 1135. When Henry II did become king in 1154, the English accepted him as the heir to Henry I through Stephen. In this way the civil war ended, by requiring that Henry bypass his father's rights to the Anglo-Norman realm.

6

Observations on the Twelfth-Century *Historia* of Alfred of Beverley

John Patrick Slevin

One of England's lesser known twelfth-century historical writers is Alfred, sacrist of the collegiate church of Beverley in the East Riding (ER) of Yorkshire, and author-compiler of a Latin prose narrative recounting the history of Britain from its supposed foundation by the Trojan Brutus to the time of Henry I. The work is arranged in nine *capitula*, 'chapters'. The first five abbreviate Geoffrey of Monmouth's *Historia Regum Britanniae* (*HRB*), incorporating the newly discovered British history within a narrative that draws also on the accounts of conventional historical authorities of the time: Bede's *Historia Ecclesiastica*, Paul the Deacon's *Historia Romana*, and Orosius' *Historiarum Adversus Paganos* amongst others. Compiling his work only a decade or so after the appearance of Geoffrey's history (*c.* 1148 x *c.* 1151–1153, see below), Alfred is the first historical writer to attempt to integrate the *HRB* within a comprehensive history of Britain; Henry of Huntingdon's 1139 epitomization of that work in the form of the *Epistola Warino Britoni* (*Letter to Warin the Breton*) is inserted only as a stand-alone piece in book eight of the *Historia Anglorum*. Only one printed edition of Alfred's history exists. This was published in 1716 by the Oxford antiquary, Thomas Hearne,[1] who attached to the work the title '*Aluredi Beverlacensis Annalium*': thus 'Alfred's Annals' is how the compilation has, misleadingly, come to be known.[2] The compilation is not written in annalistic form and its chapters each address an historical period with a given theme. In his prologue Alfred gives us his reasons for designing the work in this way:

---

[1] *Aluredi Beverlacensis Annalium, sive Historiae de gestis regum Britanniae*, ed. T. Hearne (Oxford, 1716). Hereafter Hearne, *ABA* with chapter references in Roman numerals. This history is now available in digital format in *Eighteenth Century Collections Online* (Gale Cengage Learning). Document no. CW 1017100S, Aluredi Beverlacensis Annales, Sive de Gestis Regum Britanniae, libris ix, 1716.

[2] The secondary title *Historiae de Gestis Regum Britanniae* provided by Hearne, indicates that he may not have been entirely satisfied with the term 'annalium' to describe the work. This title is closer to the description supplied in the rubric of the manuscript used to prepare his edition, Oxford, Bodleian MS Rawlinson B200, *Hystoria de Gestis Regalibus Regum Britanniae*.

... For in this work, described as if in a little notebook, the scholarly reader will be able to learn of events which can otherwise only be read about scattered here and there in the writings of several different authors, covering more than two thousand years, from the first inhabitants of Britain until the times of the Normans. The reader will also be able to find the events of different times divided into chapters, for ease of reading.[3]

Alfred's history has attracted very little interest from modern scholarship and what little has been written has often been unflattering. J.S.P. Tatlock described Alfred as a 'dullard' and his '*Annales* unimportant'.[4] Charles Gross described the work as 'a worthless compilation' and John Taylor called the history 'uninformative'.[5] However, as Alfred is one of a relatively small group of secular clerks writing history in twelfth-century England – in Yorkshire, for example, there is otherwise only Hugh the Chanter and Roger of Howden – his neglect is surprising. The purpose of this essay is to present a summary of results of recent research that suggest Alfred's to be a text of considerable historiographical interest.[6] The topics to be considered are the manuscript transmission and reception of the text, date of composition, sources used, an assessment of the character of the work and its place in twelfth-century Anglo-Norman historical writing, concluding with comments on authorial purpose and Alfred's probable intended audience. What is known of the author and his milieu in twelfth-century Beverley first, however, requires brief discussion.

What we know of Alfred derives from three principal sources: the surviving charters in which he appears as a witness, internal evidence from the history, and his commemoration in later historical and hagiographical sources. Five surviving charters (Appendix 2) show Alfred as active during the period of Archbishops Thurstan, William fitz Herbert and Henry Murdac with his last attestation dating to no later than 1154. In *c.* 1157 a 'Robert', sacrist of Beverley, attests a charter of Watton Priory (ER, Gilbertine) and it would appear that by that date Alfred may have been dead.[7] In the history Alfred talks of the removal of the Flemings by King Henry to Rhos in Dyfed, Pembrokeshire (*c.* 1110) as being 'in our own time' and he is recalled in a miracle story collection of late twelfth- or possibly thirteenth-century provenance: 'The sacrist of the church at the time was Alfred of good memory, an old man and wise in the laws of the

---

3   '... A prima habitacione Britanniae usque ad Normannorum tempora per annos amplius quam duo milia in hoc opusculo quasi in brevi tabella depicta studiosus lector agnoscere, et diversorum temporum gesta leccione capitulatim distincta poterit invenire.' Hearne *ABA*, i.3.

4   J.S.P. Tatlock, *The Legendary History of Britain* (Berkeley, CA, 1950), 210.

5   Charles Gross, *A Bibliography of English History to 1485*, ed. E.B. Graves (Oxford, 1975), 405, John Taylor, *Medieval Historical Writing in Yorkshire*, Borthwick Institute of Historical Research, *St Anthony's Hall Publications* 19 (York, 1961), 8.

6   This article is based on research undertaken in the course of preparing a doctoral dissertation, J.P. Slevin, 'The Historical Writing of Alfred of Beverley' (unpublished Ph.D dissertation, University of Exeter, January 2014).

7   *Beverley Minster Fasti: Being Biographical Notes on the Provosts, Prebendaries, Officers and Vicars in the Church of Beverley Prior to the Dissolution*, ed. Richard T.W. McDermid (York, 1993), 113.

church.'[8] These three circumstantial details therefore suggest that Alfred may have been born before the turn of the twelfth century. The charters show Alfred witnessing in favour of the religious houses of Bridlington (ER, Augustinian), Warter (ER, Augustinian), and Watton and he is described as *magister* in a charter of Archbishop William fitz Herbert, confirming privileges to the town of Beverley first granted by Archbishop Thurstan in *c.* 1143. In his latest attestation, a charter preserved in the fifteenth-century Rufford cartulary with its witness list, Alfred witnesses a grant of land by William Tyson in Averham, Nottinghamshire, to the Cistercian abbey of Rufford (Notts) alongside 'Ernaldo filio Alveredi'.[9] Whilst the name Ernaldus does not immediately follow that of Alfred – he is the twelfth named and Alfred is the third – there are reasonable grounds to consider Ernaldus to be the son of Alfred the sacrist. If so, then Alfred was like many of the secular clergy of the period: a family man, either married or living in concubinage.

In later medieval Beverley and York, Alfred's memory was preserved in artefacts which promote the rights and privileges of those institutions. The late fourteenth-century Beverley cartulary contains a tract, elaborately set off within the volume, setting out the ancient liberties of Beverley as supposedly conferred by King Æthelstan, 'cognomento niger'.[10] In its introductory rubric the work is attributed to Alfred who it describes as 'a man of venerable life and an ardent student of the scriptures and sacrist of the aforementioned church', and whom it also states to have translated the work into Latin.[11] This second reference to Alfred's biblical expertise is noteworthy because a familiarity with exegesis is suggested in the character of Alfred's historical writing, to be discussed later in this essay.[12]

In York, from about the same time as the Beverley cartulary and during the pontificate of Archbishop Thomas Arundel (1388–1396), Alfred is recalled in an historical artefact of importance to the cathedral. Two York tablets – large folding wooden (oak) boxes each consisting of three panels (triptychs) – survive, upon which are fastened parchments containing historical notices for display in the minster.[13] On the left hand panel of the larger triptych are historical notices

---

8   'Sacrista ejusdem ecclesiae tunc temporis fuit Alveredus, bonae memoriae, senex, ecclesiastica institutione sagax,' *The Historians of the Church of York and its Archbishops*, ed. J. Raine (3 vols., London, 1879–1894), i, 304. For Raine's comments on the date of the miracle story, see i, lv.

9   See *EYC*, xii, 134 and also in *Rufford Charters*, ed. C.J. Holdsworth, Thoroton Society Record Series (4 vols., Nottingham, 1972–1981), i, 167.

10   King Æthelstan is described as 'cognomento niger' in a second historical artefact from Beverley dating from about the time of the Beverley cartulary, the vicars' cartulary. See Oxford, University College MS 82, 8.

11   'vir vitae venerabilis et praenominatae ecclesiae Sacrista, Scripturarum studiosus indagator,' London, BL, Additional MS 61901, fols. 60v–69r.

12   See below, 120–122.

13   On the date of the tablets see Raine, ed. *Historians of the Church of York*, ii, xxviii. N. Ker and A.J. Piper, *Medieval Manuscripts in British Libraries* (Oxford, 1992), 824–826, list the tablets as Adds., 533 and 534.

from Geoffrey of Monmouth, Henry of Huntingdon, William of Malmesbury, 'Martinus in chronicis de pontificibus',[14] and 'Alfridus beverlacens thesaurarius'.[15] The remaining panel of material consists of papal bulls, archiepiscopal grants and indulgences, privileges in favour of the church of York, and notices of its metropolitan status over the Scottish bishops. The smaller panel contains biblical material, including an account of the seven ages of man. The panels were observed on display in the Minster by John Leland in 1534, who defaced portions of panel text relating to papal authority in Britain.[16]

Ten manuscript witnesses of the history have been identified, including extracts, fragments, and early modern transcripts (Appendix 1).[17] None originate from the time of Alfred. The earliest witness, London, BL, Cotton Cleopatra A.I, a volume associated with Furness Abbey (Cistercian, Lancashire), dates from approximately a century and a half after the work left Beverley. It contains a history from Brutus down to 1298, and appears to have been compiled very shortly after that date.[18] Folios 7r, 10r and 12r–115v of the codex contain extensive extracts from all nine chapters of Alfred's *Historia* with occasional additions and expansions noted.[19]

The text as we have it from Hearne's 1716 edition of the history is based exclusively on Oxford, Bodleian, MS Rawlinson B 200. This manuscript was loaned to Hearne by the bibliophile Thomas Rawlinson (1681–1725) in a collaborative publishing venture in early 1716 and by July, Hearne had printed some 148 copies for circulation to subscribers.[20] Neil Ker considered

---

[14]   A reference to Martin of Troppau's highly popular thirteenth-century chronicle of the popes and emperors. Currently printed in Martini, *Oppaviensis Chronicon Pontificum et Imperatorum*, ed. I. Weiland, MGH *SS*, 22 (1872), 377–475. I am indebted to Professor E. van Houts for drawing my attention to this.

[15]   Much of the text of the panels is badly damaged including the nine lines of text attributed to Alfred of Beverley. A research programme enabling the text to be fully recovered using ultra-violet photography has been under consideration. see Richard Hall, 'York Minster Tables', *Yorkshire Archaeology Today* (Sept, 2004), 3.

[16]   Leland's defacement is noted in James P. Carley, 'Leland, John (c. 1503–1552)', *Oxford Dictionary of National Biography*, 33 (Oxford, 2004), 297–301.

[17]   Correspondence between the sixteenth-century bibliophiles William Claxton of Wynyard, County Durham, and John Stow in 1594 provides evidence of a further witness of Alfred's history. Claxton informs Stow that he has in store for him a folio-size manuscript containing Ailred of Rievaulx's *Life of Edward the Confessor* and Alfred of Beverley's *History* 'unto the xxjth yere of Henry the first'. See A.I. Doyle, 'William Claxton and the Durham Chronicles' in *Books and Collectors 1200–1700, Essays Presented to Andrew Watson*, James P. Carley and Colin C.G. Tite eds. (London, 1997), 335–55 at 337.

[18]   T.D. Hardy, *Descriptive Catalogue of Materials Relating to the History of Great Britain and Ireland to the End of the Reign of Henry VII* (3 vols., London, 1862–1871), iii, 258–259.

[19]   See, for example, fols. 39r–41r, 44r, 50v, 66r–67r, 72v.

[20]   *Remarks and Collections of Thomas Hearne, Volume V*, ed. D W. Rannie (Oxford, 1901), 172. Correspondence between Hearne and Rawlinson makes it clear that Hearne printed his edition from the Rawlinson MS only. On February 12, 1716, Hearne wrote to Rawlinson, 'I take great care of your M.S. of Aluredus Beverlacenis which you have bound very finely … You insinuated that Aluredus hath been printed already. If so, I will not undertake him. But perhaps you may be mistaken.'

the manuscript to have originally formed part of a larger volume containing works of Bede and William of Malmesbury, which may have originated in the ownership of John de Newton, treasurer of York minster (1393–1414).[21] In de Newton's will, three historical tracts of Bede, William of Malmesbury, and Alfred of Beverley, in one volume, were among a very large collection of books bequeathed to the chapter of the metropolitan church of York for the purpose of establishing a library by de Newton.[22]

Oxford, Bodleian, MS Rawlinson B 200 preserves a version of Alfred's history which ends in the year 1129 at the words '*a rege acceperat*', describing Henry I's gift of the bishopric of Winchester to his sister's son Henry, brought up since infancy as a monk in Cluny. The majority of manuscript witnesses, however, extend Alfred's history to the death of Henry I in 1135 (Figure 1, nos. 3, 4, 5, 6, 10). One of the three witnesses ending at the year 1129, Aberystwyth, NLW, Peniarth MS 384 – a codex possibly originating from the Cistercian abbey of Jervaulx (Yorkshire, NR) – also has a continuation to 1135 added in a later fifteenth-century hand.[23]

From the 1360s, Paris, BnF, MS Lat. 4126, a manuscript associated with the Carmelite priory of Hulne, Northumberland contains extracts from the final chapter of Alfred's history (fols. 242v–252r) commencing with the words 'Incipiunt excerpta de gestis regum Normannorum in Anglia secundum Alfridum Beverlacensum', and ending at the death of Henry I in 1135. On fol. 211v one reads 'Ora pro Popilton qui me compilavit Eboraci' and the codex appears to have used the resources of the York Austin Friars library in its compilation. Twelve of the items in the manuscript are found in the Austin convent's collections, which very probably was the source of Populton's copies.[24]

A copy of Alfred's history was also in the possession of the Benedictine Abbey of Chester in the 1320s and was extensively quarried by Ranulf Higden

---

21 N.R. Ker, ed., *Medieval Libraries of Great Britain: A List of Surviving Books*, 2nd edition (London, 1964), 216. These works now exist as separate volumes: Oxford, Bodleian MS Rawlinson C 162, consisting of Bede's *Historia Ecclesiastica, Ymago Mundi*, and *Epistola Cuthberti de obitu venerabilis Bedae Presbyteri*, and Oxford, Bodleian MS Rawlinson B 199, William of Malmesbury's *De gestis pontificum Anglorum*.

22 *Testamenta Eboracensia*, ed. W. Raine, Surtees Society (Durham, 1836), 366. For further discussion of John de Newton as a book owner, and his ownership of Bodl. MS Rawlinson B 200, see J.B. Friedman, *Northern English Books, Owners and Makers in the Late Middle Ages* (Syracuse, 1995), 114–115, 203–206.

23 Aberystwyth, NLW, unpublished notes on Peniarth MS 384. Visible under ultra violet light at the top of fol. 1 is an erased inscription 'Liber de .... vall', suggesting 'Jorevall.' See, Ker, ed., *Medieval Libraries*, 105. The common form of ex libris inscription from Jervaulx is 'Liber sancte Marie de Jorevalle or (Jorevallis)'. The additional text is a verbatim copy of that found in Paris, BnF, Lat. 4126 and in all but one detail, to that also contained in London, BL, Cotton Cleopatra A.I. It states in its entry for the year 1133 that it was Adelulph to whom Henry I gave the newly created bishopric of Carlisle.

24 *The Friars' Libraries, Corpus of British Medieval Library Catalogues*, ed. K.W. Humphreys (London, 1990), xxviii, 159–60.

in his widely disseminated *Polychronicon*, which first appeared in *c*. 1327.[25] Higden names 'Alfridus Beverlacensis thesaurarius' in his prefatory list of forty authorities on which he has drawn to compile his history and subsequently names and quotes him some forty-four times in his account.[26] In book one of the *Polychronicon*, the *mappa mundi* – a part of the work contributing greatly to its wide appeal[27] – Alfred is particularly influential. For several of the central elements of Higden's geo-historic survey of Britain – its marvels and *mirabilia*, its famous rivers, its shires and provinces, the periods of its history, the establishment of the seven Saxon kingdoms, and its bishoprics – Alfred is the principal authority quoted. Some 170 years after Alfred had singled out the Flemings as a potential sixth people of Britain, Ranulf reworked Alfred's comment, naming the Flemings as the seventh of the island's peoples.[28] In his description of Britain's cities, whilst Higden quotes Bede first, it is to Alfred that Higden turns to supply the names of the cities. Higden's reception of Geoffrey of Monmouth's British history in the *Polychronicon*, appears to have been decisively influenced by Alfred. Higden frequently uses Alfred as an authority supporting the historical account of 'Gaufridus', and his direct interventions questioning the historicity of elements of the *Arthurania* in Geoffrey's account, appear to have taken a lead from Alfred's own questioning interventions in his history.[29]

From the second half of the sixteenth century London, BL, MS Cotton Vespasian A.V consists of a miscellany of historical excerpts from English chronicles, amongst which are notes made by William Lambarde (d. 1601), lawyer of Lincoln's Inn and member of Archbishop Matthew Parker's circle of bibliophiles and antiquaries, from a copy of Alfred's history owned by William Darrell, canon of Canterbury. The notes, on fols. 18r–19v, are taken from all sections of the history and dated 1568. That Lambarde was interested in Alfred and studied the text closely is shown by his use of it in his *A Perambulation of Kent, Conteining the Description, Hystorie and Customes of that Shire* (1576). Here he compared Alfred's account of the death of Earl Godwine in the history with that of Ailred of Rievaulx in his *Vita Ædwardi* (*c*. 1162–1163).[30]

---

[25]   John Taylor, *The Universal Chronicle of Ranulf Higden* (Oxford, 1966), 96. The chronicle survives in some 120 manuscripts attesting its wide dissemination in the later medieval period.
[26]   Additional citations of Alfred are frequently to be found in the collection of manuscripts used to prepare the RS printed edition and noted by the editors in the footnotes.
[27]   A.S.G. Edwards, 'The Influence and Audience of the *Polychronicon*: Some Observations', *Proceedings of the Leeds Philosophical and Literary Society* 17, 6 (1978–1981), 113–19.
[28]   *Polychronicon Ranulfi Higden Monachi Cestrensis*, ed. C. Babington and J.R. Lumby, RS 41 (9 vols., London, 1865–1886), ii, 152.
[29]   Compare, for example, both Higden's and Alfred's questioning why King Arthur's exploits were not reported more widely in the historical sources. *Polychronicon* v, 332–334 and Hearne, *ABA* v, 76.
[30]   William Lambarde, 'A Perambulation of Kent. Conteining the Description, Hystorie and Customes of that Shire. Written in the Year 1570. First Published in the Year 1576' (London, 1826), 99. Alfred's account of the death of earl Godwine whilst dining with King Edward the Confessor, the result of ordeal by bread (Hearne *ABA* viii, 121), appears to have gone unnoticed in scholarship. See for example C.E. Wright, *The Cultivation of Saga in Anglo-Saxon England* (Edinburgh, 1939),

A number of conclusions can be drawn from this brief survey of the surviving manuscripts and witnesses of Alfred's history. All early witnesses are associated with northern ecclesiastical centres: York Minster, the Austin friars' convent at York, Furness and Chester abbeys, Jervaulx and possibly also Rievaulx, indicating a strongly northern circulation of the work. William Lambarde's notes from a copy of the history from Canterbury in 1548 do not necessarily signal a southern circulation of the text, but rather that books were being actively exchanged and studied by Elizabethan bibliophiles and antiquaries engaged in the recovery of the past, and that Alfred's was a sought after text at the time.[31] Six surviving manuscripts extend Alfred's history from 1129 to 1135. The additional entries from 1130 to 1135 comprise text taken only from two of Alfred's principal sources in the history: the Durham *Historia Regum* and Henry of Huntingdon's *Historia Anglorum*. It therefore seems likely that this text did form part of the history that left Beverley in the twelfth century. The entries from 1130 to 1135 are, however, in the form of brief annals and have the appearance of hurried composition. In marked contrast to all previous eight chapters of Alfred's *Historia*, the text terminates with no summarizing commentary on the historical period just narrated, nor with recapitulated list of kings given. This suggests that either the work was left off prematurely, possibly due to illness, death, or the call of other duties, or that the work may not have survived in its entirety.

Alfred's *Historia* is commonly assigned to the year 1143 in modern scholarship, a date attached to the work by Antonia Gransden in her influential survey of Insular medieval historical writing, *Historical Writing in England c. 550–c. 1307*.[32] However, information supplied by Alfred himself in the prologue to the history, and his use of source material within the text itself, indicate that Alfred worked on his history several years after this date, almost certainly over

---

233–236, 296–298 and more recently *The Warenne (Hyde) Chronicle*, ed. and trans. Elizabeth M.C. van Houts and Rosalind C. Love (Oxford, 2013), xix–xx.

[31] For the interest of sixteenth-century antiquaries and bibliophiles in recovering and sharing manuscripts of the past see in particular, *The Recovery of the Past in Early Elizabethan England*, ed. Timothy Graham and Andrew G. Watson (Cambridge, 1998). The considerable Tudor and Elizabethan antiquarian interest in Alfred is discussed in Slevin, 'Historical Writing', 264–285.

[32] A. Gransden, *Historical Writing in England c. 550–c. 1307* (London, 1974), 212 and see also A. Gransden, 'Prologues in the Historiography of Twelfth-Century England' in *England in the Twelfth Century*, ed. D. Williams (Woodbridge, 1990), 55–81, reprinted in *Legends, Traditions and History in Medieval England*, ed. A. Gransden (London, 1992), 125–51 at 133. Gransden's argument for dating the work to 1143 mirrors that which was first proposed by Hardy, *Descriptive Catalogue*, II, 172–173. Recent reiteration of 1143 as the date of compilation is found in E. Oksanen, *Flanders and the Anglo-Norman World 1066–1216* (Cambridge, 2012), 178; Neil Wright, 'Twelfth-Century Receptions of a Text: Anglo-Norman Historians and Hegesippus', *ANS* 31 (2010), 177–95 at 178. See also R. Sharpe, *A Handlist of The Latin Writers of Great Britain and Ireland before 1540* (Turnhout, 1997), no. 105 at 54; R. William Leckie, Jr, *The Passage of Dominion: Geoffrey of Monmouth and the Periodization of Insular History in the Twelfth Century* (Toronto, 1981), 132.

the period *c.* 1148 x *c.* 1151 x 1153.[33] Alfred describes the circumstances giving rise to his history in the following opening words to his prologue:

In the days of our silence we could not render unto God the things that were God's. We were forced to render unto Caesar the things that were Caesar's for we withdrew from divine services because a large number of people had been excommunicated at that time, under the decree of the Council of London, and, worn down by royal taxation, we lived weary lives. The oppression which had troubled me long and sorely continued to assail me and, as the pillars of our church were driven from their sees by royal edict, I nearly fell into a state of despair, for I was almost alone.[34]

Four items of information relevant to date of compilation are supplied in these lines. First, Alfred describes a suspension of Divine Office at Beverley triggered by a large number of excommunications. Second, he tells us that the suspension of Divine Office had been mandated by a decree of the council of London. Third, he describes how the 'pillars of our church' had been driven from their sees by royal edict.[35] Fourth he claims that a burdensome royal tax had been imposed on Beverley. A brief examination of the London council and the decretal to which Alfred might be referring, and to events which took place in the Yorkshire church in the 1140s, will make clear that whilst Alfred was almost certainly referring to prior disciplinary legislation introduced at a London council, the excommunications, suspension of church services, exile of senior clergy and imposition of royal tax on Beverley which he also describes, took place during the years 1148 to 1151, not in 1143.

Amongst the legatine and general councils of King Stephen's reign (1135–1154), three produced significant legislation for the protection of church property and clergy against the violence of the anarchy and laid out disciplinary sanctions to be taken against disturbers of the peace. These were the legatine councils of Alberic of Ostia (London 1138), the Westminster council in March 1143 of the bishop of Winchester, Henry of Blois (1129–71),

---

[33] Not all earlier scholars shared Gransden's (and Hardy's) view on the date of Alfred's history. See, for example, *The Historians of the Church of York and its Archbishops*, ed. J. Raine, RS 71 (3 vols., London, 1879–1894), i, liv, and H.S. Offler, 'Hexham and the *Historia Regum*', *Transactions of the Architectural and Archaeological Society of Durham and Northumberland*, II (1970), 51–62, at 61, note 41. Both considered that the work originated *c.* 1150.

[34] 'In diebus silencii nostri, quando non poteramus reddere deo quae dei erant, et tamen cogebamur reddere Caesari quae Caesaris erant, quod propter praesentem excomunicatorum multitudinem secundum Londoniensis concilii decretum a divinis cessabamus et regiis exaccionibus afflicti vitam taediosam agebamus, grassante oppressione qua, expulsis ad regis edictum de sedibus suis ecclesiae nostrae columpnis, diu graviterque vexatus sum, pene en desperacionem cum pene solus essem decidi.' Hearne, *ABA* i, 1–2.

[35] The expression 'pillars of the church' was used by chroniclers to describe the most senior clergy. See for example how Henry of Huntingdon describes the attending clergy at the 1129 legatine council of Archbishop William de Corbeil in London in 1129. 'Hi columpne regni erant et radii sanctitatis hoc tempore.' *Henry of Huntingdon, Historia*, 484. Henry in this passage refers to Archbishops William and Thurstan of York and the bishops of Lincoln, Salisbury, London, Rochester, Chichester, Bath, Worcester, Norwich, St David's, and Ely.

and the London council of Archbishop Theobald of March 1151.[36] It is the Westminster council of Henry of Blois in March 1143 that took the most drastic measures against disturbers of the peace and protection of the clergy, introducing some seventeen canons specifically related to this theme.[37] Canon 5 prescribed the mandatory suspension of the service of Divine Office and the ringing of bells in 'town, hamlet, or countryside' where any excommunicate person was present. Canon 2 also prescribed the suspension of Divine Office in locations where clerks had been seized and held captive. Canon 8 stipulated that heavy penalties be imposed on clerks who failed to enforce the suspension of the Divine Office.[38] These canons are therefore closely related to the circumstances Alfred describes in the prologue – an enforced idleness brought on by the suspension of celebration of Divine Office which resulted from the presence of excommunicates. As no similar legislation is known to have been introduced in the London councils of 1129 or of 1151, there are good grounds to believe that it was the London council of March 1143 that Alfred referred to in his comments.[39]

The passage of disciplinary legislation is one matter but its implementation another, and there is no evidence whatever of a serious disruption in the chapters of York or Beverley in 1143 which resulted in interdicts, excommunications, and the suspension of Divine Office. Nor is there evidence that the leader of the church of York and Beverley at the time, Archbishop William fitz Herbert, was driven from his see by order of King Stephen in that year or that a fine was imposed on Beverley by the king; indeed Stephen is not known to have visited Yorkshire in 1143.[40]

On the other hand, the events described in Alfred's prologue precisely describe the crisis which engulfed the Yorkshire church between mid-1148 and January 1151 and which followed the deposition of Archbishop William fitz Herbert and election of Henry Murdac in July 1147.[41] The newly elected and consecrated archbishop was, according to John of Salisbury, elected in open defiance of King Stephen's express wishes.[42] He was denied access to both his see and temporalities by the king and was effectively driven from

---

[36]   F. Barlow, *The English Church 1066–1154* (London, 1979), 130–131.

[37]   Barlow, *English Church*, 131.

[38]   *Councils and Synods with other Documents Relating to the English Church*, ed. D. Whitelock, M. Brett and C.N.L. Brooke, (2 vols., Oxford, 1964–1981), i, 794–804.

[39]   Whitelock, *Councils and Synods*, i, 795, note 1. The editors suggest that Alfred's prologue remarks referred to this particular council.

[40]   The itinerary of King Stephen in 1143 is set out in *Regesta*, iii, xlii–xliii.

[41]   The crisis has most recently been surveyed in Christopher Norton, *St William of York* (Woodbridge, 2006). See in particular 118–131. It is earlier discussed in David Knowles, 'The Case of Saint William of York', in D. Knowles, *The Historian and Character* (Cambridge, 1963), 76–97 and see also D. Baker, 'Viri Religiosi and the York Election Dispute', *Studies in Church History* 7 (1971), 87–100.

[42]   John of Salisbury's *Historia Pontificalis. Memoirs of the Papal Court*, ed. and trans. Marjorie Chibnall (London, 1956), 5.

it. John of Hexham describes how Murdac excommunicated his leading opponents in York, William of Aumale and Hugh du Puiset, the treasurer of York Minster and the archdeacon of the East Riding. Hugh reacted by issuing counter excommunications on Murdac and his supporters.[43] John tells us that Hugh du Puiset caused ecclesiastical services to be continued in York, but later in 1148, on his remove to Winchester, opposition to Murdac moderated and the archbishop's interdict appears to then have been implemented. In late 1149 for example, Eustace, son of King Stephen, visited York and found ecclesiastic services discontinued whereupon he compelled the clergy to 'fulfil all the divine services'.[44]

Whilst John of Hexham makes no mention of a suspension of ecclesiastical services at Beverley, Alfred's testimony suggests that amongst those excommunicated by Murdac were opponents resident in Beverley and, as both William of Aumale and William fitz Herbert had strong East Riding and Beverley associations, this would appear likely. William of Aumale's central holdings in Yorkshire were in the strategically important land of Holderness in the East Riding, of which Beverley was chief town and ecclesiastical centre.[45] William fitz Herbert had served as archdeacon of the East Riding from 1109 and owned estates in the East Riding in Londesborugh and Weaverthorpe and also a residence in Beverley, granted to his father Herbert the Chamberlain by Archbishop Thomas II *c.* 1109–1111.[46] Finally, John of Hexham tells us that in 1149 King Stephen visited Beverley and imposed a fine on the town for harbouring Archbishop Murdac against his wishes.[47] John does not specify when in that year Stephen went to Beverley, but the king's movements in the north during the summer of 1149 are well attested in other chronicle sources. Henry of Huntingdon relates that in 1149 Stephen came to York with an army and stayed there throughout the month of August.[48] The *Gesta Stephani* also reports Stephen's visit to Yorkshire in 1149.[49] Alfred's statement about a royal tax on Beverley indicates that at least the prologue of his history must have been written after August 1149.

From within the history itself, Alfred's use of sources shows him to be at work on his history in the later 1140s. At the conclusion of chapter six, Alfred, borrowing from Henry of Huntingdon's introductory description of Britain in the *HA*, writes

---

43   John of Hexham, 'Historia Continuata', ed. T. Arnold in Symeon, *Opera*, ii, 284–332 at 322.
44   'Historia Continuata', 324, and see 306 note b. John incorrectly supplies the year 1150 for this event. In his chronicle he had placed Archbishop Thurstan's death in 1141, instead of 1140, and from that point on, the chronicle is consistently one year ahead.
45   See Barbara English, *The Lords of the Holderness 1086–1260* (Hull, 1979), 16–28.
46   Burton, ed. *Episcopal Acta* V, no. 15, at 17 and see Norton, *St William*, 10–15.
47   John of Hexham, 'Historia Continuata', 323.
48   *Henry of Huntingdon, Historia*, 755. Stephen's itinerary during 1149 is set out in *Regesta* iii, xliii.
49   *Gesta Stephani*, 216–217.

But in the western part of Britain called Wales there are three additional bishoprics: one at St Davids, another at Bangor and a third at Glamorgan i.e. Llandaff. These three are without cities on account of the desolation of Wales, which was all that was left to the Britons after they had been conquered. In our time the bishop of St David's received from the pope the pallium which in ancient days had been at Caerleon, but he very soon lost it.[50]

In her 1996 edition of the *HA*, Diana Greenway identified the various stages of the making of the text. In this particular passage she identified that the phrase, 'in our time' was added in 1140 (version three) but the words, 'he very soon lost it' were only added in the fourth recension of the *HA* dating from 1147 or a little later.[51] The words remained in later versions of the *HA*, and so it is quite possible that Alfred was borrowing from version five of the *HA*, representing the largest group of manuscripts of the *HA*.[52] This version takes Henry's account to the enthronement of Robert de Chesney as bishop of Lincoln in January 1149, and Greenway suggests Henry may have brought the *HA* up to that date to present it to Bishop Robert.[53] At present, it is not possible to be certain whether Alfred used version four or five of the *HA*, but further collation of Alfred's identified borrowings with specific items of content which Henry added at the version four and version five stage, may well provide answers to this question. What is clear from the concluding passage of chapter six, however, is that Alfred was at work at his *Historia*, quarrying a text circulating no earlier than 1147 and possibly as late as 1149. In addition, Alfred's more than thirty references to King Henry in the history, without once referring to him as King Henry I, strongly suggest that work on the history was concluded before the accession of Henry II in December 1154.

The 1143 compilation date of Alfred's history, first proposed by T.D. Hardy and reiterated by Antonia Gransden, conflated two separate historical events: the passage of disciplinary legislation at the council of Westminster of spring 1143 and the crisis in the Yorkshire church which took place over the years 1148–1151. It failed to consider important information supplied by Alfred concerning a royal tax imposed on Beverley and the leaders of the church driven from their see by royal command. It can be shown that Alfred worked with a version of Henry of Huntingdon's *HA*, in circulation only from 1147, or quite

---

50 'Sed in occidentali parte Britanniae, quae vocatur Walia III. supersunt episcopatus, unus apud Sanctum David, alius apud Bangor, tercius apud Glamorgan. Sunt tamen hii tres nullarum urbium post desolacionem Walliae, quae sola devictis mansit Britannis. Tempore autem nostro recepit episcopus Sancti David palleum a papa, qui scilicet olim fuerat apud Keer legion, sed statim amisit.' Hearne, *ABA* vii, 97.

51 Henry of Huntingdon, *Historia*, 18–19 and see note 25. Bernard, bishop of St David's (1115–1148) claimed metropolitan status for his church and the statement probably refers to a papal ruling of June 1147 that Bernard owed obedience to Canterbury.

52 The sixth and final version of the Henry of Huntingdon's *Historia* was composed after the coronation of Henry II in December 1154 and as Alfred appears to have completed the history before this date (see below) his use of the final version of the HA can therefore be ruled out.

53 *Henry of Huntingdon, Historia*, lxxvi.

possibly, with version five which circulated from 1149. We can be confident therefore that work on the history was undertaken during the period of Interdict in the church of Beverley, from mid to late 1148 until at least January 1151. Alfred's literary activities may have concluded in 1151 after the resumption of church services in Beverley, but there is no clear evidence of this. The terminus date for the *Historia* appears to be December 1154. Moreover, the work as we have it today appears to have been prematurely concluded.

Figure 1 below provides a summary of the principal sources used and their textual contribution to the history.[54] At least thirteen texts have been quarried. The Durham *Historia Regum* represents the largest single source, with the final three chapters of the history being almost entirely dependent on that work. Text originating in Geoffrey of Monmouth's *Historia Regum Britanniae*, Bede's *Historia Ecclesiastica*, the dynastic accounts and genealogies in the preliminary section of the chronicle of John of Worcester, the *Historia Anglorum* of Henry of Huntingdon, and the *Historia Brittonum* of the pseudo-Nennius are extensively quarried. An impressive range of classical, late antique, and hagiographical texts is also consulted, including: Orosius, *Historiarum Adversum Paganos*; Paul the Deacon, *Historia Romana*; Suetonius, *Lives of the Caesars*; Aethicus

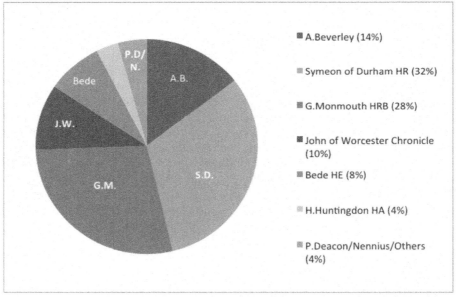

Figure 1. Alfred's borrowings by source in the *History*

---

[54] Alfred's textual borrowings from his sources expressed as the percentage of the total text word count. The main borrowings are: approximately 12,700 words taken from Durham *Historia*; 11,300 from *HRB*; 4,000 from John of Worcester, *Chronicle*; 3,300 from Bede *EH*; 1,300 from Henry of Huntingdon, *Historia*; 900 from Paul the Deacon *Historia Romana*. Alfred himself supplies some 5,800 words of original text.

Ister, *The Cosmography*; Hegesippus's Latin translation of Josephus's *Jewish War*; Constantius, *Life of St Germanus;* Sulpicius Severus, *Life of St Martin of Tours*. In addition, Alfred names, but does not use, Pompeius Trogus and quotes Solinus's *Collectanea Memorabilia*, taking the quotation from the *HA* of Henry of Huntingdon, not directly from Solinus. Alfred cites and appeals to Gildas as a historical source seven times in the history but five of these are spurious citations recycled from the *HRB* and two are from Bede. Alfred shows no direct knowledge of Gildas's *De Excidio Britanniae* in the history.

Of special note, given Alfred's knowledge of contemporary historical writers, is his lack of knowledge of – or his failure to use – the works of William of Malmesbury. Only one instance in the narrative hints at Alfred's familiarity with William's writings. In chapter eight, Alfred employs a phrase from Hegesippus to describe King Æthelred's attempts to bribe the Danes by payment of the Danegeld, 'when King Æthelred, unable to do by steel, tried to drive off by silver'.[55] This same phrase from Hegesippus is used by William of Malmesbury in the *Gesta Regum* to describe the bribing of the Danes in order to buy peace by King Æthelred.[56] Alfred's use of the phrase, however, is not identical to William's. In the *Gesta Regum* it is Archbishop Sigeric who bribes the Danes, though William implies it is on behalf of King Æthelred.[57] Alfred attributes the act of bribery directly to King Æthelred himself.

Although Beverley had possessed a library since the days of the Anglo-Saxon Archbishop Cynesige (d. 1060),[58] it has left no medieval literary legacy of note. Thus the question arises, from where and by what means did Alfred assemble his impressive inventory of texts? Alfred had access not only to recently produced texts – version four or five of the *HA* and the *HRB* for example – but to texts which appear to be quite rare at the time. The *Cosmography* of Aethicus Ister for example, which provides detail for the prefatory geo-historic description of Britain, is a work listed in few surviving library catalogues from the period.[59] Of contemporary chroniclers only Ralph Diceto cites and uses the *Cosmography* in his *Abbreviationes Chronicorum* (*c.* 1180) when relating the story of how Alexander captured and imprisoned the two giants, Gog and Magog.[60]

[55] 'unde rex Agelredus quos ferro nequibat, eos argento repellere temptavit', Hearne *ABA* viii, 114.
[56] See Wright, 'Twelfth-Century Receptions ', 190–193. William's fondness for this particular antithetical phrase of Hegesippus and his use of it in both the *Gesta Regum* and *Gesta Pontificum* is discussed. Wright also discusses Alfred of Beverley's use of Hegesippus in the article (at 178–179) but considers only a second Alfredian borrowing from Hegesippus, used to open his prefatory description of Britain (Hearne *ABA* I, 3).
[57] William of Malmesbury, *GR* I, 270.
[58] Raine, *Historians of the Church of York* ii, 354.
[59] The work is listed in a late twelfth-century catalogue from the Benedictine abbey of Bury St Edmunds. See *English Benedictine Libraries. The Shorter Catalogue, Corpus of British Medieval Library Catalogues* ed. R. Sharpe et al. (London, 1996). Bury St Edmunds, B13. 49, 59.
[60] *Radulfi de Diceto Decani Lundoniensis Opera Historica*, ed. W. Stubbs (2 vols., London, 1876), i, 48. The Cosmography is not among the works which appear to have been known at first hand by William of Malmesbury. See R. Thomson, *William of Malmesbury* (Woodbridge, 1987), 197–207.

How then might Alfred have obtained his books? The community of church dignitaries, canons, and lay aristocratic patrons which surrounded him in Beverley and York were likely an important source. The composition of this group can be partially observed in the witness lists of the five surviving charters where Alfred acted as attestor (Appendix 2). The co-witnesses number seventy in total, of which fifteen are senior clergy and the remainder a cross section of the landowning aristocracy of the East Riding of Yorkshire. Among the ecclesiastical witnesses are the dignitaries of the chapters of York and Beverley and abbots and priors of East Riding religious houses. Prominent among these are William of Sainte-Barbe, dean of York and later bishop of Durham (1143–1152), William d'Eu the precentor (*c.* 1140–1178) [61] and Robert Butevilain, archdeacon and later dean of York (1158–1186). Robert is described as *magister* in a charter of Henry Murdac in favour of Kirkstall abbey. [62] One of the co-attestors of this charter is Nicholas de Trailly, the York canon whom Geoffrey Gaimar, in the epilogue of the *Estoire des Engleis*, had singled out as a source of expertise on English history who could vouchsafe the veracity of what was written in the *Estoire*. [63] Nicholas was a contemporary of Alfred and had also witnessed a charter of Archbishop Henry Murdac in favour of Fountains abbey alongside an officer of the church of Beverley. [64] Lay witnesses include William of Aumale (*c.* 1110–1179), who, in addition to the Cistercian abbey of Meaux (1151), had founded the priory of Thornton (1139), the abbey of Bytham (1147) and was co-founder of North Ormsby priory (1148–1154). [65] Other witnesses of note are Robert de Stuteville III (d. 1183), a benefactor of Meaux abbey and probable founder of Keldholme priory, [66] and Everard de Ros, nephew of Walter Espec, Lord of Helmsley and one of William of Aumale's principal tenants in the lordship of Holderness in the East Riding. [67] Everard's presence as a witness alongside Alfred places Alfred within touching distance of a leading literary patron of the period. Everard's uncle, Walter Espec, founder of the Augustinian priory of Kirkham (*c.* 1121) and Fountains (1132) and lover of history, was the magnate who lent Lady Constance fitz Gilbert the copy of Geoffrey of Monmouth's *HRB* which Geoffrey Gaimar himself claims have used as a source text for his *Estoire des Engleis*. [68] Alfred attests with two monastic leaders in the region: Adam,

61   D. Carpenter, 'The Dignitaries of York Minster in the 1170s: A Reassessment', *Northern History* 43 (March, 2006), 21–31. Based on the evidence of two previously unpublished charters, it has been established that William d'Eu survived until 1178 or later.

62   *English Episcopal Acta V*, no. 121.92–95.

63   *Geffrei Gaimar, Estoire des Engleis*, ed. Ian Short (Oxford, 2009), line 6482, 350.

64   *English Episcopal Acta V*, no. 114, 87–88.

65   Paul Dalton, 'William le Gros, Count of Aumale and Earl of York (*c.* 1110–1179)', *Oxford Dictionary of National Biography* 59 (Oxford, 2004), 122–123.

66   Hugh M. Thomas, 'Stuteville, Robert (III) de (d. 1183)', *Oxford Dictionary of National Biography* 53 (Oxford, 2004), 259.

67   Paul Dalton, *Conquest, Anarchy and Lordship, Yorkshire 1066–1154* (Cambridge, 1994), 182.

68   Gaimar, *Estoire*, lines 6435–6483, 348–50.

first abbot of the Cistercian abbey of Meaux and formerly monk of Fountains (1151–1160) and Ivo, abbot of Warter priory, which during its Arrouaisian phase (*c.* 1142–*c.* 1197), assumed the title of abbey.[69]

Archbishop Henry Murdac is a channel through which books may have reached Beverley. The archbishop, with access to both York and Cistercian centres of learning in the region, was a regular visitor to Beverley over the period of Alfred's literary activity, evidenced by King Stephen's fine on the town in August 1149 and charters issued in front of the assembled Beverley chapter over the period 1151–1153.[70] The archbishop was temporal lord of Beverley with an archiepiscopal residence in the town, and it was at Beverley that he died on October 14, 1153.[71] Henry's scholarly and pedagogical background is attested in contemporary sources. St Bernard of Clairvaux in a letter to Henry of *c.* 1125 describes him as 'magister' and encourages him to leave the world of books and learning and join him at Clairvaux. The letter ends with references to two of Henry's pupils who had become monks at Clairvaux.[72] John of Salisbury in the *Historia Pontificalis* recounts how Henry was included in a select group of the most learned churchman to meet Bernard of Clairvaux during the council of Reims in 1148 to debate Bernard's reservations on the Gilbert of Poitiers commentaries of the *De Trinitate* of Boethius.[73] John of Hexham tells us that Henry had served in the church of York under Thurstan, 'with honours and riches both in the church of York and in the adjoining province'.[74] The archbishop is remembered in the *Chronica Pontificum Ecclesiae Eboracensis* as 'professor probatissimus'.[75]

A centre of scholarly activity, with which Alfred is associated, lay close at hand and may also have provided books.[76] The prior of the Augustinian priory of Bridlington, some twenty miles north-east of Beverley, was Robert I 'the Scribe' (*c.* 1147/50–*c.* 1160), author of *The Bridlington Dialogue* and glosses on Exodus, the Minor Prophets, and St Paul. Robert's commentary on the Minor Prophets was requested by Gervase, abbot of the Cistercian abbey of Louth Park in Lincolnshire, founded in 1139 by Bishop Alexander

---

[69]   Burton, *The Monastic Order in Yorkshire 1069–1215* (Cambridge, 1999), 96.
[70]   *English Episcopal Acta V*, nos. 128, 129.99–102.
[71]   John of Hexham, 'Historia Continuata', 331–332. From the 1160s the archiepiscopal residence in Beverley was known as the Dings. See R. Horrox, 'Medieval Beverley' in *VCH, A History of the County of York East Riding*, ed. K.J. Allison, vol. 6, *The Borough and Liberties of Beverley*, 2–62 at 14.
[72]   Christopher Holdsworth, 'St Bernard and England', *ANS* 8 (1985), 138–53 at 144. This letter is described by Holdsworth as one of St Bernard's warmest and happiest of all.
[73]   *John of Salisbury's Memoirs of the Papal Court*, ed. Chibnall, 16–17.
[74]   John of Hexham, 'Historia Continuata', 317–318. 'sub venerabili archiepiscopo Turstino tam in Eboracensi ecclesia quam in circumjacenti provincia ex dono parentum honoribus et divitiis locupletatum'.
[75]   Printed in *Historians of the Church of York*, ed. J. Raine, ii, 388–421 at 388.
[76]   See Appendix 2 charter 1. Alfred was a co-attestor of the confirmation of an agreement of mutual confraternity between the canons of the church of Beverley and those of Bridlington, *c.* 1135 x 1140.

of Lincoln. Bridlington was therefore linked with other communities with scholarly interests, extending beyond the East Riding of Yorkshire and into Lincolnshire.[77] Bridlington's scholarly interests are attested by its eight or possibly nine surviving books from the period and a book list from Bridlington is preserved in a late twelfth-century glossed copy of the gospel of St Mark (BL MS Harley 50) which lists some seventy-eight major titles and some forty 'parvi libelli' books contained in the priory's 'magnum armarium'.[78] Among the books contained in the list are several of authors used or cited by Alfred in his *Historia* including Orosius *Historia Adversus Paganos,* Solinus *Collectanea Rerum mirabilium,* Bede *HE,* Henry of Huntingdon *HA,* and Geoffrey of Monmouth *HRB.*[79]

What then are the defining characteristics of Alfred's history and where might the work be placed in the context of twelfth-century historical writing? The work adopts a narrative approach wherein a continuous account of Britain's history is built on a series of chapters each addressing themed historical periods. The text is not dominated by a chronological outlook which, for one eminent scholar of medieval historiography, is the characteristic that distinguishes a 'history' from a 'chronicle'.[80] Fixed dates are used sparingly and the chronological thread is maintained principally by use of synchronism, regnal years to date events and by summarizing king lists for each of the periods narrated.[81] In chapter nine, which covers the reigns of William I, William Rufus, and Henry I, only two fixed dates are provided: the date of the accession of William I, incorrectly given as 1065, and the death of William Rufus given as 'On Thursday, 2 August, in the eighth indiction.'[82] Annalistic entries are used only in book seven, when Alfred begins to compile from the Durham *Historia Regum* (*HR*), a text organized in this fashion, but in chapters eight and nine the history resumes its system of reporting events by regnal years.

Whilst concise, the narrative remains firmly based on the Latin literary and rhetorical tradition. A prologue opens the account containing several suitable *topos*, including one of modesty, a classical rhetorical technique advocated by

---

77   A. Lawrence, 'A Northern English School? Patterns of Production and Collection of Manuscripts in the Augustinian Houses of Yorkshire in the Twelfth and Thirteenth Centuries', in *Yorkshire Monasticism: Archaeology, Art and Architecture from the Seventh to the Sixteenth Centuries,* ed. L.R. Hoey (Leeds, 1995), 145–53, at 147.

78   *The Libraries of the Augustinian Canons, Corpus of British Medieval Library Catalogues* 6, ed. T. Webber and A.G. Watson (London, 1998), 8 and see Ker, ed. *Medieval Libraries,* 12–13.

79   *The Libraries,* ed. Webber and Watson, Bridlington A4, 9–24. Orosius *Historia Adversus Paganos* no. 37; Solinus *Collectanea Rerum Mirabilium* no. 86; Bede *Historia Anglorum* no. 75; Henry of Huntingdon *Cronica Henrici* no. 54; Geoffrey of Monmouth, *Historia Brittonum* no. 76.

80   Antonia Gransden, 'The Chronicles of Medieval England and Scotland', in *Legends, Traditions and History in Medieval England* (London, 1992), 199–238 at 199–201.

81   A total of thirty-nine fixed dates are supplied in the text as follows: cc. 1–5 contain 5; c. 6 contains 12; c. 7 contains 12; c. 8 contains 8. c. 9 contains 2.

82   'Anno M.C.IIII Nonas Augusti feria Vᵃ Indiccione VIII'. The continuation text from 1130 to 1135 found in the manuscripts listed in Appendix I is supplied annalistically.

Cicero and Quintilian to disguise the guile and art of the orator *calliditas occulta*.[83] Classical sources are quoted to adorn the narrative and invest it with *elocutio*, language appropriate to the serious nature of the narrative. Alfred opens the history with an arresting quotation from the late fourth-century Latin translation of Flavius Josephus' *Jewish War*, known to medieval audiences as *Hegesippus*, describing Britain's remote location at the edge of the civilized world, but its incorporation within it by the Roman conquest.[84] Rhetorical tropes such as *similitudo* are used, where the orator invokes comparison with a subject silently, in order to arouse the suspicions of his audience. Alfred employs *similitudo* to raise questions in his readers' minds about the credibility of Geoffrey of Monmouth's account of the four royal roads of Britain supposedly built by the British king Belinus when his account is silently compared to that of Henry of Huntingdon in the *HA*.[85] The rhetorical practice of paraphrase: rendering a set piece in different styles, using alternative vocabulary in the process of abbreviation, is employed throughout. In Alfred's abbreviation of the *HRB* there are some sixty-seven instances where Geoffrey's vocabulary and syntax have been altered stylistically, whilst the original sense has been accurately retained.[86] Good rhetorical practice is also evident in the manner in which the text of the history is designed to imprint itself on the memory, for example, in the text's organized structure and in the formulaic endings of each chapter. The presence of explanatory linking comments, opening and closing each chapter, where readers are reminded of what has just been covered and what is about to come, also indicates this intent. In rhetorical theory, the impression of the *inventio*, the argument or case, on the *memoria*, was one of the five constituent elements of speech or text.[87]

Alfred's rhetorical practices may in part be indebted to the work which appears to have exercised a decisive influence on the making of his history, the *HA* of Henry of Huntingdon, but Alfred's more modest literary enterprise has its own distinctive character. If the *HA* embraces expansion, amplification, and embellishment as a rhetorical strategy, adorned with invented speeches, poetry, letters, and interlaced digressions, Alfred, with no sacrifice

---

[83] E.R. Curtius, *European Literature and the Latin Middle Ages* (London, 1953), 83–85. For tropes and figures of speech used in rhetorical practice see M. Kempshall, *Rhetoric and the Writing of History 400–1500* (Manchester, 2011), 28–29.

[84] Hearne, *ABA* i, 3. 'Haec insula Britannia extra orbem est posita, sed Romanorum virtute in orbem est redacta …' 'This island of Britain was situated beyond the known world, but, by the valour of the Romans, brought within it.'

[85] Hearne, *ABA* i, 17–18.

[86] For the skills of abbreviation and paraphrasing as essential elements of medieval training in rhetoric see D. Greenway, 'Authority, Convention and Observation in Henry of Huntingdon's *Historia Anglorum*', *ANS* 19 (1996), 105–21 at 106–109.

[87] Kempshall, *Rhetoric*, 19. Constituent elements in addition to *memoria* were *inventio*, convincing or persuasive argument; *dispositio*, the order and arrangement of the argument; *elocutio*, the choice of language appropriate to the argument; *pronuntiatio*, the manner of presentation or delivery of the argument.

to the requirement of elegant Latin composition, adopts the reverse strategy
of abbreviation and conciseness.[88] Another marked feature of Alfred's history
is its non-parochial outlook. It exhibits little interest in either the church of
Beverley or York and, as such, the work cannot be categorized as a local,
institutional, or even regional history.[89] References to Beverley occur only
three times in the text and these all in one passage. Here Alfred, at this point
in the narrative dependent on the Durham *Historia Regum* (*HR*) as his source,
reports King William I's 'Harrying of the North' in 1069–1070 and tells the
story of a miraculous intervention of St John of Beverley to protect refugees
fleeing to the sanctuary of Beverley.[90] Alfred's insertion of this local interest
story is out of character, a spontaneous reaction to the text in front of him.
The Durham text relates the story of how Bishop Æthelwine of Durham (d.
1071–2) and members of the Durham community flee William's destructive
campaign in and around York in 1069, carrying the body of St Cuthbert
with them, describing an odyssey which eventually brings them to the safety
of Holy Island, aided by the miraculous intervention of Cuthbert. Alfred
is sufficiently moved by this story of the Durham community's relationship with their patron saint that he substitutes an equivalent story of his
own Beverley saint. Most matters of interest or relevance to the church of
Beverley and York which are reported in the *HR*, however, are overlooked.
Alfred omits the Durham compiler's report of the elevation of Thomas II,
provost of the church of Beverley, to the Archbishopric of York, in 1108
and the eulogy at his death in 1114. No reference to Archbishop Thurstan
of York is made in the history, even though the archbishop was a benefactor
of Beverley, a contemporary probably known to Alfred personally, as lord
of Beverley and a figure of national importance. The interest of the history
remains single-mindedly focused on the *gesta* of the kings and princes of first
Britain and then England.

Allied to a non-parochial outlook is a highly secular cast of mind. This
is made particularly evident by Alfred's handling of the Durham text. Most
ecclesiastical matter of `interest to the Durham compiler – the deaths and
appointments of senior clergy, monastic or church foundations, the translation
of saints, papal and Insular councils and their legislation – is filtered out.
Dramatic episodes involving kings and princes, however, are rarely overlooked.
The account of King Edgar rowed on the river Dee by Britain's eight sub-kings
as an act of homage (973),[91] the death of the tyrant Swein killed by the ghost

---

[88]   For amplification and embellishment as a rhetorical strategy and its reverse, abbreviation, see
Greenway, 'Authority, Convention and Observation', 108.

[89]   For a discussion on the character and nature of local histories see Elizabeth M.C. van Houts,
Local and Regional Chronicles, Typologies des Sources du Moyen Âge Occidental 74 (Turnhout,
1995), 13–16 and John Hudson, 'Local Histories' in *The Oxford History of Historical Writing Vol
2: 400–1400*, ed. Sarah Foot and Chase F. Robinson (Oxford, 2012), 457–75.

[90]   Hearne, *ABA* ix, 129–130.

[91]   Hearne, *ABA* viii, 112.

of St Edmund (1014),[92] the capture and death of Alfred, brother of Edward the Confessor at the hands of Earl Godwine (1036),[93] the trial by bread and death of earl Godwine (1053),[94] the loss of Prince William and other children of Henry I in the shipwreck of 1120 are all reported in full.[95] Prophetic episodes of national importance are also retained, for example, St Dunstan's prophecies both at the birth of King Edgar – forecasting a time of peace (943)[96] and at the consecration of King Æthelred – predicting the loss of the kingdom to a foreign power (1016).[97] In addition to the preference for reporting matters of secular rather than ecclesiastical interest, the *Historia* exhibits another Alfredian characteristic: guardedness and neutrality in the reporting of events and people. Alfred pointedly omits the prophecies of Merlin in his abbreviation of Geoffrey of Monmouth's *HRB*, diplomatically commenting, 'they are too long to be included here'. But that he had read and understood their political significance is shown by his immediately preceding comment, 'he [Merlin] prophesied many things concerning the future of the British Kingdom'.[98] In chapter nine of the history, reporting the post-Conquest period, issues of political and ecclesiastical controversy which are reported in detail by the Durham compiler such as clerical marriage, investiture, the Canterbury–York controversy, are all avoided by the expedient of omission. When the Durham compiler comments pejoratively or describes critically the actions or motives of people and individuals, Alfred either omits or moderates the comment. So while the Durham compiler describes the slaughter of the Norman garrison in York of 3,000 soldiers in September 1069 as an act of 'divine vengeance', Alfred reports the event but passes over the comment.[99] The ransacking of the kingdom's monasteries, ordered by William I in 1070, the Durham compiler tells us, was due to William's 'rapacity and harshness'. Alfred reports the event but omits the phrase 'propter illius austeritatem et depopulationem'.[100] The account of King Malcolm III's cruel campaign in the north in 1070 is retained but the Durham compiler's comment that the Scots were 'more savage than wild beasts' is omitted as is the description of Malcolm's implacable cruelty and responsibility for encouraging even greater enslavement of the native population.[101] In 1093 the Durham compiler describes how William count of Eu broke his oath of fealty to his legitimate sovereign Robert of Normandy, 'overcome by great lust for gold', and defected to William Rufus, 'his greatest

---

92 Hearne, *ABA* viii, 115.
93 Hearne, *ABA* viii, 118–119.
94 Hearne, *ABA* viii, 121.
95 Hearne, *ABA* ix, 148.
96 Hearne, *ABA* viii, 110–111.
97 Hearne, *ABA* viii, 116. This prophecy of Dunstan, made at Æthelred's consecration, was recalled in the *HR* at his death in 1016.
98 Hearne, *ABA* v, 52
99 Hearne, *ABA* ix, 128.
100 Hearne, *ABA* ix, 130.
101 'bestiis crudeliores Scotti', Hearne, *ABA* ix, 130

corruptor'.[102] Alfred reports the events, but omits these two critical comments. In 1097 the *HR* reports how William Rufus set out for Wales with a second army with the intention of killing all male inhabitants. Alfred reports the campaign but excludes the comment about its genocidal intention.[103] This guardedness of reporting contrasts sharply with the more uninhibited expression in the monastic text from which he was excerpting his material. In the politically charged and public environment in which he composed his history Alfred, it would appear, chose to use his words with care.

A feature of Alfred's *Historia* which has attracted some scholarly comment is his effort to reconcile Geoffrey of Monmouth's British history with the accounts of conventional authorities. Antonia Gransden, who described Alfred as 'a would-be historian',[104] commented that Alfred 'made no systematic attempt to evaluate the relative reliability of his sources'.[105] However, as Alfred's sources on the twenty-nine occasions when Geoffrey's account are so tested (Appendix 3) were Bede, Suetonius, Eutropius, Orosius, and hagiographical sources such as Sulpicius Severus's *Life of St Martin* and Constantius's *Life of St Germanus*, this comment would appear wide of the mark. Alfred had little else to compare Geoffrey's account against, and the sources he consulted were, in any case, of unimpeachable authority. The very act of systematically collating one historical account against another to test its veracity, moreover, is rare in the historical writing of the time and therefore significant. It demonstrates that writers of the period were well aware of the need to distinguish between *fabula* (fiction) and veracity in a work of literature and also shows that amongst some of the very earliest audiences of Geoffrey's history, the work was greeted, at least by some, with considerable doubt, if not with open scepticism.

Alfred's collations also help us place his historical writing. In his textual cross-examination Alfred often exhibits a detailed knowledge of the authors cited and the relationship of one author to another. When he quotes a passage from Bede to compare it with Geoffrey's version of events, Alfred demonstrates knowledge of the source of Bede's information; for example 'Haec Beda secundum Orosium'[106] or 'Haec Beda, cui astipulatur et Eutropius in Romana Hystoria, scribens ita'[107] or 'Scribit autem et Beda, sequens Orosium, his consona de Claudio ita'.[108] He carefully notes points of difference between, for example, Geoffrey's account of the death of the emperor Marcus Aurelius Bassianus (Caracalla) and that of the Roman History: 'There is a discrepancy on the place

---

[102] Hearne, *ABA* ix, 140.
[103] Hearne, *ABA* ix, 142.
[104] Gransden, *Historical Writing*, 212.
[105] Gransden, 'Bede's Reputation', 19.
[106] Hearne, *ABA* iii, 34. 'These things Bede says following Orosius'.
[107] Hearne, *ABA* v, 55. 'These thing says Bede. Eutropius in his Roman History agrees with him writing as follows ...'.
[108] Hearne, *ABA* ii, 28. 'Bede, following Orosius, writes these things about Claudius, which are in agreement'.

and the circumstances of Bassianus' death. The Roman History says "He died in Osdroena near Edessa engaged in an expedition against the Parthians."'[109]

An interest and facility in comparing texts against each other for the purposes of arriving at a harmonized account suggests scholastic training and familiarity with grammatical tools such as *accessus ad auctores*, used, amongst other subjects, in medieval exegesis.[110] Alfred was remembered as a student of the scriptures in the later sources, it will be recalled, and his manner of textual collation of the Galfridian material in the text lends support to this view. Familiarity with biblical exegesis is further suggested by critical vocabulary employed in the text. Alfred's use of the Latin word 'status' to define the nine historical periods of his account is a case in point. Alfred seems to mean 'state' or 'era', but the term is nowhere found or used for historical periodization in his principal historical sources. It is, however, encountered in scholastic theology and *accessus* treatises for the study of the Bible at the time.[111] For example, in the works of the influential contemporary theologian, Hugh of Saint Victor (1096–1141), the term is found frequently and in his major work, *de Sacramentis Christianae fidei* (*c.* 1134), the term 'status' is used to denote historical periods. The treatise is organized on historical lines where Hugh based his thinking on a division of human history into three stages in a continuous process of ascent towards God after man's fall.[112] The term *status* (*statibus, statu*) is encountered some forty times in the text with instances where the term carries a clear sense of historical periodization.[113] Book one, part six, chapter ten of *de Sacramentis,* for example, is entitled *Tribus Statibus Hominis* and describes the three states of man: man before sin, man after sin, and man after the resurrection of the dead.[114]

---

[109] 'Discrepat a morte Bassiani, et de loco mortis, Romam Hystoria. "Defuncto est," inquid, "in Hosdroena apud Edissam, moliens adversus Parthos expedicionem,."' Hearne, *ABA* iii, 34.

[110] The practice of 'accessus ad auctores' is recently discussed in Kempshall, *Rhetoric*, 25–28, 413, 432.

[111] Bede opens the concluding paragraph of the penultimate chapter of the *EH* (v. 23) with the words, 'hic est inpraesentiarum universae status Brittaniae' ('This is the state of the whole of Britain at the present time') but the word is not used in the same historical periodizing sense that Alfred employs it.

[112] Hugh's historical thinking applied to scriptural study is explored in R.W. Southern, 'Aspects of the European Tradition of Historical Writing: 2. Hugh of St Victor and the idea of Historical Development', *TRHS*, 5th series, 21 (1971), 159–79 at 166.

[113] A search on the *Patrologia Latina* electronic data base in the volume devoted to the printed writings of Hugh of St Victor (vol. 176) shows frequent use of the term status in others of Hugh's treatises.

[114] Hugh's belief that history was an essential tool for the study of theology is attested by his *Chronicle* (*c.* 1130), a schoolbook of history entitled in most of the extant manuscripts, 'de tribus maximis circumstantiis gestorum, id est personis locis temporibus'. It described the three chief conditions of history, people, place and time and was used in the curriculum of the abbey of St Victor. The influence and dissemination of Hugh's handbook in England in the twelfth century was formerly considered to have been limited as only Ralph de Diceto was known to have made extensive use of it. The recent discovery of six copies of Hugh's *Chronicle* in the British Library, all of English provenance, has led to reappraisal of this view. See Julian Harrison, 'The English

There are some grounds to believe, therefore, that in Alfred's concise, orderly compilation we can observe traces of the new scholarly tools of textual analysis applied to the writing of history. In this sense the *Historia* might serve as an example of what Bernard Guenée described as the shift from eloquent to erudite historiography which occurred over the course of the twelfth century; history, as Guenée put it, written by the technician, rather than by the rhetor.[115] Yet Alfred's history also looks back. One of the reasons for compiling the *Historia*, he tells us in the prologue, was to present a history which gathered together accounts 'scattered here and there in the writings of several different authors'.[116] In this assimilative sense, the *Historia* shares similar interests to the historical narratives of the first half of the twelfth century which sought to systematize the materials for early Insular history or, in the words of James Campbell, were interested in 'bringing things together and sorting them out'.[117] Alfred's history is also assimilative in a cultural sense. The text suggests an interest in the cultural and ethnic identities of Britain at the time. The prefatory geo-historical description of Britain ends by describing the five different peoples who inhabit the island of his day and the precise locations where these peoples live on the island is carefully noted. Alfred goes on to wonder about a sixth people, the Flemings, who may be on the point of emerging on the island.[118] From such comments and remarks, an impulse for the writing of the *Historia* might have been to answer what was felt to be a pressing need; to supply an account of the island's past which integrated the various separate existing accounts of its peoples and spoke for them as one.

Because the Kingdom of the English came into being in Britain when the kingdom of the Britons lapsed, and because the learned and venerable Bede, when writing his own History of the English, covered the period from the time of Julius Caesar until his own times, I decided to collect together several things from his *History* too. After Bede several people across the English church also examined the times of the Kings

Reception of Hugh of Saint-Victor's Chronicle', *British Library Electronic Journal* (2002), Article I, 1–29. Harrison has shown that at least fifteen religious communities owned copies of the handbook, including convents of rich intellectual heritage.

[115] Bernard Guenée, 'L'histoire entre l'éloquence et la science. Quelques remarques sur le prologue de Guillaume de Malmesbury à ses Gesta Regum Anglorum.' *Comptes rendus des séances de l'Académie des Inscriptions et Belles-Lettres* (1982), 357–70, at 369.

[116] 'Quod quae sparsim in plurimorum leguntur scriptis'. Hearne, *ABA* i, 3.

[117] See James Campbell, 'Some Twelfth-Century Views of the Anglo-Saxon Past', in his *Essays in Anglo-Saxon History* (London, 1986), 209–28 at 220. The interest of English monks during the period 1090–1130, primarily in the Benedictine communities, in collecting, sifting, and organizing historical evidence from the past in order to understand the present, is discussed by Sir Richard Southern in 'Aspects of the European Tradition of Historical Writing: iv. The Sense of the Past', *TRHS*, 5th series, 23 (1973), 243–63. Also see Martin Brett, 'John of Worcester and his contemporaries', in *The Writing of History in the Middle Ages*, ed. R.H.C. Davis and J.M. Wallace Hadrill (Oxford, 1981), 101–26. For interest in collecting historical information on the Britons at that time, see Leckie, *Passage*, 18–19.

[118] Hearne, *ABA* I, 10.

most diligently and ensured that the deeds of these kings were expertly investigated and recorded. Some of this material has, after careful research, been included in this little work.[119]

From the structure of the account, its narrative arrangement, content, and tone of voice, we can draw tentative conclusions on authorial purpose and intended audience. As Alfred tells us in the prologue, the work was specifically planned as a series of self-contained chapters. The formulaic openings and conclusions, with summarizing commentary reminding readers what has been and what is about to be narrated, suggest a work intended to be serially read; to be put down and picked up again. None of the chapters exceed eight thousand words, permitting readings perhaps at single sittings, perhaps in the communal refectory which was then a constituent part of the church of Beverley.[120] The intended audience of the text therefore appears to have been internal: the canons, church dignitaries and officers of the church of Beverley, and visiting clergy some of whom were certainly, like Alfred, family men. The strongly secular viewpoint of the narrative, its interest in narrative story-telling and the clear, uncomplicated Latin sentence structures, suggests also that the intended audience was likely to have included local secular aristocracy. Alfred's awareness of his audience is revealed both in his prologue comments suggesting that his Beverley colleagues themselves acted as his 'patron', encouraging him to undertake the history, and also in the lesser-noted comments which draw to a close his abbreviation of the *HRB* at the end of chapter five of the history.

So I want to entreat the reader that, if he considers what I have laboured over, in one way or another, for the benefit of myself and those like me who cannot aspire to the

---

[119] 'Quia vero deficiente regno Britonum exortum est in Britannia regnum Anglorum, et venerabilis doctor Beda a tempore Julii Caesaris hystoriam Anglorum texens ad sua usque tempora eam perduxit, eciam de ipsa plura colligere animus mihi fuit. Similiter et post Bedam plures per Anglorum ecclesias regum tempora diligencius perscrutantes, ipsorum gesta sollerti indagine annotare curaverunt, de quibus non nulla studiosius investigata huic opusculo sunt inserta.' Hearne, *ABA* i, 3.

[120] The anonymous chronicler of the archbishops of York, a work whose early section is believed to date from shortly after the death of Archbishop Thurstan (1140) reported that Archbishop Ealdred (1062–1069) established a common dormitory and refectory for the canons of Beverley, *Chronica Pontificum Ecclesiae Eboracensis, Pars Prima*, in *Historians of the Church of York*, ed. Raine, ii, 312–87 at 353. For a survey of the medieval church of Beverley see *Memorials of Beverley Minster: The Chapter Act Book of the Collegiate Church of S. John of Beverley, A.D. 1286–1347*, ed. A.F. Leach (2 vols., Durham, 1898–1903), i, ix–lxxv and on communal living specifically, see xxix. It has been argued that a conservative church of Beverley resisted the Norman reformed model of secular chapters longer than other Yorkshire secular establishments and that the Beverley canons lived communally until the end of the twelfth century, see D.M. Palliser, 'The Early Medieval Minster', in *Beverley Minster: An Illustrated History*, ed. R. Horrox (Cambridge, 2000), 23–35 at 28. There is evidence, however, that territorial-based prebends in Beverley may have been established from the early years of the archiepiscopate of Roger de Pont l'Eveque (1154–1181). See 'Beverley Minster Fasti', ed. R.W.T McDermid, *Yorkshire Archaeological Society*, Record Series 149 (Leeds, 1990), xix–xx.

heights, less than pleasing, he should at least not deter simple and uneducated people from reading it, by his criticism.[121]

Alfred's history therefore is a work of considerable interest in Anglo-Norman historiography. It is an example of historical writing undertaken by a secular clerk at a time when most historical writing still originated in monastic communities. The range of literary resources available to a compiler in a regional ecclesiastical institution with an otherwise little-known intellectual tradition attests to the extent of the spread of learning and literature in mid-twelfth-century England. The text is an important witness at the midway point of the twelfth century to the transmission of several of the most important twelfth-century Anglo-Norman historical texts from which it freely borrows, and from which it absorbs and serves to disseminate ideas in a concise and clear manner. Alfred's is the first Latin history to integrate Geoffrey of Monmouth's British history into a continuous narrative of the island past, whilst demonstrating critical historical awareness. Alfred appreciates the tensions which exist between Geoffrey's version of British history and those of conventional accounts and he edits his account to provide a more convincing chronology.[122] Open scepticism and silent doubts distinguish his handling of the *HRB*. A generation before William of Newburgh's famous denunciation of Geoffrey's history in the preface to his *Historia Rerum Anglicarum* (*c.* 1196), Alfred had more modestly voiced the essence of William's concerns.

Alfred is also the earliest Insular Latin chronicler to promote a number of the influential historical ideas of Henry of Huntingdon's *HA*, amongst which is the theory of the establishment of the seven English kingdoms – the heptarchy – after the coming of the Saxons to Britain. The establishment of the seven English kingdoms giving way to the emergence of one *regnum* under the West Saxon kings is an idea very powerfully promoted in Alfred's history, forming chapter six of the work. The dynastic accounts and royal genealogies of the Saxon kingdoms, contained in the preliminary sections of the Worcester Chronicle, are extensively quarried and influence deeply Alfred's portrayal of the emergence of one kingdom under West Saxon dominion. The Worcester material is also significant in shaping Alfred's views of the Saxon kings.[123] Alfred emphasizes the view that King Æthelstan was the first of the English kings to hold undisputed national sovereignty, an idea which he appears to have absorbed from the dynastic

---

[121] 'Unde lectorem exoratum esse volo, ut quod michi meique similibus qui ad alta aspirare non possumus, utcumque elaboravi, si sibi minus gratum judicat, saltem parvulos et idiotas ab ejus leccione derogando non abigat.' Hearne, *ABA* v, 76.

[122] Alfred's awareness of the tensions existing between the 'Bedan' and 'Galfridian' versions of early Insular history and his editorial strategy to provide a seamless transition from the sovereignty of the British to the English kings on the island is illuminatingly discussed in Leckie, *Passage*, 45–46, 86–92. Leckie's commentary on Alfred of Beverley represents perhaps the most serious scholarly attention the work has received to the present.

[123] The Worcester dynastic accounts and royal genealogies are presently only available printed in *Monumenta historica Britannica, or, Materials for the History of Britain from the Earliest Period. Vol. 1, Extending to the Norman Conquest*, ed. H. Petrie (London, 1848), 616–644.

accounts and royal genealogies from the Worcester Chronicle. Chapter eight of the history, themed the 'status monarchiae Angliae', runs from King Æthelstan to Harold. Alfred notes in the opening lines of the book that Æthelstan's father, Edward the Elder, died as king of the West Saxons, as if to underscore that in Æthelstan's succession a turning point in the island's history had been reached. The statement describing Æthelstan as 'first of the English to obtain gloriously the monarchy of all England' is repeated three times in the *Historia*, and is found in the preliminary section of the Worcester Chronicle, next to Æthelstan on the West Saxon genealogical tree.[124] It is repeated in the Deira dynastic account – with Alfred reproducing the words *verbatim*.[125] Both in the preliminary accounts and genealogies and in the main chronicle, the Worcester text describes Æthelstan as '*gloriosus*', and '*strenuus*', terms which Alfred repeats, adding also the word '*potentissimus*', to describe Æthelstan.[126] Alfred's extensive reworking of the Durham *HR* from book seven onwards in the history is also important. It sheds light on the considerably different mindsets and concerns of writers of history in secular and monastic institutions at the time. It also provides rare evidence on the state of the *HR* in Beverley at *c.* 1150, a midway point between its leaving Durham in *c.* 1129 and its appearance in its sole surviving copy in Cambridge, Corpus Christi College, MS 139.

That Alfred has a strong sense of Britain's island identity and its multiple ethnicities is attested by the geo-historical description of Britain and its peoples with which he begins his *Historia,* and which was later to exercise consider-able influence on Ranulf Higden and successor chroniclers and topographers.[127] A sense of kingdom is suggested also by the employment of Henry of Huntingdon's explanation of the evolution of the naming and identity of the island: first Albion, then Britain, and finally Anglia, an idea Alfred uses early in book six of the history.[128] With well over eighty percent of the text reworked from his sources, Alfred's is a highly derivative work, a scissors and paste production *par excellence*, but it is of no less historical interest for that. In the words of an eminent medievalist describing a similar compiler-author of the time, Symeon of Durham, 'the scissors were quite deftly wielded: the paste was of good quality'.[129]

---

[124] 'primus Anglorum tocius Angliae monarchiam gloriose optinuit'. The notice states 'Strenuus et gloriosus rex Athelstanus solus per totam Angliam primus regum Anglorum regnavit.' Petrie ed., *Monumenta* 634, note 2. This notice is best observed in Oxford, Corpus Christi College, MS 157, 53. For the most recent discussion on Insular twelfth-century views of King Æthelstan see Sarah Foot, *Æthelstan. The First King of England* (New Haven, CT, 2011), 227–223.

[125] Petrie ed., *Monumenta*, 640, and Hearne *ABA* viii, 93.

[126] Hearne *ABA* vi, 79, 93; viii, 93.

[127] How the idea of Britain resonated powerfully in the medieval mind is discussed by in R.R. Davies, 'Island Mythologies', in *The First English Empire, Power and Identities in the British Isles, 1093–1343* (Oxford, 2000), 31–53.

[128] Hearne *ABA* vi, 78.

[129] H.S. Offler, *Medieval Historians of Durham: Inaugural Lecture as Professor of Medieval History Delivered in the Applebey Lecture Theatre, on March 14, 1958* (Durham, 1958), 7.

Appendix 1. Manuscripts of the history of Alfred of Beverley

	Date	Manuscript	Short Description
1	s.xiv/xv	Oxford, Bodleian, MS Rawlinson B 200	T. Hearne's edition was printed from this manuscript, once owned by John de Newton, treasurer of York Minster (d. 1414).
2	s.xv	Aberystwyth, NLW, MS Peniarth 384	There is some evidence to suggest a Jervaulx provenance for this book. A later xv. hand extends the history from 1129 to 1135.
3	s.xvii	Aberystwyth, NLW, MS Wynnstay 11	Transcript of NLW, MS Peniarth 384, made in 1663 by William Maurice of Llansilin. **New witness.**
4	s.xiv	Bibliothèque national de France, MS lat. 4126	Folios 242v–252r contain c.9 of Alfred's history. The work was commissioned by the Carmelite Robert Populton, prior of Hulne Northumberland, in 1364. Text continues to 1135.
5	s.xiii/xiv	London, BL, MS Cotton Cleopatra A.I	This volume, dating from c1300 from the Cistercian abbey of Furness, contains from folios 12r to 115v an almost complete copy of Alfred's history with some expansions noted on folios 39–41, 44r, 50v, 66r–67r, 72v. **New witness.** The text continues to 1135.
6	s.xvii	London, BL, MS Harl. 1018, art. 1	A late seventeenth-century transcript of Alfred's history which entered the Harley collection in 1707 from the collection of Edward Stillingfleet, bishop of Worcester (d. March 1699). The narrative extends to 1135.
7	s.xvii	Cambridge, Trinity College, MS O.2. 52	A seventeenth-century transcript. The manuscript was one of the collection of five hundred volumes bequeathed in 1738 by Roger Gale, Hearne's contemporary antiquary (d. 1744), to Trinity College Cambridge. Supplies a copy of chapter 6 to early chapter 9 of the history.
8	s.xvi	London, BL, MS Cotton Vespasian A.V	A miscellany of historical excerpts from English chronicles. Folios 18r–19v contain notes made by William Lambarde (d. 1601) from a copy of Alfred of Beverley's history owned by William Darrell, canon of Canterbury. The notes are taken from all sections of the history and dated 1568.
9	s.xv	London, BL, MS Cotton Vespasian D.IV	A fifteenth-century collection of five items. That occupying folios 73v–125r, with the rubric, 'Godfridi Malmesburiensis a Saxonicum adventum' is cc. vi–ix of Alfred's history. The text continues to 1129 ending at the word, 'acceperat.' First half of s.xv.
10	s.xvii	Glasgow University Library, MS Hunter 318 (s.xvii), art.1	The manuscript catalogue[1] describes this MS as follows: 'a s.xvii MS bound volume containing A. of Beverley's history, prologue of Robert de Torigni, Henry of Huntingdon's letter to Warin, Nennius's Historia.' It notes that the Rev. J. Stevenson refers to the MS in his edition of Nennius (pp.xxvii and 4) stating that he considered it a transcript of Ff.i.27 in University Library Cambridge.' Text extends to 1135.

[1] J. Young and P. Aitken, A Catalogue of the Manuscripts in the Library of the Hunterian Museum in the University of Glasgow (Glasgow, 1908), 252–254.

Appendix 2. Charters attested by Alfred of Beverley

	Where Printed	Date	Details of Charter	Names of Principal Witnesses
1	EYC I, no. 104	c. 1135–1143	Confirmation by Thurstan Provost and the Beverley Chapter of alms to canons of Bridlington priory as was originally granted by Thomas, Provost and the canons of his time.	William dean of York, Simon, Ralph, Roger canons of Beverley. *Aluredus Sacrista.* Total witnesses 14. 5 ecclesiastic, 9 lay.
2	EYC I, no. 105 EEA V. no. 86	c. late 1143–1147	Grant by Archbishop William fitz Herbert as first granted by Archbishop Thurstan to the town of Beverley of free burgage as per York.	Earl William of Aumale and Robert de Stuteville (III), Everard de Ros. Thurstan provost, Ivo abbot of Warter, Simon, Ralph canons of Beverley, *Magistro Alfrido sacrista.* Total witnesses 20. 5 ecclesiastic, 9 lay.
3	EYC II, no.1108 EEA V. no. 129	Jan. 1, 1151–Oct. 14, 1153	Notification by Archbishop Henry Murdac before the Beverley chapter of confirmation of the gift of Eustace fitz John to the nuns of Watton priory. To support 13 canons of the order of Sempringham to minister to nuns.	Adam abbot of Meaux. William cantor and Robert archdeacon of York. Canons of Beverley; Aildwardus, Ralph, Simon, Roger, Willelmus Morin. *Aluredus sacrista,* Warin clerk of the counts, William of Warter, Hugh and Richard Murdac and their sons Hugh and Stephen Total witnesses 26. 8 ecclesiastic, 18 lay.
4	EYC X. no. 67 EEA V. no.128	c. 1151?	Confirmation by Archbishop Henry Murdac and notification to Robert the dean and the chapter of York of the grants made to the church of St James and the canons of Warter priory for the construction of an abbey by William de Roumare, earl of Lincoln, and family.	William cantor and Robert the archdeacon of York. Aeldwardus, Ralph, Simon, Nicholas, William, Philip canons of Beverley. *Alveredus Sacrista.* Total witnesses 8, all ecclesiastic.
5	EYC XII, no. 109 Rufford II no. 303	1146–1154	Grant in free alms by William Tison to Rufford Abbey (Cistercian) of land in 'Arthes' in Averham, Nottinghamshire.	Simon et Roger Canons of Beverley. *Alveredo sacrista,* *Ernaldo filio Alveredi* Stephano Murdac. Total 17 witnesses. 3 ecclesiastic, 14 lay.

Appendix 3. Alfred's collations of the *HRB* with other historical authorities

Location in *Historia*	Collations of Geoffrey of Monmouth's version of events
Chapter 1. p. 16	Roman History. Eutropius, *Breviarium ab Urbe Condita*
Chapter 1. p. 17	H. Huntingdon, *Historia Anglorum*
Chapter 2. p. 26	Bede, *Historia Ecclesiastica*, Orosius, *Historiarum Adversum Paganos*
Chapter 2. p. 27	Suetonius (*Lives of Caesars*), Roman History
Chapter 2. p. 28	Bede, Orosius
Chapter 2. p. 29	Suetonius
Chapter 2. p. 29	Roman History
Chapter 2. p. 29	Roman History
Chapter 3. p. 31	Bede
Chapter 3. p. 33	Bede
Chapter 3. p. 34	Roman History
Chapter 3. p. 34.	Roman History
Chapter 3. p. 35	Bede, Orosius
Chapter 3. p. 35	Roman History
Chapter 3. p. 36	Bede
Chapter 3. p. 37	Bede
Chapter 3. p. 37	Eutropius in Roman History
Chapter 3. p. 38	Eutropius
Chapter 3. p. 39	Bede, Roman History
Chapter 3. p. 40	Roman History
Chapter 3. p. 40	Bede
Chapter 3. p. 40	*Vita S. Martini* (Sulpicius Severus)
Chapter 4. p. 42	Bede
Chapter 4. p. 46	Roman History
Chapter 5. p. 50	Roman History
Chapter 5.p. 50	Bede, Roman History
Chapter 5. p. 51	*Vita St. Germani* (Constantius)
Chapter 5. p. 55	Bede, Eutropius
Chapter 5. p. 74	Bede

7

Bethell Prize Essay

Helena, Constantine, and the Angevin Desire for Jerusalem[*]

Katherine L. Hodges-Kluck

In the second half of the twelfth century, English interest in the Holy Land was intimately linked to the dynastic claims of the Angevin kings. Historians and hagiographers writing in the shadow of the Angevin court deliberately shaped a narrative of Angevin rule that laid claim to the royal legacy of Britain, the imperial legacy of Rome, and the spiritual legacy of Jerusalem. In particular, these writers reimagined legends about the Roman emperor Constantine the Great (r. 306–337) and his mother, Helena Augusta (d. 328/9), in ways that turned them into exemplary twelfth-century English monarchs. This process of reimagining, I argue, had two distinct phases. In the middle decades of the twelfth century, Anglo-Norman authors drew upon Helena's and Constantine's legacies in Britain to legitimize Henry II's (r. 1154–1189) right to rule England. By the beginning of the thirteenth century, in turn, Angevin depictions of Britain's fourth-century Roman rulers began to show influences from the memory of events surrounding the Third Crusade (in particular the Muslims' capture of the True Cross and Jerusalem in 1187) and of English participation in the crusading movement. While a Christian longing to protect the sacred sites and relics of the Holy Land from the Muslims was felt throughout Europe, in England that longing took the shape of a distinctive crusading ideology built

[*] This paper is an expanded version of a talk given at the Haskins Society Conference in Northfield, MN, in November 2014. I am grateful for the insightful questions and comments of the conference attendees, and would especially like to thank Bill North, Bob Berkhofer, Robin Fleming, Laura Gathagan, and Nick Paul. Many thanks also to Jay Rubenstein and Stefan Hodges-Kluck for their assistance in reading drafts of this article. Research for this article was supported by the Galen Broeker Summer Travel Fellowship from the University of Tennessee History Department, the Anne Marie Van Hook Memorial Summer Travel Fellowship and the Jimmy and Dee Haslam Dissertation Prize from the UT Marco Institute for Medieval and Renaissance Studies, and the Graduate Student Fellowship from the UT Humanities Center. All translations are my own unless otherwise noted. I have previously published as Katherine L. Thompson Newell.

upon the Angevins' appropriation of England's Romano-British past – a past to which the Angevin kings sought to connect themselves through genealogy and cultural inheritance.

While Angevin interest in Roman Britain took many forms, the legends about Helena and Constantine proved especially adaptable to twelfth-century events. Helena's historic connection to Britain was tenuous at best. She was probably born somewhere in Asia Minor and may have been an innkeeper or a prostitute before she became the wife (or, more likely, the consort) of the Roman tetrarch Constantius Chlorus (r. 293–306). Their son, the future emperor Constantine the Great, was born in Naissus (present-day Niš, Serbia) around 272. Constantius later separated from Helena in 298 so that he could marry Theodora, the daughter of his senior emperor Maximian. It was through Constantius, however, that Helena's story first became linked with the history of Roman Britain. Under the Tetrarchy, Constantius was responsible for ruling the provinces of Gaul and Britannia. He waged campaigns against the Picts in northern Britain and died at York in 306. Constantine was subsequently proclaimed Augustus by the Roman legion in York upon his father's death. Contemporary sources say nothing about what Helena was doing or where she was from 298 to 306. Most likely she was in Trier, only reuniting with her son after he had returned east from Britain. There is no evidence that Helena herself ever set foot on the island.[1]

Constantine appointed his mother Augusta in 324, and from 326 until her death in 328/9, she oversaw the construction of new churches in the eastern Roman provinces on his behalf.[2] One of the locations for these building projects was the city of Aelia Capitolina, the Roman outpost built in the second century over the ruins of Jerusalem.[3] It was there that Helena, according to legend, aided either by Jerusalem's bishop Macarius or by a Jew named Judas, reportedly discovered the True Cross, lost for nearly three centuries.[4] Constantine then oversaw the construction of the Martyrion basilica over the site where Helena had found the Cross, along with the Anastasis (Resurrection) rotunda encompassing Christ's empty tomb (the cave donated by Joseph of Arimathea) and the Triportico atrium. Dedicated in 335, these buildings together formed the

---

[1]   Jan Willem Drijvers, *Helena Augusta: The Mother of Constantine the Great and the Legend of Her Finding of the True Cross* (Leiden, 1992), 5–16, 21; Antonina Harbus, *Helena of Britain in Medieval Legend* (Cambridge, 2002), 14; Marios Costambeys, 'Helena (*c.* 248–328/9)', *Oxford Dictionary of National Biography*, Online Edition (Oxford, 2004). On the possible dates of Constantine's birth, see David Potter, *Constantine the Emperor* (Oxford, 2012), 318 at note 14. See also Colin Morris, *The Sepulchre of Christ and the Medieval West: From the Beginning to 1600* (Oxford, 2005), 18, 39–40.

[2]   Drijvers, *Helena Augusta*, 21; Harbus, *Helena of Britain*, 14; Costambeys, 'Helena'; Morris, *Sepulchre of Christ*, 18, 39–40. Morris suggests that Helena's tour of the provinces probably happened in 326.

[3]   Morris, *Sepulchre of Christ*, 5, 6, 18; Drijvers, *Helena Augusta*, 5, 36.

[4]   H.A. Drake, 'Eusebius on the True Cross', *JEH* 3 (1985), 1–22; Morris, *Sepulchre of Christ*, 17, 20–2; Susan Grace Larkin, 'Transitions in the Medieval Legends of Saint Helena', Ph.D. Dissertation (Indiana University, 1995), 28–29; Costambeys, 'Helena'.

first iteration of the Church of the Holy Sepulchre. Indeed, Colin Morris has argued that Jerusalem's central importance in medieval Christianity owed much to Constantine's construction of the Holy Sepulchre complex, and to the holy relics – including the True Cross – found during excavations for it.[5]

In England, Constantine's brief association with York left an enduring legacy. Antonina Harbus identifies the seventh-century Anglo-Saxon bishop Aldhelm (d. 709) as the first author to claim that Helena gave birth to Constantine in Britain.[6] This invented story of the emperor's British birth took root in the tenth century and gained further strength in the early twelfth.[7] Implied in these tales, of course, was the understanding that Helena was living in Britain when she gave birth to her son. In the Welsh and Anglo-Saxon traditions, she became the daughter of King Coel of Colchester (memorialized in nursery rhymes as 'Old King Cole'). Her mythical origins as a British princess thereby complimented her historical promotion to the rank of Augusta.[8]

In the first half of the twelfth century, as Helena's legend grew in popularity, she and her son Constantine became model British rulers in the works of several Anglo-Norman authors. Henry of Huntingdon (*c.* 1088–*c.* 1157) called Constantine 'the flower of Britain' ('flos Brittannie') because he was 'British by birth and by his native land: neither before him nor after did an equal come from Britain'.[9] He described Helena, 'the noble alumna of Britain', as a good British ruler who built fortified walls around London and Colchester. 'But above all the other many things', Henry added, 'she restored Jerusalem, and having cleansed it of idols, she adorned numerous basilicas.'[10] Helena, in Henry's mind, had left a lasting imprint of herself upon the physical and spiritual landscape of both western and eastern kingdoms, and her contributions were still visible in Henry's day. By referring to Helena as Britain's 'noble alumna', moreover, Henry emphasized Britain's (and, by extension, England's) importance in establishing this legacy.

Geoffrey of Monmouth (d. 1154/5), in turn, integrated Helena's legend into the larger narrative of British history, while also setting her up as the epitome of noble feminine accomplishment. Helena's beauty, he wrote, 'surpassed the girls of the land, nor could another be found anywhere who might be judged

---

5   Drijvers, *Helena Augusta*, 85; Martin Biddle, *The Tomb of Christ* (Stroud, 1999), 67–70; Drake, 'Eusebius on the True Cross', 6–7, 11–14; Morris, *Sepulchre of Christ*, 318, 501.
6   Harbus, *Helena of Britain*, 38.
7   Larkin, 'Transitions', 60–61, 65; Harbus, *Helena of Britain*, 3, 39–40.
8   Harbus, *Helena of Britain*, 1.
9   Henry of Huntingdon, *Historia Anglorum: The History of the English People* I.38, ed. Diana Greenway, OMT (Oxford, 1996), 60: 'Britannicus genere et patria: ante quem nec post similis egressus est de Britannia'.
10   Henry of Huntingdon, *Historia* I.38, 62: 'Helena uero Britannie nobilis alumna, Lundoniam muro quod adhuc superest cinxisse fertur, et Colecestriam menibus adornasse. Sed et inter alia multa Ierosolim instaurauit, mundatamque idolis, basilicis pluribus adornauit.' See also Harbus, *Helena of Britain*, 75.

more skilled than her in musical instruments or in the liberal arts'.[11] Geoffrey likely sought to create parallels between Helena and Henry II's mother, Matilda (1102–1167). Fiona Tolhurst has suggested that Geoffrey was here presenting Helena as a feminine figure who, like Matilda, had been trained to govern the kingdom.[12] Moreover, like Matilda, who held the title of Holy Roman empress, Helena served as the conduit through whom Britain's future Roman rulers could make their claims upon the kingdom.[13] In Geoffrey of Monmouth's version of the legend, therefore, Helena's importance lay not so much in her own deeds but rather in her role as unifier of Roman imperial and British royal power.

Not long after Henry II inherited the English throne in 1154, the Jersey poet and historian Wace (*c.* 1100/10–1174/83) completed a translation of Geoffrey of Monmouth's history from Latin into Anglo-Norman. Wace's *Roman de Brut*, written in 1155, drew primarily from Geoffrey's text, although Wace also incorporated other oral and written traditions into the narrative.[14] Wace was known at Henry's court: the king commissioned him to write the first vernacular history of the Norman rulers (the *Roman de Rou*) in 1160 and granted him a prebend in Rouen *c.* 1165–1169, although the poet fell out of favor a few years later.[15] The *Roman de Brut* shows Wace's early response to the rise of Angevin dynastic power in England. Following Geoffrey, his portrayal of Helena centered on her identity as the sole heir of her father Coel, whom Wace called the king of England ('Engleterre').[16] Wace drew parallels between Helena and Matilda, and by extension between Constantine and Henry II. Matilda, as the sole heir of Henry I, provided Henry II with his claim to the English crown.[17] Indeed, Matilda regularly broadcast her right to rule through the use of the title 'Matildis imperatrix Henrici regis filia' (Empress Matilda, daughter of King Henry [I]), while her son regularly referred to

---

[11] Geoffrey of Monmouth, *History of the Kings of Britain, An Edition and Translation of the De Gestis Britonum* [Historia Regum Britanniae], ed. Michael D. Reeve, trans. Neil Wright (Woodbridge, 2007), v, 97: 'Pulchritudo eius prouinciales puellas superabat, nec uspiam reperiebatur altera quae in musicis instrumentis siue in liberalibus artibus doctor illa censeretur'; Fiona Tolhurst, *Geoffrey of Monmouth and the Translation of Female Kingship*, Arthurian and Courtly Cultures (New York, NY, 2013), 118–119; Tolhurst, *Geoffrey of Monmouth and the Feminist Origins of the Arthurian Legend*, Arthurian and Courtly Studies (New York, NY, 2012), 122; Harbus, *Helena of Britain*, 3, 79.

[12] Fiona Tolhurst, *Feminist Origins*, 2 (quote), 122; and Tolhurst, *Female Kingship*, 118–119, 127. See also Larkin, 'Transitions', 112.

[13] See, e.g., Geoffrey of Monmouth, *History of the Kings of Britain*, v, 99, 101, 105. See also Tolhurst, *Female Kingship*, 108, 120–121; Harbus, *Helena of Britain*, 1, 4.

[14] Jean Blacker, 'Wace (b. after 1100, d. 1174 x 1183)', *DNB*.

[15] Charity Urbanski, *Writing History for the King: Henry II and the Politics of Vernacular Historiography* (Ithaca, NY, 2013), 83–147, at 83; Blacker, 'Wace', *DNB*. By the 1170s the monarch's patronage favored the poet Benoît de Sainte-Maure over Wace.

[16] *Wace's Roman de Brut: A History of the British*, ed. Judith Weiss (Exeter, 1999), 142.

[17] Wace's successor in royal favor, Benoît de Sainte-Maure, similarly emphasized that Matilda's position as Henry I's sole heir gave Henry II his right to the English throne. See Urbanski, *Writing History*, 184–185.

himself as Henry fitzEmpress.[18] Constantine's right to rule Britain similarly derived from his mother, who also bore the title of Empress (Augusta). The question of legitimate rule was integral for Henry II, who devoted great amounts of energy to establishing both the legality and the stability of his new dynasty.[19] Wace therefore presented Constantine as the just and rightfully elected ruler of Britain. After his 'barons' ('barnage') and 'knights' ('chevaliers') proclaimed him king (i.e. emperor), Wace explained, Constantine ruled wisely, upholding justice throughout his lands.[20] Constantine thus became the model of legitimate succession, through the female line, to the British/English throne.

According to Layamon, an English monk who some fifty years later translated Wace's *Roman de Brut* into early Middle English, Wace dedicated his *Roman de Brut* to 'Eleanor, who was Henry the high king's queen'.[21] There is no reason to disbelieve that Eleanor, a famous patron of the arts, at least would have been familiar with the poem. Indeed, Wace's Helena also functioned as a mirror for Eleanor: Helena's name was generally rendered in Old French as Heléne or Eleine, which was similar to the Provençal name Aliénor. As Geoffrey of Monmouth had done, Wace emphasized Helena's learning and other accomplishments. She was well lettered as well as esteemed for her beauty. Indeed, the poet suggested that Constantius was a lucky man for marrying Coel's daughter, for no woman of that time was her equal in worthiness or intelligence.[22] Moreover, just as Helena had supposedly inherited Britain from her father Coel, so had Eleanor inherited Aquitaine from her father, Duke William X. Eleanor had even been to Jerusalem for eleven months in 1148–1149, although the visit never granted her the same reputation for piety that Helena had achieved. Eleanor and Henry II were married in 1152, and in February 1155 – the same year that Wace completed the *Roman de Brut* – Eleanor gave birth to their son Henry, named after his father the king. It is tempting to think that Eleanor and Henry II would have recognized themselves in Wace's descriptions of the heiress Helena's marriage to the great warrior-emperor Constantius and the subsequent birth of their son Constantine. The similarities would likely not have been lost on contemporary readers.

---

[18] Urbanski, *Writing History*, 79–80.
[19] Urbanski, *Writing History*, 387–1 and especially 401. For a discussion of how the Norman historian Dudo of Saint-Quentin used Constantine as a model of legitimate rule for the Normans, see Benjamin Pohl, '*Translatio imperii Constantini ad Normannos*: Constantine the Great as a Possible Model for the Depiction of Rollo in Dudo of St. Quentin's *Historia Normannorum*', *Millennium: Yearbook on the Culture and History of the First Millennium* 9 (2012), 297–339, especially 306, 311, 313. See also Benjamin Pohl, 'Constantine and the Normans: Legitimising myths of Roman imperial heritage in (Anglo) Norman historiography, *c.* 1000–1154', in *Proceedings of the Conference Figures of History: The Exemplary Past in Nordic, Norman and German Historiography c. 1050–1200*, ed. Sigbjørn Sønnesyn (2014/15), forthcoming.
[20] Wace, *Roman de Brut*, 143–144 at 143.
[21] Layamon, *Brut*, ed. Frederic Madden (3 vols., London, 1847), i, 3: 'Aelienor þe wes Henries quene; / þes heȝes kinges'.
[22] Wace, *Roman de Brut*, 142. See also Tolhurst, *Female Kingship*, 186.

Wace's *Roman de Brut* reflects the Angevins' reception of the Helena and Constantine legends in the first years of their dynasty. As they had done with Helena, the Anglo-Norman authors had created a British Constantine, building upon his acclamation as emperor at York in 306 and suggesting that he and his future deeds owed their success to his British origins. Thus these authors sought to reinforce Helena and Constantine's connections to English soil and bloodlines. Nor did Constantine's Roman connections necessarily undermine his association with Britain: Susan Larkin suggests that the emperor's 'dual ancestry' from Britain and Rome would have appealed to twelfth-century audiences, who were themselves often of mixed heritage.[23] If the Romano-British Constantine could be English, so could an Anglo-Norman or Anglo-Angevin. As Wace put it, Constantine 'loved the Britons for his mother, / and the Romans for his father'.[24] This statement can also be seen as a reminder to Henry II, son of an Anglo-Norman mother and an Angevin father, to love all of his subjects equally.

Importantly, where Geoffrey of Monmouth and Henry of Huntingdon had left Helena's discovery of the True Cross out of their histories, Wace restored it. After Constantine became emperor, Wace wrote, his 'good mother, Helena, traveled to Jerusalem'.[25] Wace focused on the Judas version of the story, describing how Helena had demanded that the Jews reveal to her the place where Christ had died. He noted how one of the Jews showed her the site and concluded by stating simply that it was thus that Helena found the Cross, 'which had long been concealed'.[26] On the whole, however, Wace and the other Anglo-Norman historians showed only a limited interest in Helena and Constantine's activities in the Holy Land. Indeed, up through the middle of the twelfth century, England had played – to quote Christopher Tyerman – only a 'minimal and peripheral' role in the crusades, with the greatest English military success occurring at the capture of Lisbon in 1147, rather than in Jerusalem.[27] The growing popularity of the crusading movement meant that by the 1130s English authors were devoting more attention to affairs in the Holy Land, but Jerusalem still played a background role in English narratives about Helena and Constantine.[28]

Contemporary events in the Holy Land, however, brought a new sense of relevance to legends about Helena's and Constantine's actions in Jerusalem. On 4 July 1187 Ayyubid Muslim forces soundly defeated the Christian army at the Horns of Hattin in the Latin kingdom of Jerusalem. Guy of Lusignan, king of Jerusalem (r. 1186–1192), was taken captive along with a number of

---

23   Larkin, 'Transitions', 110.
24   Wace, *Roman de Brut*, 144: 'Les Bretuns ama pur sa mere / E cels de Rome pur sun pere'.
25   Wace, *Roman de Brut*, 144.
26   Wace, *Roman de Brut*, 144: 'Qui lonc tans ot esté celée'. On iconography of Judas and his role in the *Inventio crucis* story, see Sara Lipton, *Dark Mirror: The Medieval Origins of Anti-Semitic Iconography* (New York, NY, 2014), 86–90.
27   Christopher Tyerman, *England and the Crusades, 1095–1588* (Chicago, IL, 1988), 15.
28   Tyerman, *England and the Crusades*, 223, 25, 32.

other Christian leaders. The Muslim army also seized a fragment of the True Cross from the Franks.[29] The True Cross had been an important Christian relic since Helena's legendary fourth-century discovery of it, but it had acquired particular importance after the crusader capture of Jerusalem in 1099, and had gradually replaced the Holy Sepulchre as the focal point of crusader devotion over the course of the twelfth century.[30] Islamic sources similarly understood the Cross's importance. The Arab historian Ibn al-Athīr (1160–1233) wrote that the capture of the Cross represented one of the 'greatest misfortunes' suffered by the Frankish army, while the Persian scholar Imad al-Din (1125–1201) noted that 'In their [the Christians'] eyes, its capture was more important than the loss of the king [of Jerusalem]; it was the worst thing that happened to them on the field of battle'.[31] Word of this defeat spread rapidly throughout Christendom. From one end of Europe to the other, Christians lamented the loss of the True Cross, seeing it as representative of the larger threat hanging over Jerusalem and the Holy Land. The French chronicler Rigord claimed that the Cross's capture caused children born that year to have fewer teeth; in Rome Pope Urban III reportedly died of shock upon hearing the news.[32]

After the Muslims captured the True Cross at Hattin in 1187, a call went out across Christendom to rescue it and restore it to its rightful home in Jerusalem.[33] Christians could not allow the very wood sanctified by Christ's dying body now to be defiled by its Muslim captors. Yet, while Christians everywhere longed to free the True Cross and Jerusalem, England's Angevin rulers believed that the relic and the holy city were specifically part of their own family's dynastic heritage. Henry II's grandfather, Fulk V of Anjou, had visited the Holy Land in 1120 and in 1129, and he donated a fragment of the True Cross to the monastery

---

[29] [Roger of Howden], *Gesta Regis Henrici Secundi Benedicti Abbatis: The Chronicle of the Reigns of Henry II and Richard I, AD 1169–1192*, ed. William Stubbs, RS (2 vols., London, 1867), i, 331 (hereafter Roger of Howden, *Gesta*); Anne-Marie Eddé, *Saladin*, trans. Jane Marie Todd (Cambridge, MA, 2011), 210–211; Jay Rubenstein, *Armies of Heaven: The First Crusade and the Quest for Apocalypse* (New York, NY, 2011), 306, 308–309.

[30] Sylvia Schein, *Gateway to the Heavenly City: Crusader Jerusalem and the Catholic West (1099–1187)*, Church, Faith and Culture in the Medieval West (Burlington, VT, 2005), 83.

[31] Ibn al-Athīr, *The Chronicle of Ibn al-Athīr for the Crusading Period from al-Kāmil fi'lta'rīkh, Part 2: The Years 541–589/1146–1193, The Age of Nur al-Din and Saladin*, trans. D.S. Richards, Crusade Texts in Translation (Burlington, VT, 2007), 323 (first quote) (hereafter Ibn al-Athīr, *Chronicle*); Compare Amin Maalouf, *The Crusades through Arab Eyes*, 192; Imad al-Din, quoted by Jonathan Phillips, *Holy Warriors: A Modern History of the Crusades* (London, 2010), 130 (second quotation).

[32] *Oeuvres de Rigord et de Guillaume le Breton*, ed. H. Francoise Delaborde (2 vols., Paris, 1882), i, 82–83: 'Et nota quod ab eodem anno Domini quando crux Dominica in transmarinis partibus eodem Saladino capta fuit, infantes qui ab eo tempore nati sunt, non habent nisi xx duos dentes aut tantum xx, cum antea xxx aut xxx duos habere consueverant.' See also Eddé, *Saladin*, 212; Jonathan Riley-Smith, *The Crusades: A Short History* (New Haven, CT, 1987), 109.

[33] Ralph de Diceto, *The Historical Works of Master Ralph de Diceto, Dean of London*, ed. William Stubbs, Cambridge Library Collection (2 vols., Cambridge, 2012; originally published 1876), ii, 514.

of Saint-Laud in Angers. Henry later provided a new reliquary case for it.[34] On 14 September 1131 – the Feast of the Exaltation of the Cross – Fulk was crowned King Fulk I of Jerusalem at the Church of the Holy Sepulchre, rebuilt on the site of Constantine's original church. Before this, Jerusalem's Frankish kings had been crowned on Christmas day in Bethlehem.[35] The coronation ceremony for Fulk and his second wife, Melisende, thus began a new tradition in the Holy Land, one that linked an Angevin ruler of Jerusalem to the True Cross and the Holy Sepulchre in both ritual and space.[36] Saladin's capture of the Cross in 1187 and the fall of Jerusalem later that year, together with the subsequent Angevin participation in the Third Crusade, led to increased interest within England in the stories of Helena's and Constantine's activities in the Holy Land. The Angevin kings had a stake in the fate of the relic – and, more broadly, the fate of Jerusalem – not just because they were Christians, but also because they believed, as Angevins and as Englishmen, that protecting the True Cross and the holy city was part of their royal prerogative inherited from Helena and Constantine as well as from Fulk.

The English chronicler Roger of Howden dwelt on the Angevin kings' relationship to Fulk V of Anjou in both his *Gesta Regis Henrici Secundi* and his *Chronica*. Roger described the arrival of Heraclius, the patriarch of Jerusalem, who came to England in 1185 to request military aid for the Holy Land from Henry II and his court. In his description of the patriarch's plea, Roger inserted a reminder that England's kings were directly related to the royal families of both England and Jerusalem. Roger (or his scribe) mistakenly wrote that Fulk was the brother (rather than the father) of Geoffrey Plantagenet, thus collapsing two generations into one. Geoffrey, in turn, 'begot Henry [II] king of England, from she who was the empress of Rome [Matilda], daughter of King Henry [I] the elder, son of William the Bastard, who subdued England and conquered it'.[37] Then, just in case his descriptions of these connections had not been clear enough, Roger began his next paragraph with a reference 'to this Henry, the son of Matilda the empress, the son of Geoffrey the brother [*sic*] of Fulk the king of Jerusalem'.[38] Roger's account of Jerusalem's patriarch beseeching England's king for aid thus contained this repeated reminder that the Angevin royal family was heir (in theory, if not always in reality) to England and Rome through Henry I and his daughter Matilda, and to Jerusalem through the Angevin counts Geoffrey and Fulk. These statements neatly parallel the

---

34   Nicholas L. Paul, *To Follow in their Footsteps: The Crusades and Family Memory in the High Middle Ages* (Ithaca, NY, 2013), 117, 126, 216–217; Schein, *Gateway to the Heavenly City*, 84; Jaroslav Folda, *Crusader Art: The Art of the Crusaders in the Holy Land, 1099–1291* (Burlington, VT, 2008), 71.

35   Folda, *Crusader Art*, 31.

36   The Angevin kings of England were descended from Fulk by his first marriage to Ermengarde of Maine (d. 1126).

37   Roger of Howden, *Gesta*, 331. Compare Roger of Howden, *Chronica Magistri Rogeri de Houedene*, ed. William Stubbs, RS (4 vols., London, 1868–71), ii, 299.

38   Roger of Howden, *Gesta*, 331. Compare Roger of Howden, *Chronica*, ii, 299.

Angevin interest in Helena and Constantine, whose British legends helped to reinforce Angevin claims to the triad of England, Rome, and Jerusalem. It was no coincidence that Roger chose to insert this reminder of these familial connections into his narrative about Heraclius's journey to seek the aid of a Western prince to come to Jerusalem's aid. The overall effect was to present the current Angevin king (Henry II or his son, Richard I) as the true heir to, and future liberator of, Jerusalem.

Roger wrote in the early 1190s, simultaneous with the events of the Third Crusade. A decade or so after the crusade, a new group of English writers further sought to link Helena's and Constantine's British stories to their spiritual and physical accomplishments in Jerusalem. The monk Layamon, writing around the beginning of the thirteenth century, embellished upon Helena's achievements in the Near East in his *Brut*.[39] In Layamon's rendition of British history, Helena's relationship with Jerusalem became much more important than it had been in the *Brut's* sources. Indeed, Layamon repeatedly emphasized that Helena ruled both Britain and Jerusalem. Where Geoffrey of Monmouth and Wace had introduced her simply as King Coel's daughter, Layamon wrote, 'The maid was called Helena; / subsequently she was queen / in the land of Jerusalem, / to the joy of the people'.[40] But Layamon reminded his audience that Helena also 'was this land's [i.e. Britain's] queen ... / she descended from Britons'.[41] When Layamon's narrative reached Helena's arrival in Jerusalem in 326, he praised her as 'the lady Helena, / the holy queen'.[42] This statement served as a reminder to Layamon's audience that Helena's influence extended over both the secular and spiritual realms.[43] Layamon then elaborated on Wace's version of the Jerusalem story. He described how Helena sought the assistance of the Jews, asking their help to locate the Cross. In this version, rather than frightening the Jews with threats of prison, Helena simply offered them money, and they brought the Cross to her.[44] This version of the story reflects the stereotypes about greedy Jews that were developing in England (and in Europe more broadly) during the late twelfth and early thirteenth century.[45] Helena, in Layamon's retelling, took advantage of this greed in order to find the Cross. Then, Layamon wrote, she was glad, 'as she never was before in her life', and settled in Jerusalem, living

[39] E.G. Stanley, 'Layamon (*fl.* 13th cent.)', *DNB*; Le Saux, *Layamon's Brut: The Poem and Its Sources*, Arthurian Studies XIX (Woodbridge, 1989), 142–143.
[40] Layamon, *Brut*, ii, 30: 'Þ[e] mæide hehte Elene / seoððen heo wes quene / i þan londe of Jerufalem / leoden to bliſſen'. See also Tolhurst, *Female Kingship*, 239–240.
[41] Layamon, *Brut*, ii, 36: 'Elene; / wæs þiſſes londes queen ... / icomen heo wes of Brutten'.
[42] Layamon, *Brut*, ii, 40: 'þa læuedi Ælene; þa halie quene'.
[43] Tolhurst argues that Layamon's emphasis on Helena's deeds in Jerusalem 'displaces Geoffrey of Monmouth's theme of female kingship with that of queenly service to God'. Tolhurst, *Female Kingship*, 241.
[44] Layamon, *Brut*, ii, 401.
[45] Gavin I. Langmuir, *Toward a Definition of Antisemitism* (Berkeley, CA, 1990), 10; Anna Sapir Abulafia, *Christian–Jewish Relations, 1000–1300: Jews in the Service of Medieval Christendom* (Harlow, 2011), 88–92. See also Larkin, 'Transitions', 121.

near the Cross for many years.[46] These descriptions ultimately reinforce the message that Helena had been a powerful figure in Jerusalem, but her power originally derived from the land of Britain – the geographic extremes of East and West united under Helena's leadership.

Helena's importance to the Angevins cannot be understood simply as a product of fanciful historical imaginations. Celebrated for her connection to the Cross and Jerusalem, she, along with her son, also played a significant role in Angevin spirituality. Reading Abbey, for example, claimed possession of several relics of the True Cross, and the abbey's cartulary, compiled during Richard I's reign, listed relics of Constantine and Helena directly after those of Nicodemus and Mary Magdalen, respectively.[47] Not surprisingly, Helena's cult was especially popular in northern England, particularly around York, one of the towns most closely linked to the legends about her and Constantine. The cult of the Cross, by contrast, was more popular in the southern part of the kingdom. Indeed, churches in the north were dedicated to Helena two to three times more often than churches in the south, but the north only had about a quarter as many churches dedicated to the Cross or the Rood (the tree from which the Cross was fashioned). In Yorkshire, some thirty churches were dedicated to Helena with about the same number in Lincolnshire.[48] There were at least three such churches in twelfth-century York: St Helen-on-the-Walls, Aldwark; St Helen's Fishergate; and St Helens, Stonegate. York was, of course, the city where Constantine had been proclaimed emperor in 306, and the church of St Helen-on-the-Walls, expanded twice in the Angevin period, proudly touted itself as the site of his father Constantius' tomb.[49] Farther south, in Essex, a late twelfth-century inclusion in the foundation charter (*c.* 1120–1130) for the Abbey of St John in Colchester claimed that 'Helena ... [was] born and educated in this city.'[50]

Helena's and Constantine's spiritual legacies in Jerusalem were further memorialized in northern England through the iconography of the Kelloe Cross. This historiated monumental stone cross from the twelfth-century parish church of St Helen's in Kelloe, near Durham, has been dated to *c.* 1200.[51] The three scenes carved into the stone depict recognizable moments in the *Inventio crucis* legend. The reliefs are topped by a wheel style cross head bearing the inscription from Constantine's famous vision of the cross before the battle of the Milvian

---

[46] Layamon, *Brut*, ii, 41: 'swa heo nes neuere ær on liue'. See also Harbus, *Helena of Britain*, 84.

[47] London, British Library, Egerton MS 3031, fols. 6v, 7v–8r.

[48] Frances Arnold-Forster, *Studies in Church Dedications, or England's Patron Saints* (3 vols., London, 1899), i, 188–189.

[49] Arnold-Forster, *Church Dedications*, 188; John Cherry, Review of J.R. Magilton 'The Church of St Helen-on-the-Walls, Aldwark', *JEH* 33 (1982), 328.

[50] *Cartae ad Colecestrense Coenobium in agro Esseriense spectantes*, quoted in Larkin, 'Transitions', 108: 'Traditur tamen Helena ... ex hac civitate natam et educatam; Harbus', *Helena of Britain*, 67–69.

[51] I would like to thank Diane Reed, Church Warden for St Helen's Parish, for generously showing me around the church in July 2014, and Gabriel Fidler for his assistance and company on the visit.

Figure 1. Kelloe Cross wheel-style cross head,
St Helen's Church, Kelloe, Co. Durham.

Figure 2. Kelloe Cross upper panel, St Helen's Church, Kelloe, Co. Durham.

Bridge in 312, '*in hoc vinces*' (Figure 1). The topmost image shows a crowned figure, reclining on a couch with hand raised, while from above an angel makes the sign of blessing (Figure 2). Barbara Baert identifies this scene as depicting Constantine's vision.[52] The middle scene on the Kelloe Cross is of two facing figures, both crowned, who most likely represent Constantine and Helena. The figure of Helena holds a cross in her hands (Figure 3). The bottom carving again depicts two standing figures – a woman holding a sword, and 'a bearded man with a Jewish cap' and a shovel – flanking a cross topped with an inscribed tablet like the one commissioned by Pilate to identify the cross on which Christ died (Figure 4).[53] This panel is quite clearly representative of the Judas variant of the Helena legend. At their feet are people cured by the power of the Cross.

This iconography of the *Inventio crucis* story is displayed in a distinctly insular fashion, carved into one of the massive stone crosses that had formed part of the northern English landscape since Anglo-Saxon times. Baert also suggests that the Kelloe Cross might once have held a relic of the True Cross.[54] If this were the case, it would have helped to further cement the associations between Jerusalem, the True Cross, and the British origin legends of Helena and Constantine. The monumental stone cross and its possible True Cross relic gave these legends a tangible presence in Kelloe. The images could have been recognized by all members of the parish, clerical and lay alike, and the towering presence of the cross, coupled with liturgical celebrations centered around it, would have reminded Angevin viewers that the person responsible for finding the symbol of Christ's Passion had (they believed) been born just down the road.[55]

Religious texts also served as reminders of Helena's importance in the twelfth-century Anglicized history of the finding of the True Cross. Although on the Continent she had long been the subject of hagiographical works (derived from a ninth-century *vita* by the German hagiographer Altmann[56]), the first life of Helena to be written in England was the *Vita Sancte Helene*, composed sometime around 1198–1207 by the Cistercian monk Jocelin of Furness (fl. 1199–1214).[57] Jocelin's residence at Furness Abbey, on the Lancashire coast, placed him in that northern part of England that was so thoroughly steeped in the stories of

---

[52]   Barbara Baert, '*In Hoc Vinces*: Iconography of the Stone Cross in the Parish Church of Kelloe (Durham, ca. 1200)', *Archaeological and Historical Aspects of West-European Societies: Album Amicorum Andre van Doorselaer*, ed. Marc Lodewijckx, Acta Archaeologica Lovaniensia Monographiae 8 (Leuven, 1996), 341–62 at 341, 343; compare 'Appendix 1: The *Vita Sancte Helene* of Jocelin of Furness (Cambridge, Corpus Christi College, MS 252)', in Harbus, *Helena of Britain*, Appendix 1, 158 (hereafter Jocelin, *VSH*).

[53]   Baert, '*In Hoc Vinces*', 341–346 (quotation at 341). On the *Inventio crucis* iconography and the tradition of depicting Jews as bearded and wearing hats, see Lipton, *Dark Mirror*, 13–54, 87–90, esp. 88–89.

[54]   Baert, '*In Hoc Vinces*', 347.

[55]   Compare Harbus, *Helena of Britain*, 87, 93. See also Carl Watkins, '"Folklore" and "Popular Religion" in Britain during the Middle Ages', *Folklore* 115 (2004), 140–150 at 145–146.

[56]   Helen Birkett, *The Saints' Lives of Jocelin of Furness: Hagiography, Patronage and Ecclesiastical Politics* (York, 2010), 72.

[57]   Harbus, *Helena of Britain*, 96–97, see also 46–47, 66.

Figure 3. Kelloe Cross middle panel, St Helen's Church, Kelloe, Co. Durham.

Figure 4. Kelloe Cross lower panel, St Helen's Church, Kelloe, Co. Durham.

Helena and Constantine. His *vita* presents a late twelfth- or early thirteenth-century synthesis of Helena's eastern Roman history with her British legend, resulting in a portrait of an English saint who earned her holy reputation in both Britain and Jerusalem. Jocelin depicted Helena as an ideal ruler who combined wisdom, learning, and piety. She was the 'propagator of the Christian faith and the defender of the church of the saints'.[58] Her father was the British king Coel, and her mother (who is not mentioned in the early twelfth-century histories) was 'by birth and in appearance most illustrious'. More notably, Jocelin emphasized that she was 'the sister of three magnates of Britain'.[59] Here, even more than in the earlier accounts of Helena's life, the stress is placed upon her parentage, derived from both her paternal and her maternal ancestry. Jocelin was not leaving room for anyone to dispute the reality of Helena's British ancestry.

Jocelin's Helena, like Geoffrey of Monmouth's, possesses the personal traits that were valued in elite women of the twelfth century. She excels at the study of letters, and is reputed to be 'incomparable in composing refrains and in singing', surpassing both 'her countrymen and foreigners'. She is 'humble and modest, prudent, unaffected and calm, liberal and clever, altogether lovable and precious'.[60] She also acts like a good twelfth-century Christian ruler ought. Jocelin repeats Henry of Huntingdon's story that Helena was responsible for building fortified walls around London and Colchester. Moreover, he adds, upon Constantius's death, she 'governed the realm of Britain, and administered justice and law in the land'.[61] She upheld the Christian faith, exalted the Church, spurned idolatry, suppressed Judaism, and strove to eliminate heresies of all kinds.[62] Importantly, in this list of attributes, Jocelin refers to his subject as 'our Helena' ('Helene nostre').[63] He assumes that his audience will associate themselves with Helena, presumably by virtue of a shared Anglo-British heritage.[64] Calling her 'our' further reinforces a personal and communal connection to Helena, bringing her out of distant history and placing her within a modern Angevin context. At the same time, treating Helena in this fashion collapsed the temporal barrier between Roman Britain and Angevin England, helping to co-opt a contested historical legacy.[65]

---

58   Jocelin, *VSH*, 153: 'Christiane fidei propagatricem et propugnatricem ecclesia sanctorum'.
59   Jocelin, *VSH*, 154: 'Puellam quoque genere ac specie clarissimam sororem trium magnatum Britannie'.
60   Jocelin, *VSH*, 154: 'proficiebat in studiis litterarum … In musicis eciam instrumentis et cantilenis componendis et canendis supra omnes patriotas et peregrinos magistra dicebatur inconperabilis … Fuit humilis et pudica, prudens, simplex et pacifica, liberalis atque faceta, cunctis amabilis ac preciosa.'
61   Jocelin, *VSH*, 157: 'regnum Britannie gubernabat, faciensque iudicium et iusiciam in terra'. See also Birkett, *The Saints' Lives of Jocelin of Furness*, 75.
62   Jocelin, *VSH*, 155: 'Helene nostre decor occasionem prebuit promocioni Christiane fidei, ecclesie Dei exaltacioni, ydolatrie euacuacioni, Iudaice secte depressioni, plurimarum heresium <elininacioni>.'
63   Jocelin, *VSH*, 155.
64   Compare Harbus, *Helena of Britain*, 103.
65   Martin Aurell, *The Plantagenet Empire, 1154–1224*, trans. David Crouch (Harlow, 2007),

Jocelin's depiction of Helena's husband Constantius further emphasizes the centrality of Britain in relation to the western Roman Empire. The Furness monk describes how Constantius often had to travel throughout the many territories that he governed west of the Alps, yet 'he loved Britain above all the realms of the world'.[66] This statement needs only slight alteration to apply to the Angevin kings, who governed not only England but also extensive western territories on the Continent. Jocelin's Constantius served as a reminder that England was the heart of the Angevin realm, legitimizing the rule of the Angevin kings as heirs to the Roman legacy in England and directing royal devotion toward the island kingdom.

Jocelin goes on to describe how Pope Sylvester baptized Helena, who had earlier been tempted by Judaism but wholeheartedly devoted herself to upholding Christian doctrine after baptism.[67] She helped Constantine build Constantinople, served as a judge in debates between Jews and Christians, and supported her son at the Council of Nicaea in 325.[68] It is not difficult to imagine early readers recognizing modern parallels to Late Antique history. In particular, Jocelin was likely drawing on Eleanor of Aquitaine as a model of the powerful queen who actively supported her sons' causes, particularly that of Richard while he was in the East. Jocelin then describes Helena's arrival in Jerusalem. Accompanied by soldiers and backed by the wealth of the imperial treasury, Helena took the journey 'for the sake of visiting and repairing the holy places and of investigating and discovering the symbols of the dominical Passion'.[69] Jocelin recounts how Helena and Judas the Jew discovered the True Cross, whereupon Judas converted to Christianity.[70]

After detailing the discovery of the Cross, Jocelin praises Helena's construction of churches in Jerusalem. In particular, he emphasizes the construction of a temple on Golgotha and 'another around the sepulchre of the Lord'.[71] Helena also repaired and built churches at the Mount of Olives and other locations in Jerusalem, as well as in Nazareth, Bethlehem, and throughout Judea more broadly. Moreover, she 'eliminated' the Jews and 'pagans' from all of Judea.[72] These achievements would have resonated with Jocelin's post-Third Crusade English audience. These were, after all, the same people who responded to news of the loss of the True Cross by massacring the Jews in England, notably at York in 1190.[73] Helena, Jocelin tells us – with the support of her son Constantine –

146–147, 149, 153.

[66] Jocelin, *VSH*, 157: 'Super omnia regna terrarum Britanniam dilexit'.

[67] Jocelin, *VSH*, 160–161.

[68] Jocelin, *VSH*, 164–169.

[69] Jocelin, *VSH*, 169: 'uenit Ierosolimam causa uisitandi ac reparandi loca sancta atque inuestigandi et reperiendi dominice passionis insignia'.

[70] Jocelin, *VSH*, 169–172.

[71] Jocelin, *VSH*, 172.

[72] Jocelin, *VSH*, 172–173, at 173: 'Iudeos quoque et Gentiles in Christum credere contempnentes non solum ab Ierosolima sed eciam a Iudee finibus eliminauit'.

[73] Sethina Watson, 'Introduction: The Moment and Memory of the York Massacre of 1190', in *Christians and Jews in Angevin England: The York Massacre of 1190, Narratives and Contexts,*

successfully Christianized the Holy Land, driving the Jews and 'pagans' from the land and thereby restoring it to its former glory.

Ultimately, for Jocelin, Helena's accomplishments in Jerusalem were her most important. He drives this point home, explaining how he had read in an ecclesiastical history (probably that of Rufinus) that Helena had acquired grain from Egypt to help feed the Jerusalemites in times of famine: 'But', Jocelin concludes,

> our Helena, it seems to me, is worthily judged with greater praise in respect to Jerusalem, for by her constant urging, care, and effort that city was entirely restored inside and out, [and] the wood of life, once found, was exalted as a vine for the sustenance of the faithful, as a fruit of life-giving nourishment.[74]

Much of Jocelin's *Vita Sancte Helene* was derived from other sources, but here his own voice sounds clearly as he offers his opinion about the sanctity of his subject.[75] Right away, he reiterates that she is 'our Helena', reminding his audience that the saint belongs to England, even when she is in Jerusalem. Jocelin used these reminders about Helena's connection to England to emphasize certain points in his narrative. In all, he called her 'our Helena' five times: once in reference to her attributes as a good ruler in Britain; once as praise for her impact on Jerusalem; twice to compare her with the Queen of Sheba; and once to state that no daughter of Eve was her equal, other than the Virgin Mary.[76]

Ultimately, Jocelin crafted an image of Helena that showed her as a model in battles against Jewish and pagan error. He took care to emphasize that the restoration of Jerusalem and the discovery of the True Cross were Helena's most important contributions to history. At the time he wrote, of course, at the end of the twelfth century, arguably the most celebrated fragment of the True Cross had been again lost, this time not buried but captured by the Muslim armies of Saladin. Like the second-century pagan Roman emperor Hadrian, Saladin had leveled many of the Christian buildings in Jerusalem, and replaced them with 'pagan' temples.[77] Jocelin's *Vita Sancte Helene* reminded the Angevins that it was their duty and their obligation to imitate Helena, rescue Jerusalem from the heathen easterners, and restore the True Cross to its proper glory.

Like his mother, the historical Constantine had also played an important role in shaping Jerusalem's history. Obviously, Constantine was best remembered for his vision of a cross in the sky at the Milvian Bridge in 312, inspiring

---

ed. Sarah Rees Jones and Sethina Watson (York, 2013), 114; Joe Hillaby, 'Prelude and Postscript to the York Massacre: Attacks in East Anglia and Lincolnshire, 1190', in *Christians and Jews in Angevin England*, ed. Sarah Rees Jones and Sethina Watson (York, 2013), 43–56 at 54; Abulafia, *Christian–Jewish Relations*, 93–95.

[74] Jocelin, *VSH*, 173: 'Sed, ut michi uidetur, ampliori preconio nostra Helena erga Ierosolimitas digniter iudicatur cuius instancia sollitudine [sollicitudine?] et opere tota ciuitas illa interius et exterius restaurabatur, lignum uite ad sustenacionem fidelium, fructum uitalis alimonie, inuentum exaltabatur.'

[75] Birkett, *The Saints' Lives of Jocelin of Furness*, 59.

[76] Jocelin, *VSH*, 155, 173, 175, 177. See also Harbus, *Helena of Britain*, 103.

[77] Ibn al-Athīr, *Chronicle*, 334. See also Eddé, *Saladin*, 218–227; and Folda, *Crusader Art*, 67.

legions of artists to have the sign of the cross depicted in artistic representations of his victories.[78] In the twelfth century, the symbolism of the cross also helped to reinforce the parallels between Constantine and twelfth-century crusaders. When Heraclius, the patriarch of Jerusalem, visited Henry II's court in 1185 in an attempt to convince the English king to undertake a crusade, he presented Henry with a 'banner of the Holy Cross' ('vexillum sanctae crucis'), the standard of the kingdom of Jerusalem.[79] The same terminology was used to describe Constantine's fourth-century banner. For instance, in his *vita* of Helena, Jocelin of Furness praised the 'banner of the Holy Cross' ('uexillum Sancte Crucis') that Constantine had carried with him into battle at the Milvian Bridge.[80] The standard that Henry II received from Heraclius thus not only symbolized the power of Jerusalem, but specifically invoked Constantine's victory, seen by later generations as a victory for Christianity. An Angevin king carrying such a standard could have imagined himself as a new Constantine, coming to Jerusalem's rescue.

In Jocelin of Furness's hands, Constantine also became a model ruler for English crusader kings. Geoffrey of Monmouth – who praised Constantine's lion-like pursuit of justice – and Henry of Huntingdon had already set Constantine up as a hero in opposition to the persecutor emperors Diocletian, Maximian, and Maxentius.[81] For Jocelin, Constantine's defeat of these pagan emperors took on an even greater significance: Constantine became a pseudo-crusader, protecting Christendom from oppression at the hands of pagan tyrants. While Constantius and then Helena and Constantine were ruling peacefully in the west ('orbis occidui'), in the east ('orbe orientali') people were suffering the 'darkness of persecutions, proscriptions, [and] every sort of torture and death' at the hands of Constantine's pagan predecessors and contemporaries.[82] By highlighting the evil actions of the pagan tetrarchs – and emphasizing their oriental identity – Jocelin justified Constantine's departure from the idyllic island of Britain. The western, Christian ruler was morally obligated to stamp out oriental threats to a nascent Christendom. Indeed, Jocelin emphasized that God had sent Constantine 'from Britain to the eastern parts' of the world in order to spread Christianity throughout the empire.[83] The west, Jocelin implied, was prosperous and peaceful; England's king therefore ought to travel to the eastern part of the world, where

---

[78]   Drake, 'Eusebius on the True Cross', 17.
[79]   *The Historical Works of Master Ralph de Diceto*, ed. William Stubbs, Cambridge Library Collection (2 vols., Cambridge, 2012, originally printed London, 1876), ii, 33.
[80]   Jocelin, *VSH*, 159.
[81]   See, e.g., Geoffrey of Monmouth, *History of the Kings of Britain*, 94–97; Henry of Huntingdon, *Historia*, 56–61.
[82]   Jocelin seems to have conflated Maximian and his son Maxentius into one person. Jocelin, *VSH*, 164: 'In orbe orientali, principantibus, Dyocliciano uel Maximiano siue Maxencio, inualuerunt tenebre persecucionis, proscripcionis, suppliciorum et mortium genera multimoda'.
[83]   Jocelin, *VSH*, 164: 'Confitebatur crebro quod dominus a Britannia ad orientales partes adduxerit illum qualemcumque famulum suum ut eius diebus proparetur Christianissimus per uniuersum Romanum imperium'.

Christianity was under threat. Constantine thus became a model for the Angevin kings, who ought similarly to lead armies into the east, both to expand their own empire and to save Christendom from the oriental threats to its survival.

These ideas undoubtedly represent a post-Third Crusade ideology, but it is possible to suggest that a writer like Jocelin also would have been thinking about England's role in the next round of crusades. Pope Innocent III, after all, had wanted Richard I to take part in what became the Fourth Crusade, and later pressured John to do the same.[84] John did eventually take the cross in 1215, although for political expediency more than anything else.[85] It is in this context, then, that we should understand the increasing popularity of the Anglo-British version of Helena's and Constantine's legends. Writers like Layamon and Jocelin of Furness dreamed of an Angevin ruler whose responsibilities were to both England and the Holy Land. Following their model, a king like John could imagine himself as a new Constantine, riding out from England to rescue Jerusalem and restore Christendom.

Helena and Constantine had, over the course of the twelfth century, become increasingly part of the narrative of England's royal and imperial history. Their popularity as important figures from England's British past developed in tandem with the Angevins' increasing interest in events in the Holy Land. As Anglicized hero-saints, these fourth-century Romans came to reflect modern Angevin ideals of English kingship rooted in dynastic heritage, alongside a responsibility to the land where Christ had suffered and died. In the twelfth century, the Muslims posed a very real threat to both the salvific history of the Cross and the fate of the Holy Land. Saladin's armies had captured the most famous fragment of the True Cross at Hattin in July 1187, occupied Ascalon in September, and conquered Jerusalem by November. After 1187, it was therefore impossible to retell the story of Helena and Constantine's activities in the East without calling to mind violent and shocking memories of these recent events. Indeed, events in Palestine, especially in 1187, transformed what had been a long-established and relatively innocuous set of hagiographic ideas and made them all at once extraordinarily relevant to current events. By the early years of the thirteenth century, the recovery of Jerusalem and the True Cross from the Muslims formed a vital part of the triumphal narrative of England's Romano-British past and Angevin present. If Helena and Constantine could rule and protect both Britain and Jerusalem, then surely the Angevin kings could – and should – do the same.

---

[84] Vincent Ryan, 'Richard I and the Early Evolution of the Fourth Crusade', in *The Fourth Crusade: Event, Aftermath, and Perceptions*, ed. Thomas F. Madden, Crusades Subsidia 2 (Burlington, VT, 2008), 3–13. For examples of Innocent's letters to John about crusading, see *Selected Letters of Pope Innocent III Concerning England, 1198–1216*, ed. C.R. Cheney and W.H. Semple (London and New York, 1953), nos. 4, 19, 51, 68, 72, and 78.
[85] *Magna Carta*, clauses 52, 53, and 57.

8

The Revolts of the Embriaco and the Fall of the County of Tripoli

Jesse W. Izzo

Late in the year 1288 two Franks whose identities are unknown to us traveled from Tripoli to see al-Mansur Qalawun, the Mamluk sultan of Egypt. They told him that the knights and burgesses of this city in the northern sector of the Latin Kingdom of Jerusalem had made common cause with Genoa, and now '[t]he Genoese will pour into Tripoli' and '[T]hey will rule the waves, and it will happen that those who will come to Alexandria will be at their mercy ...'.[1] They then warned the sultan of the dire consequences this would have for the merchants of the chief Nile port and, therefore, for the revenues and commercial well-being of the sultanate. Finally, they pointed out that the intervention of the Genoese would mean a significant strengthening of Tripoli's defenses, doubling or even tripling the number of warships it could muster if needed, such that if Qalawun did not seize the city immediately he might find it considerably more difficult to do so later.[2] The sultan took these warnings seriously and he began preparations for an assault on Tripoli that would result in its capture in April of the following year.[3]

This essay examines a prolonged period of internal strife that plagued the County of Tripoli from the late 1250s until the loss of the Holy Land to the Mamluks in 1291. It highlights the Embriaco family and their relationship to the House of Antioch-Tripoli while offering a case study of the complex web of local, regional, and trans-regional interests entangling the Franks of Syria during

---

[1] *Cronaca del templare di Tiro: 1243–1314: la caduta degli stati crociati nel racconto di un testimone ocular*, ed. and trans. Laura Minervini (Napoli, 2000), 192–195 (hereafter, Templare di Tiro); *The 'Templar of Tyre', Part III of the 'Deeds of the Cypriots'*, trans. Paul Crawford (Aldershot, 2003), 98 (hereafter Crawford, *The 'Templar of Tyre'*).

[2] Templare di Tiro, 192–195.

[3] 'Annales de Terre sainte', ed. Reinhold Röhricht, *Archives de l'Orient Latin* (2 vols., Paris, 1884), ii, 460 (hereafter, ATS); Templare di Tiro, 196–199. Arabic sources do not agree on the precise date. See Linda S. Northrup, *From Slave to Sultan: The Career of Al-Manṣūr Qalāwūn and the Consolidation of Mamluk Rule in Egypt and Syria (678–689 A.H./1279–1290 A.D.)* (Stuttgart, 1998), 153–154; Joshua Prawer, *Histoire du Royaume latin de Jérusalem* (2 vols., Paris, 1975), ii, 536–537.

the late thirteenth century. By this time the Frankish presence in the region had been eroded by Mamluk conquests to just a few coastal cities and hinterland fortresses. How, then, had it come to pass that two Franks pleaded with the sultan of Egypt to attack the city of Tripoli, commercial and administrative heart of the eponymous county?[4] The answer must be located in a series of revolts undertaken by the Embriaco lords of Jubail against the comital family.

The first of these revolts began in 1258 and was led by Bertrand Embriaco. It quickly collapsed following Bertrand's death a year later. A second revolt broke out in 1277 against Bohemond VII, this time led by Guy II Embriaco, a cousin of the deceased Bertrand, and was quelled in the winter of 1283 after the capture and execution of Guy and his followers.[5] The third and final revolt, led by Bertrand's son Bartholomew Embriaco, occurred soon after the death of Bohemond VII in 1287 when the House of Antioch-Tripoli was overthrown in favor of a short-lived commune in Tripoli of which Bartholomew was mayor. This revolt ended in 1289 with Qalawun's conquest.

Jean Richard has written extensively about these events from the vantage point of what he has dubbed 'des questions féodales',[6] while Joshua Prawer has analyzed the Commune of Tripoli in the context of other communal movements in the Kingdom of Jerusalem. Gian Luca Borghese has shed light on Angevin involvement in the county in the 1270s and 1280s; and Georg Caro and Roberto Lopez have written on Genoese activities there.[7] Finally, Robert Irwin has written about a number of what he has called '*curiosa*' – intriguing and possibly misinformed references to strife among the Franks of Tripoli in this period by Muslim chroniclers writing in Arabic.[8] However, these disparate elements have not been gathered together previously for the purpose of analyzing and comprehending the Embriaco-comital struggle in its totality – how it propagated across multiple generations and became intertwined with various regional and trans-regional commercial and political rivalries.

---

[4]   The Franks of the Kingdom of Jerusalem made what was in effect their last stand at Acre in the spring of 1291.
[5]   Now prince of Antioch in name only, as the principality had been lost to the Mamluks in 1268.
[6]   Joshua Prawer, *Crusader Institutions* (Oxford, 1980), 76–79; Jean Richard, 'Le comté de Tripoli dans les chartes du fonds des Porcellet', *BEC* 130.2 (1972), 339–82; Jean Richard, 'Les comtes de Tripoli et leurs vassaux sous la dynastie antiochénienne', in *Crusade and Settlement*, ed. Peter W. Edbury (Cardiff, 1985), 213–24; repr in Richard, *Croisades et états latins d'orient: points de vue et documents* (Brookfield, VT, 1992).
[7]   Gabriella Airaldi, 'Je suis Bertrand de Gibelet', in *Chemins d'Outre-Mer* (2 vols., Paris, 2004), i, 25–30; Michel Balard, 'I genovesi in Siria-Palestina (secc. XI–XV)', in *Genoa: una 'porta' del Mediterraneo* (Genoa, 2005); Gian Luca Borghese, *Carlo I d'Angiò e il Mediterraneo: poltica, diplomazia e commercio internazionale prima dei Vespri* (Rome, 2008), 181–204; Georg Caro, *Genua und die mächte am Mittelmeer 1257–1311. Ein Beeitrag zur Geschichte des XIII. Jahrhunderts*, (Halle A.S., 1895–99), 121–133; Roberto S. Lopez, *Benedetto Zaccaria: ammiraglio e mercante nella Genova del Duecento* (Genoa, 2004), 131–160.
[8]   Robert Irwin, 'The Mamlūk Conquest of the County of Tripoli', in *Crusade and Settlement: Papers Read at the First Conference of the Society for the Study of the Crusades and the Latin East and Presented to R.C. Smail*, ed. Peter W. Edbury (Cardiff, 1985), 246–250.

There has been little investigation of what this struggle can reveal about the attitudes, values, and concerns typical of the Frankish nobility of Syria in the thirteenth century. In the course of the events described below we are made to witness a set of chauvinisms and loyalties that defined the nobility residing there. These include a resentment of foreign (i.e. non-Syrian or Cypriot) meddling, pronounced anti-clericalism and suspicion of female power, and the importance not only of family ties but corporate affiliation (in this instance, among Templar confrères). Also evident is a regular willingness to make common cause with Muslims against fellow Franks, a reality that defies any simple understanding of politics and war in the Holy Land in this period as driven exclusively – or even primarily – by hostility between Latin Christianity and Islam.

The most detailed source for the revolts is the Old French prose narrative of the so-called Templar of Tyre.[9] The anonymous chronicler, possibly a member of the lesser nobility in the Kingdom of Jerusalem, spent many years in the service of the powerful and politically active Montfort family at Tyre. Later he was the secretary and personal confidante of William of Beaujeu, the last Templar grand master to serve in the Holy Land before it was lost to the Mamluks. The Templar likely completed his chronicle by the end of the first decade of the fourteenth century while living in Cyprus, where he fled in 1291 during the Mamluk siege of Acre, at which he had been present.[10] The Genoese annals, certain Arabic chronicles, and the *Eracles* continuation of the History of William of Tyre also shed light on events.[11] Documentary records that deal directly with the revolts are fairly scant – there is, for example, no extant archive from the County of Tripoli – but papal letters, trial testimony, and certain key charters do augment the picture offered by the narrative sources.

The Embriaco were a family of Genoese extraction with deep roots in Syria. William of Embriaco had played a decisive role in the Frankish conquest of Tripoli in 1109, and his successors became lords of Jubail as well as other important fiefs in Tripoli.[12] In the thirteenth century they were the most prominent family in the county apart from the ruling family itself. For its part, the House of Antioch had been established in the course of the First Crusade.[13] Tripoli came into the family's hands in 1187 and became its principal seat after the fall of Antioch to the Mamluks in 1268. These two prominent, long-established

---

9   For the Templar of Tyre see Crawford, *The 'Templar of Tyre'*, 1–14 and Minervini's introduction in Templare di Tiro, 1–23; Charles Grivaud, 'Literature', in *Cyprus: Society and Culture 1191–1374*, ed. Angel Nicolaou-Konnari and Chris Schabel, (Leiden, 2005), 240–44.

10   Crawford, The 'Templar of Tyre', 2–5.

11   *L'estoire de Eracles empereur et la conqueste de la terre d'Outremer,* in *RHC occid.* (Paris, 1859), ii, 1–481 (hereafter, *Eracles*); *Iacobi Auriae annales*, ed. G. Pertz in *MGH SS* 18, (Hanover, 1863), 288–356 (hereafter, *Annales Ianuenses*).

12   Airaldi, 'Je suis Bertrand de Gibelet', 26; Balard, 'I genovesi in Siria-Palestina', 10. On the Embriaco family in Syria, see E. Rey, 'Les Seigneurs de Giblet', *Revue de l'Orient Latin* 3 (1895), 398–422.

13   For the establishment of Antioch, see Thomas Asbridge, *The Creation of the Principality of Antioch, 1098–1130* (Woodbridge, 2000).

families were closely connected to each other by blood and marriage in the late
thirteenth century. Henry Embriaco, lord of Jubail in the 1250s and a pivotal
figure in the events investigated below, was the eldest son of Alix of Antioch, a
half-sister of Bohemond IV of Antioch-Tripoli.[14] Henry's son, Guy II, another
key figure in the revolt of the Embriaco, was not only a blood relative of the
comital family but also a first cousin by marriage to Bohemond VI.[15]

Initial hostilities between the Embriaco and counts of Tripoli must be viewed
in the context of two other quarrels among the Franks in Syria. The first of these
concerned the regency of the Kingdom of Jerusalem, over which the House of
Antioch-Tripoli sought to exert control. After the death of Henry I of Cyprus
in 1253, Jerusalem lacked a hereditary royal-regent who was of age.[16] Hugh II,
Henry's son by Bohemond's sister, Plaisance of Antioch, was still an infant –
and the kingdom was therefore governed by a series of vassal-regents chosen
by the High Court over the course of the next five years. The barons of the
High Court first chose John of Ibelin, lord of Arsur, for this dignity.[17] Hugh II
remained in Cyprus, but if he were ever to come to Syria, it could be argued that
he should be named royal-regent with Plaisance as his warden-regent. There was
at this time no precedent for installing a minor in the regency, so Plaisance and
Bohemond VI were not prepared to press Hugh's claim. Instead, they looked to
guarantee their influence on the government at Acre by marrying Plaisance in
1254 to John of Arsur's son, Balian.[18]

John of Arsur was replaced as vassal-regent by his cousin and political rival,
John of Jaffa, in 1255 for reasons that are not altogether clear. However, the
very next year John of Arsur had been returned to the vassal-regency again.
Bohemond VI and Plaisance could not help but fear they had backed the wrong
man and began proceedings to secure a papal annulment of the marriage between
Plaisance and Balian. Unsurprisingly, this poisoned the relationship between the
Ibelins of Arsur and Bohemond and Plaisance. John of Arsur was returned to the
vassal-regency in 1256, possibly in exchange for an agreement to help defend

---

[14]   They were children of Bohemond III.

[15]   Guy's mother-in-law and Bohemond VII's mother were sisters (daughters of Hetoum I of
Armenia). See Crawford, *The 'Templar of Tyre'*, 71, note 6.

[16]   A royal-regent, like a monarch, had to be confirmed by the High Court and was the nearest
blood relation who was living in the East and of age. A royal-regent who was not yet of age
could have a warden-regent, who was the closest living relative of the royal-regent; he or she
also needed to be confirmed by the High Court. A vassal-regent, on the other hand, was an
individual chosen by the High Court from among the barons of the king of Jerusalem to be the
head of government. There could only be a vassal-regent when a hereditary monarch or royal-regent had died and the High Court had not yet confirmed a new monarch or royal-regent. Both
kinds of regents, as well as various other types that do not concern us here, are referred to in the
sources as *baillie*. Jonathan Riley-Smith, *The Feudal Nobility and the Kingdom of Jerusalem,
1174–1277* (Hamden, CT, 1973), 210–218.

[17]   Like the various kinds of regent, a monarch's or regent's lieutenant is also referred to as a
baillie in the sources.

[18]   Hans Eberhard Mayer, 'Ibelin *versus* Ibelin: The Struggle for the Regency of Jerusalem,
1253–1258', *Proceedings of the American Philosophical Society* 122 (1978), 25–67.

his cousin's County of Jaffa. At this time he decided to facilitate Plaisance and Hugh II's coming to Syria and support Hugh II's candidacy for the royal-regency in hopes of regaining an influential role for himself at Acre.[19] Doing so would negate the need for a vassal-regent and thus eject John of Arsur from power yet again. Plaisance and her son arrived in the city on 1 February 1258, and the High Court confirmed Hugh as regent with Plaisance as his warden-regent, a style in which she remained until her death in 1261.[20]

These maneuverings over the regency were enmeshed with a Genoese–Venetian war fought in the Levant primarily between 1256 and 1261 commonly known to scholars as the War of St Sabas. It was nominally fought over a property fronting the harbor of Acre that had formerly belonged to a Greek monastery of that name, but this dispute must be understood as only one facet of the broader struggles between the two maritime republics that were playing out across the Mediterranean throughout the thirteenth century.[21] In the course of the war the Genoese were expelled from their quarter in Acre, which the Pisans and Venetians subsequently destroyed.[22]

The local nobility leapt at the chance to exploit the Genoese–Venetian rivalry to further their own individual interests. Philip of Montfort, lord of Tyre, summarily expelled the Venetians from that city, where their exemptions and privileges had been growing throughout the thirteenth century. Similarly, Bohemond VI supported the Venetians as a way to roll back the many privileges and exemptions the Genoese had historically enjoyed in Tripoli.[23] John of Ibelin, lord of Arsur, backed the Genoese at first but later switched his support to the Venetians, likely at the insistence of Plaisance and Bohemond, who paid for 800 troops at Acre to be placed under the lord of Arsur's command.[24]

The Embriaco supported the Genoese. Henry Embriaco, lord of Jubail, sent 200 archers and a 100-oar ship called *Poindor* to Acre and also stayed for several days in the Genoese quarter of Acre.[25] During one violent engagement that took place some time in 1258 a Genoese band was raiding outside their quarter and was confronted in a street called *La Carcaisserie* by Bohemond VI and a contingent of his knights. Bohemond ordered one of his chief vassals, Bertrand II, a cousin of Henry Embriaco and a scion of a junior branch of the

---

[19] ATS, 446–447; *Eracles*, 443. See Mayer, 'Ibelin *versus* Ibelin', 37–38 for a detailed discussion of these events.

[20] Francesco Amadi, *Chroniques de Chypre d'Amadi et de Strambaldi*, ed. R. de Mas–Latrie, (2 vols., Paris, 1891–1893), ii, 203–5 (hereafter, Amadi); ATS, 447–448; Marino Sanudo Torsello, *The Book of the Secrets of the Faithful of the Cross*, trans. Peter Lock (Aldershot, 2011), 349 (hereafter, MST); Templare di Tiro, 64–67.

[21] David Jacoby, 'New Venetian Evidence on Crusader Acre', in *The Experience of Crusading 2*, ed. Peter Edbury and Jonathan Phillips (Cambridge, 2003), 241.

[22] Amadi, 204–205; *Eracles*, 443; MST, 349–350; Templare di Tiro, 72–73.

[23] Templare di Tiro, 66–67; David Jacoby, 'New Venetian Evidence', 243–245.

[24] *Continuation de Guillaume de Tyr, de 1229 à 1261, dite du manuscrit de Rothelin*, in *RHC occid.* (Paris, 1859), ii, 634.

[25] Templare di Tiro, 64–67, 74–77.

Embriaco family, to charge them.[26] Bertrand 'prayed him to be excused, for he had a treaty' with the Genoese; Bohemond insisted; Bertrand finally acquiesced to charge, but as he rode forward he pulled up and turned his lance around so the blunt end rather than the point faced forward and called out his name to signal to the Genoese that he was a friend and kinsman. Bohemond was livid at this act of defiance and henceforth he seems to have treated the entire Embriaco clan with deep suspicion and antipathy.[27]

The animosity stirred up in the war of St Sabas and the disfavor shown by the count after the episode involving him and Bertrand exacerbated older tensions in Tripoli stemming from another issue: the significant influence of the so-called 'Roman' party in the county stretching back more than a generation. In 1238 Bohemond V of Antioch-Tripoli had married Lucy of Conti, a grand-niece of Pope Innocent III. Lucy exerted significant influence in her husband's domains.[28] According to the Templar of Tyre, she was resented by the local nobility because she was a foreigner and because she encouraged the immigration of, and gave preferment to, her family and other 'Romans' who began to flood the county.[29] She particularly inflamed local sentiment against her by installing her brother, Paul of Segni, as the bishop of Tripoli while she was regent for her son Bohemond VI after her husband died in 1252.[30] Documentary evidence corroborates the Templar's assertion: the need for the establishment of a council made up of thirteen members – six representatives of the barons, six of Bohemond's court, and the count himself – indicates there were tensions between the count and his vassals that could not be resolved through the normal feudal institutions and hence called for recourse to this ad hoc arrangement.[31]

Clearly this effort at resolving differences between the count and his chief vassals failed, for many broke out in arms during the course of the following year (1258).[32] They were led by Bertrand Embriaco and William of Antioch, Bertrand's cousin and the lord of Botron. According to the Templar, they had support from the Hospitallers while the Templars supported the prince, 'though they did not show this publicly'.[33] In a skirmish outside the city of Tripoli, the count's forces were defeated and Bohemond was wounded. He vowed to have

---

26   The 'Porcellet' branch of the family. See Richard, 'Porcellet', 348–366.
27   Templare di Tiro, 74–77; Crawford, *The 'Templar of Tyre'*, 25–26.
28   *Les registres de Nicholas III*, ed. Jules Gay and S. Vitte (Paris, 1898–1904), no. 520 (hereafter, Nicholas III); Richard, 'Les comtes de Tripoli', 215–216.
29   Templare di Tiro, 74–77; Crawford, *The 'Templar of Tyre'*, 30–31.
30   Nicholas III no. 520; Templare di Tiro, 74–77, Bernard Hamilton, *The Latin Church in the Crusader States: The Secular Church* (London, 1980), 237.
31   Joseph Delaville Le Roulx, *Documents concernant les Templiers extraits des archives de Malte* (Paris, 1882), doc. 19, pp. 26–30 (the dating of the document is in error, rectified in *Regesta Regni Hierosolymitani* and *Additamentum*, ed. Reinhold Röhricht, (Oeniponti, 1893; 1904 (hereafter, RRH), no. 1201). See Richard, 'Les comtes de Tripoli', 216–217 and 'Porcellet', 354 at note 3.
32   Templare di Tiro, 74–77; Richard, 'Les comtes de Tripoli', 216.
33   Templare di Tiro, 76–77; Crawford, *The 'Templar of Tyre'*, 31.

his revenge and exacted it by contracting some of Bertrand's own peasants to ambush and murder him while he was out riding with another knight. Bertrand was decapitated, and his head was brought back to Bohemond as a trophy.[34] Although Bertrand's father Hugh tried to continue the Embriaco rebellion in his son's stead, the loss of their leader robbed the rebels of their appetite for war. The Templars helped to mediate a truce.[35]

Certainly Bertrand's death was the primary reason for the end of the revolt, but the increased external threats of both Mongols and Mamluks at this juncture must also have served as a temporary cure to local antagonisms. In the 1260s the Mamluks adopted a more aggressive stance to the Franks than any Muslim power had since the days of Saladin. In 1263 Sultan Baybars captured Nazareth, Mount Tabor, and Bethlehem. In 1265 he took Caesarea, Haifa, and Arsur, and in 1266, he took the great Templar fortress of Safad. Jaffa, Beaufort, and Antioch all fell in 1268. In 1271 the sultan captured the fortresses of Chastel Blanc, Crac des Chevaliers, Gibelcar, and Montfort, all in the north of the kingdom.[36] Not until 1271 did the Franks gain a reprieve from Baybars's onslaught – from that year until his death he turned his attentions primarily to fighting the Mongols and the Armenians of Cilicia. When he died in 1277 uncertainty over the succession in Cairo militated against any immediate major actions against the Franks. Thus, although the resumption of hostilities in Tripoli was principally the consequence of internal developments – the death of Bohemond VI and the actions of his widow during Bohemond VII's minority – it is likely no coincidence that the Franks of Tripoli resumed their internal struggles at precisely the moment Mamluk pressures temporarily abated.

Following the death of Bohemond VI in 1275, his cousin, Hugh III of Cyprus,[37] attempted to land at Tripoli to take up the regency for the young Bohemond VII, but was rebuffed.[38] Instead, Bohemond VI's widow, Sibylla of Armenia, introduced as regent Bartholomew, bishop of Tortosa.[39] It has been suggested that Bohemond VII's mother, an Armenian princess, may have done so in part to counter growing Angevin influence in the county.[40] There had been ties between the Angevin court and Tripoli during the reign of Bohemond VI, and Charles of Anjou purchased a claim to the crown of Jerusalem in 1277. He wasted no time in sending Roger of San Severino to Acre to inaugurate his

---

34 Templare di Tiro, 76–77.
35 Delaville Le Roulx, doc. 19, pp. 26–30; RRH no. 1201; Templare di Tiro, 78–79; Richard, 'Les comtes de Tripoli', 216–217.
36 For Mamluk conquests in this period under Sultan Baybars, see Peter Thorau, *The Lion of Egypt: Sultan Baybars I and the Near East in the Thirteenth Century*, trans. P.M. Holt (London, 1992), 142–192.
37 ATS, 455; Hugh III's father, Henry of Antioch, was the brother of Bohemond VII's grandfather, Bohemond V.
38 *Eracles*, 467; MST, 359.
39 Templare di Tiro, 144–145.
40 Borghese, 191–192. For Bartholomew, Bishop of Tortosa, see Hamilton, *The Latin Church*, 235, 237–241.

regime there and made significant efforts to tie the County of Tripoli to him.[41] According to the Templar of Tyre, the knights of Tripoli were displeased by having a churchman set above them in the regency, but at least for the moment they accepted him as a counterweight to both the Roman and Angevin elements in the kingdom.[42]

Once Bohemond came of age in 1277 he embraced the Angevins, presumably against his mother's wishes. There were frequent embassies from the count to the Angevin court. Bohemond VII's sister, Lucy, married Narjot of Toucy, admiral of Apulia,[43] and another sister of Bohemond's also married a man of the Angevin court. In 1278 Bohemond's own marriage to Marguerite, daughter of the viscount Louis of Beaumont, kinsman of Charles of Anjou, was sealed by proxy with a dowry of ten thousand bezants per year drawn from the rents of Tripoli.[44]

Bohemond had warm relations with the Embriaco at first. According to the Templar of Tyre, Guy II Embriaco, lord of Jubail, 'had great love' for Bohemond VII and was married to his first cousin.[45] Bartholomew, son of Bertrand of Embriaco, witnessed an act at the comital palace in Tripoli in 1277, suggesting goodwill between Bohemond and their chief vassals.[46] However, this amity was destroyed after Bohemond broke a promise to Guy that his brother could have the hand of a local heiress in marriage.[47] After making this promise, the count changed his mind and instead allowed the heiress to marry the nephew of the bishop of Tortosa at the latter's request.[48] Aggrieved by this betrayal – and likely the meddling of the prelate under whose regency the knights of Tripoli already chafed – the lord of Jubail hastily compacted his brother's marriage and fled to the Templar house at Acre where he became a confrère of the order. William of Beaujeu gave Guy thirty knights to defend Jubail against the reprisal by Bohemond that the lord knew was coming.[49]

This led to nothing short of what Jean Richard has called a diplomatic revolution with respect to the Embriaco family and the so-called Roman party in Tripoli, who had been at loggerheads in 1258–1259.[50] Paul of Segni, the bishop

---

[41] MST 361–362; Templare di Tiro, 150–151; Borghese, 190–194; Reinhold Röhricht, *Geschichte des Königreichs Jerusalem* (Innsbruck, 1898), 975–976.

[42] Templare di Tiro, 142–143; Borghese, 192.

[43] Borghese, 191.

[44] Borghese, 191–194.

[45] Crawford, *The 'Templar of Tyre'*, 71, note 6.

[46] RRH no. 1412; Richard, 'Les comtes de Tripoli', 218.

[47] Guy's brother John married the daughter of Hugh Salamon. Templare di Tiro, 144–147; Richard, 'Les comtes de Tripoli', 218.

[48] Templare di Tiro, 144–147.

[49] Richard, 'Les comtes de Tripoli', 217–218. The two main narrative sources (*Eracles* and the Templar of Tyre) are not in agreement on dates or the order of events. Here I follow Jean Richard's convincing reconstruction: the marriage took place in 1277, the attack on the bishop of Tripoli in the winter of 1277–1278, and the Templars became involved in the conflict early in 1278.

[50] Malcolm Barber, *The New Knighthood: A History of the Order of the Temple* (Cambridge, 1994), 173; Richard, 'Les comtes de Tripoli', 215–221, esp. 218.

of Tripoli, whose influence had been so deeply resented in the 1250s, was a personal friend of William of Beaujeu (they had met at the Council of Lyons in 1274) and had also become a confrère of the Temple.[51] The common link with the Templars shared by Paul and Guy helped to unite them in opposition to Bohemond and Bartholomew of Tortosa – and also to implicate them together in the eyes of the count. In 1278 four Roman knights were killed and Paul of Segni and his retinue were assaulted in the cathedral at Tripoli by Bohemond's men, an action the exact motivation for which remains unknown but that was likely precipitated by the bishop of Tripoli and the lord of Jubail having made common cause through their Templar affiliation.[52] Paul of Segni now took refuge in the Temple, which Bohemond attacked and occupied with Muslim troops.[53] Bohemond was excommunicated and Tripoli placed under interdict by Pope Nicholas III, but the count ignored the ban.[54] In answer to the occupation of the Templar house in Tripoli, William of Beaujeu laid siege to Nephin.[55]

Over the course of the following year, amidst several truces that did not hold, Bohemond launched unsuccessful attacks against Jubail and Sidon (which belonged to the Templars) while the Templar–Embriaco alliance launched several unsuccessful attacks on Tripoli.[56] Finally, in February of 1283, the lord of Jubail, apparently at William of Beaujeu's urging, attempted to accomplish through cunning what he had not been able to by force. Guy hired a Genoese galley and came to Tripoli with some trusted allies and more than four hundred troops.[57] They lay offshore and Guy landed at night, having arranged to wait in the Templar house in the city with his men and take Bohemond by surprise.

Through an apparent miscommunication the commander of the Templars who was supposed to receive Guy and his men, a Brother Reddecoeur, was not at the Templar house. Guy and his knights panicked and fled to the Hospitaller house, but not before being discovered. Bohemond was awakened and came with his men to surround the Hospital. The commander of the Hospital brokered a settlement between Guy and Bohemond – that Guy should spend five years in prison, but after that he should be exonerated and allowed to return to his lands. Bohemond swore on the gospels to uphold the agreement, but when Guy surrendered, the prince had him seized. He ordered his men to 'put out the eyes of all the Genoese and foreigners'.[58]

---

[51]   *Eracles*, 481; Barber, 173; Richard, 'Les comtes des Tripoli', 218.

[52]   *Eracles*, 468–469; RRH no. 1424; Johannes Sbaralea, *Bullarium Franciscanum* (4 vols., Rome, 1759–1768), iii, 326–328; Richard, 'Les comtes de Tripoli', 218.

[53]   *Eracles*, 481; MST, 359.

[54]   Nicholas III nos. 104 and 520; Sbaralea, iii, 394–396; Hamilton, 238–239; Richard, 'Les comtes de Tripoli', 218.

[55]   Templare di Tiro, 146–147.

[56]   RRH no. 1444; Templare di Tiro, 146–151; Richard, 'Les comtes de Tripoli', 219; Al-Yunini, *Dhayl mir'āt al-zamān* (4 vols., Hyderabad: 1954–1961), iv, 4. Also see Irwin, 247.

[57]   Mas-Latrie, iii, 662–668.

[58]   Templare di Tiro, 156–159; Crawford, *The 'Templar of Tyre'*, 79.

As for the men of Jubail, Bohemond ordered the Embriaco lord and his followers to be thrown into a ditch which was then covered over and where they were starved to death.[59] A Muslim source claims that Guy previously had contacted Qalawun via one of his emirs in Syria and had promised to split Tripoli with the sultan if he would send him troops. Qalawun had obliged, and these, too, were now captured along with Guy and his men.[60] They were imprisoned at Maraclea and released in 1285.[61]

The death of Guy put a stop to the fighting, but the troubles in the county had not yet run their course. When Bohemond VII died in 1287, his sister Lucy was set to inherit from the childless prince. Upon receiving news of his death, she departed France with her husband, Narjot of Toucy, for the East.[62] However, the local nobility did not want her, viewing her and her husband as yet more foreign interlopers. They also could not abide another regency under Bohemond's mother, insisting rather incredibly that to govern would be too much of a burden for her because she was grief-stricken by the loss of her son.[63] Nor would they tolerate being once again under the rule of Bartholomew of Tortosa, whom she now invited back into the fold to take up the regency on her family's behalf. Instead, they proclaimed a commune dedicated to the Virgin Mary of which the local knights and burgesses chose Bartholomew Embriaco, the son of Bertrand II (the man who had defied Bohemond VI in the streets of Acre and been decapitated in 1259) and a cousin of Guy II, as their leader.[64]

The commune courted Genoese support, offering them an opportunity to outmaneuver their Venetian rivals and gain exclusive commercial access to Tripoli. The adventurer Benedetto Zaccaria came to Tripoli and succeeded in extracting from the commune unprecedented concessions in favor of the Genoese, though it is unclear to what extent he was actually acting on his own initiative and against Genoese policy.[65] Those in control back in Genoa were equivocal in their support of Zaccaria's accomplishment out of a sense of the need to preserve goodwill with Egypt in order to continue its commerce

59   Mas-Latrie, iii, 662–668; Templare di Tiro, 156–159.
60   Al-Yunini, iv, 171–172. Irwin writes of a 'quiet war' against Tripoli in the 1280s prosecuted by Qalawun through Muslim hillsmen (*jabalīyūn*) and 'dissident Embriaco gentry,' as he could not direct his full attention to the Franks because of his own rebel emir, Sunqur al-Ashqar, whom the sultan did not succeed in neutralizing until 1287. See Templare di Tiro, 186–187, Irwin, 247–249, and Northrup, 90–97.
61   Ulrich Haarmann, *Quellenstudien zur frühen Mamlukenzeit*, (Freiburg im Breisgau, 1970), Arabic, 58–59=German, 223–224 (trans. and ed. of Ibn Dawadari: *Kanz al-durar wa-jami' al-ghurar*); Ibn Taghribirdi, *al-Nujum al-zahira fi muluk Misr wa'l-Qahira*, (16 vols., Cairo, 1963–1971), vii, 316–317; Irwin, 247–248.
62   Borghese, 191–194; Templare di Tiro, 188–191.
63   Templare di Tiro, 188–191.
64   Muslim sources suggest the possibility of a rift between the two even before 1287 based on their assertion of Bartholomew's presence at Maraclea in 1285 and its lord having to be bribed by Bohemond VII: Irwin, 248–249.
65   *Annales Ianuenses*, 322; Caro, 125; Prawer, *Royaume*, ii, 532–534.

there. Nevertheless, they intended to send a podestà, Caccenimico da Volta, to Tripoli, an obvious indication they saw themselves as senior partners in their relationship to the commune and an unprecedented step for an Italian republic in Syria.[66] Some in the Commune of Tripoli now began to have second thoughts about their courtship of the Genoese, sensing they had perhaps given away too much, and were even willing to reach out to Lucy and Narjot of Toucy to help limit Genoese influence.[67]

It was at this time that the two Frankish emissaries went to Cairo to see Qalawun and promised to split control of Tripoli if he would help to eject the Genoese. The Templar of Tyre claims to have known exactly who they were but declines to name them.[68] The embassy may have been a scheme of the Venetians or Pisans, who could not abide a Genoese monopoly in Tripoli and knew the sultan would take a similarly dim view of the prospect. They equally could have been any members of the commune who feared they had relinquished self-determination through their cooperation with Genoa.[69] Whatever the case, the embassy provided an ideal pretext for the sultan to intervene, and his concern over protecting Egypt's trade revenues provided a strong motivation for him to strike before the Genoese became entrenched.[70]

But if the Franks who had gone to Cairo were in fact from the Commune of Tripoli and believed that they would receive a better deal from Qalawun than they had from the Genoese, they were sorely mistaken. William of Beaujeu attempted to forewarn the inhabitants of the city, having been informed of the sultan's intentions by one of his Muslim spies, but, unsurprisingly considering his recent partisanship, he was ignored.[71] In relatively short order Tripoli fell.[72] Bartholomew

---

66   *Annales Ianuenses*, 324, 326; Caro, 126; Lopez, 137–138; Prawer, *Crusader Institutions*, 77–79; Prawer, *Royaume*, ii, 534–535.

67   MST, 364–367; Templare di Tiro, 192–193; Caro, 128; Epstein, 179; Peter M. Holt, *Early Mamluk Diplomacy, 1260–1290: Treaties of Baybars and Qalawun with Christian Rulers*, (Leiden, 1995), 141–142; Lopez, 145–146; Prawer, *Crusader Institutions*, 76–79; Prawer, *Royaume*, ii, 534, 536–537.

68   Templare di Tiro, 192–195.

69   The Venetians had concluded treaties with Egypt in 1284 and 1288. RRH no. 1481; Eliyahu Ashtor, *Levant Trade in the Later Middle Ages* (Princeton, 1983), 10; David Jacoby, 'Le consulat vénetien d'Alexandrie d'après un document inédit de 1284', in *Chemins d'outre-mer: études d'histoire sur la Méditerranée médiévale offertes à Michel Balard* (2 vols., Paris, 2004), ii, 461–74; Prawer, *Royaume*, ii, 536–537.

70   Holt, *Early Mamluk Diplomacy*, 58–65; Northrup, 152–153. According to a later Muslim chronicler who drew on contemporary sources, Qalawun felt the Tripolitans had broken the truce of 1281, though he does not specify in what way: Ibn al-Furat, *Ta'rikh al-duwal wa 'l-muluk*, ed. Q. Zurayk, (vols. 7–9, Beirut, 1939), viii, 80; Northrup, 153. Another Muslim source asserts that Bartholomew of Embriaco had colluded with Qalawun in the latter's capture of Maraclea in 1285 and had promised to divide rule of Tripoli with the sultan if he should aid in overthrowing the comital family: Ibn Taghribirdi, *Nujum*, vii, 320–321; J.-F. Michaud and J. Reinaud, *Bibliothèque de Croisades* (4 vols., Paris, 1829) iv, 561; Irwin, 248.

71   Templare di Tiro, 194–197; Prawer, *Royaume*, ii, 537.

72   MST, 365–367; Templare di Tiro, 194–199.

Embriaco died there.[73] Lucy, Bohemond's sister, was permitted by the sultan to keep some small properties in the vicinity, while Guy II's son, Peter Embriaco, was allowed to keep Jubail. Bartholomew, bishop of Tortosa, remained in his see until the summer after the fall of Acre (1291). Jubail remained nominally in Frankish hands, though under Mamluk suzerainty, until 1302.[74]

These minor indulgences not withstanding, the County of Tripoli, like the Principalities of Antioch and Edessa before it, was now lost completely and permanently to the Franks. Meanwhile, a Genoese–Mamluk rapprochement was cemented by the treaty of 1290 in which the Genoese agreed to curtail piracy and adventurism of the kind that had led Zaccaria into Tripoli's affairs in exchange for commercial considerations in Egypt.[75] Muslim sources even state that the embassy told Qalawun (not quite truthfully) that henceforth Zaccaria would be *persona non grata* at home.[76]

Just two years after the fall of Tripoli, al-Ashraf Khalil captured the city of Acre. This conquest ended the nearly two hundred years of Frankish settlement in Syria which had resulted from the arrival of the first crusaders. The feud between the Embriaco and their lords was a manifestation of personal, familial, and corporate animosity that got swept up into broader regional and trans-regional struggles. In this way it is a microcosm of the predicament of Frankish Syria more generally in the second half of the thirteenth century, when local struggles and social tensions among the Franks of Syria became deeply enmeshed with the commercial concerns of Egypt and the Italian merchant republics.

Perhaps even more significantly, these revolts and their underlying causes shed important light on the attitudes and mentality of the Frankish nobility. These attitudes include a clear resentment of clerical intrusion on secular governance indicated by their pronounced hatred of the bishop of Tortosa and their hostility to his regency during Bohemond VII's minority. Similarly, the nobility resisted female overlordship, both in the guise of Bohemond VII's mother and his sister. Finally, they remained wary of foreign (even if Frankish) intrusion into the county's affairs and feudal relations, whether those intrusions were by 'Romans', Angevins, or Genoese. So profound were these various resentments that making common cause against fellow Franks with local Muslims, including the sultan of Egypt, was conceivable. In this way, the revolts of the Embriaco and the fall of Tripoli serve as a powerful example of the manifold complexities of politics and war in Frankish Syria in the thirteenth century.

---

[73] Ibn 'Abd al-Zahir, *Tashrif al-ayyam wa 'l-'usur fi sirat al-malik al-mansur,* ed. M. Kamil (Cairo, 1961), 165; Holt, *Early Mamluk Diplomacy,* 142; Templare di Tiro, 197–199.

[74] Steven Runciman, *A History of the Crusades* (3 vols., New York, 2002), iii, 395–407.

[75] Luigi Belgrano, 'Trattato del sultano d'Egitto col commune di Genova nel 1290', *Atti della Società Ligure di Storia Patria* 19 (1887), 163–175; *Tashrif,* 165; Steven Epstein, *Genoa and the Genoese, 958–1528* (Chapel Hill, N.C., 1996), 180; Holt, *Early Mamluk Diplomacy,* 141–151.

[76] Ibn abd al-Zahir, *Tashrif,* 165; Holt, *Early Mamluk Diplomacy,* 142; Lopez, 140, 142, 153, notes 84–85.

9

Jewish Women, Christian Women, and Credit in Thirteenth-Century Catalonia

Sarah Ifft Decker

Early in 1287, two Christian women, both widows, sought loans from Vidal, son of the late Abraham de Torre, a prominent Jewish lender in the town of Castelló d'Empúries. Beneta, widow of Pere Dalmau of Castelló, received a loan of 50 sous of Melgueil. Berenguera, widow of Guillem Bou of Vilanova de Muga, received a loan of 51 sous of Barcelona.[1] On the same day Vidal extended these loans to Beneta and Berenguera, he made an additional twelve loans, all to Christian men, for sums ranging between 9 and 101.25 sous of Melgueil. Beneta and Berenguera numbered among relatively few Catalan Christian women who sought loans from Jewish lenders without a husband or male relative by their side. However, these two widows resembled other Catalan women in that when they chose to borrow from Jewish lenders, they turned to Jewish men, rather than Jewish women.

Elsewhere in Europe, however, Jewish and Christian women interacted frequently through credit transactions. In a seminal 1978 article, William Chester Jordan argued that when Christian women in Northern France borrowed from Jewish lenders, they 'either found it more congenial or were simply constrained by circumstances to borrow from other women'.[2] In his study of two thirteenth-century *enquêtes* or notes on court cases from Picardy, he found that most Christian women borrowers chose either Jewish women lenders, or groups of lenders that included both men and women.[3] Victoria Hoyle also found significant financial interaction between Jewish and Christian women in

---

[1]   Girona, Arxiu Històric Girona, secció Castelló 2087, fols. 71v–72r (hereafter AHG, Ca). Although the text refers to Berenguera and her late husband as 'of Vilanova', this likely refers to the nearby Vilanova de Muga. The sum of 51 sous of Barcelona was equivalent to 38.25 sous of Melgueil. For conversion rate between sous of Melgueil and sous of Barcelona, see Robert I. Burns, *Jews in the Notarial Culture: Latinate Wills in Mediterranean Spain, 1250–1350* (Berkeley, CA, 1996), 8.

[2]   William Chester Jordan, 'Jews on Top: Women and the Availability of Consumption Loans in Northern France in the Mid-Thirteenth Century', *Journal of Jewish Studies* 29:1 (1978), 55.

[3]   Jordan, 'Jews on Top', 53–54.

thirteenth-century England, in a study based on the plea rolls of the Exchequer of the Jews.[4]

The Jewish women of these northern European regions possessed a high degree of financial independence, and often became prominent moneylenders. Jordan and Hoyle both demonstrate this through quantitative evidence: Jewish women participated in nearly half of the loans mentioned in Jordan's *enquêtes*, and over a quarter of the debt cases involving Jews in Hoyle's plea rolls.[5] Other scholars have relied on anecdotal evidence, particularly *responsa* literature, to demonstrate the social normalcy of Jewish women's involvement in the credit market.[6] Scholars such as Susan Einbinder and Suzanne Bartlet have reconstructed the biographies of particularly successful and well-documented women lenders, in Northern France and England respectively.[7]

In the medieval Western Mediterranean, however, Jewish women rarely engaged in moneylending. Rebecca Winer found that Jewish women acting independently extended less than four percent of loans in Perpignan.[8] In Manosque, Jewish women, either independently or alongside other lenders, participated in approximately ten percent of loans, according to a study by Andrée Courtemanche.[9] Kathryn Reyerson found no evidence of Jewish women lenders in Montpellier in the thirteenth and fourteenth centuries.[10] Yom Tov Assis names eight women among the sixty-four individual Jewish creditors of Santa Coloma de Queralt, but only one of these women lent with any frequency.[11] Only Courtemanche has examined the gender breakdown of Jewish women lenders' Christian clientele; she found that Jewish women lent primarily to men, secondarily to married couples, and much less frequently to both women acting alone and to widows with their children.[12] The marked differences scholars have already discovered between Jewish women's moneylending in Northern and

---

4   Victoria Hoyle, 'The Bonds that Bind: Money Lending between Anglo-Jewish and Christian Women in the Plea Rolls of the Exchequer of the Jews, 1218–1280', *JMH* 34 (2008), 123.

5   Jordan, 'Jews on Top', 53; Hoyle, 'Bonds that Bind', 123.

6   Kenneth R. Stow, 'The Jewish Family in the Rhineland in the High Middle Ages: Form and Function', *AHR* 92:5 (1987), 1100; Judith R. Baskin, 'Some Parallels in the Education of Medieval Jewish and Christian Women', *Jewish History* 5:1 (1991), 45; Cheryl Tallan, 'Medieval Jewish Widows: Their Control of Resources', *Jewish History* 5:1 (1991), 66; Avraham Grossman, *Pious and Rebellious: Jewish Women in Medieval Europe* (Waltham, MA, 2004), 120.

7   Susan L. Einbinder, 'Pucellina of Blois: Romantic Myths and Narrative Conventions', *Jewish History* 12:1 (1998), 29–46; Suzanne Bartlet, *Licoricia of Winchester: Marriage, Motherhood, and Murder in the Medieval Anglo-Jewish Community* (Edgware, 2009).

8   Rebecca Lynn Winer, *Women, Wealth, and Community in Perpignan, c. 1250–1350: Christians, Jews, and Enslaved Muslims in a Medieval Mediterranean Town* (Aldershot, 2006), 88.

9   Andrée Courtemanche, 'Les femmes juives et le crédit à Manosque au tournant du XIVᵉ siècle', *Provence Historique* 37 (1987), 550.

10   Kathryn Reyerson, *Business, Banking, and Finance in Medieval Montpellier* (Toronto, 1985), 73–74.

11   Yom Tov Assis, *The Jews of Santa Coloma de Queralt: An Economic and Demographic Case Study of a Community at the End of the Thirteenth Century* (Jerusalem, 1988), 36–37.

12   Courtemanche, 'Les femmes juives', 552–553.

Mediterranean Europe demand that we also question what differences existed between their clientele.

Based on data I have collected from the notarial registers of the Catalan town of Castelló d'Empúries, I argue in this essay that Mediterranean Jewish women did not predominantly lend to Christian women. Both Jewish women creditors and Christian women debtors engaged infrequently in notarial credit transactions, and members of these two groups rarely met. Further, I argue that the public, notarial credit system created a male-dominated credit market, which marginalized women of both religious identities, and prevented interactions between them. I will begin with a discussion of Castelló d'Empúries, and why this town and its sources provide an ideal site to examine Jewish women's moneylending. I will then consider, separately, the role Jewish women creditors and Christian women debtors played in Castelló's credit market during the latter half of the thirteenth century. Finally, I will consider how the notarial credit system shaped both the role of women and the nature of Jewish–Christian relations in thirteenth-century Catalonia.

Castelló d'Empúries: a dynamic local credit market

By 1260, the date of the town's earliest extant notarial register, Castelló had become the provincial capital of a semi-independent baronial enclave, the county of Empúries, and the county's economic center.[13] A public notariate, under the jurisdiction of the counts of Empúries, had arisen earlier in the thirteenth century.[14] The Jewish community of Castelló developed only after 1238, when Count Ponç Hug III issued an extensive privilege that confirmed and increased the Jews' liberties, while also protecting their financial ventures.[15] The growing community had established a synagogue by 1264 at the latest.[16] By the 1280s, Castelló had about 200 Jews, still a small community, but representing a significant proportion of the town's approximately 2,000 residents.[17] With the help of these Jewish newcomers, Castelló became a center for local credit,

[13] Stephen P. Bensch, 'A Baronial *Aljama*: The Jews of Empúries in the Thirteenth Century', *Jewish History* 22 (2006), 23–24.
[14] Stephen P. Bensch, 'Un notariat baronial: notaris i pràctiques documentals en el comtat d'Empúries al segle XIII', in *Documentació notarial i arxius: Els fons notarials com a eina per a la recerca històrica: Jornades célebrades els dies 5 i 6 d'octubre de 2006, a l'Arxiu Històric de Girona* (Barcelona, 2007), 123–33; Irene Llop i Jordana, 'Els Libri Iudeorum de Castelló d'Empúries', in *Jueus del Rei i del Comte: Homenatge a Miquel Pujol i Canelles, Girona i Castelló d'Empúries, 19 d'octubre de 2012*, Girona Judaica 7 (Girona, 2013), 48–49.
[15] Bensch, 'Baronial *Aljama*', 24, 27–30.
[16] Josep Maria Gironella, 'Noves dades sobre les sinagogues i els cementiris jueus de Castelló d'Empúries', in *Jueus del Rei i del Comte* (Girona, 2013), 80.
[17] Bensch, 'Baronial *Aljama*', 35.

and experienced considerable economic growth in the late thirteenth and early fourteenth centuries.[18]

In a recent study on Santa Coloma de Queralt, another small Catalan town, Gregory Milton argued that studying markets in smaller communities as well as large cities helps us better understand the economy of the region. Most men and women in medieval Catalonia lived in such communities, and participated in credit markets more like those of Santa Coloma or of Castelló than those of Barcelona or Girona.[19] With the growth of Jewish communities in smaller Catalan towns in the late thirteenth century, Jews as well as Christians often participated in the economic life of smaller towns.[20] Although Castelló certainly had distinctive characteristics, the town's Jewish credit market likely resembled those of the other small economic centers that proliferated throughout the region.

The wealth of documentation for Castelló in the thirteenth century makes it an especially valuable site for any study of social and economic history. Castelló boasts a particularly rich collection of thirteenth-century notarial registers; thirty-two registers, dating from 1260 to 1300, have survived. Many larger cities are less fortunate in their sources; Barcelona has only five extant thirteenth-century notarial manuals, all from the 1290s, while Girona's earliest extant register dates from 1311.

Notarial registers offer an important window onto the daily economic lives of medieval men and women. Public notariates developed in Catalonia starting in the twelfth century, and had become essential to the economic system by the mid-thirteenth century.[21] The notary transformed private transactions into publicly recognized facts, via the *instrumentum publicum*, the notarial contract.[22] Notaries played a particularly important role in credit transactions, in which the *instrumentum publicum* limited the risks associated with borrowing and lending.[23] Although participants in a transaction received official copies of their contracts, the notaries also recorded the essential information about each transaction, as well as abbreviated versions of the required legal formulae, in

---

[18] Xavier Soldevila i Temporal, *Crèdit i endeutament al comtat d'Empúries (1330–1335)* (Castelló d'Empúries: Ajuntament de Castelló d'Empúries, 2008), 47–55.

[19] Gregory B. Milton, *Market Power: Lordship, Society, and Economy in Medieval Catalonia (1276–1313)* (New York, NY, 2012), 2.

[20] Yitzhak Baer, *A History of the Jews in Christian Spain*, trans. Louis Schoffman (2 vols., Philadelphia, PA, 1961), i, 210; Assis, *Jews of Santa Coloma de Queralt*, 16; Bensch, 'Baronial *Aljama*', 31.

[21] Ignasi J. Baiges i Jardí, 'El notariat català: Origen i evolució', in *Actes del I Congrès d'Història del Notariat Català: Barcelona, 11, 12, i 13 de novembre de 1993*, ed. Josep Maria Sans i Travé (Barcelona, 1994), 133–135.

[22] Attilio Bartoli Langeli, '"Scripsi et publicavi": Il notaio come figura pubblica, l'instrumentum come documento pubblico', in *Notai, miracoli, e culto dei santi: Pubblicità e autenticazione del sacro tra XII e XV secolo*, ed. Raimondo Michetti (Milan, 2004), 68.

[23] Claude Denjean, 'Crédit et notariat en Cerdagne et Roussillon du XIIe au XVe siècle', in *Notaires et crédit dans l'occident méditerranéen medieval*, ed. François Menant and Odile Redon (Rome, 2004), 188–189.

notarial manuals, which remained in the notary's possession.[24] Clients of the notaries paid a small fee to have their documents recorded; a notary might charge five sous to record a large loan of 1,000 sous, but charged proportionally lower fees for smaller loans.[25] These fees supported the notary financially, as he received no other salary, but they were not meant to bar anyone from recording their transactions. According to a contemporary legal code, the Costums of Tortosa, members of all social strata should have access to the notary.[26]

Because ordinary men and women in Mediterranean Europe frequently employed notarial contracts to record private business and family arrangements, they constitute an invaluable source for social and economic history. They have certain advantages as sources for the study of Jewish–Christian credit, in comparison with Jordan's *enquêtes* and Hoyle's plea rolls. First, notarial sources allow us to examine credit transactions uncolored by the lens of hostility; notarial contracts present loans between Jewish creditors and Christian borrowers as simple business transactions, without acrimony. Second, notarial registers likely provide a more representative picture of lending than court cases; while registering a loan with the local notary constituted a normal act, creditors and debtors only went to court when a relationship soured. Without further data from northern Europe, we cannot determine if all types of credit transactions were equally likely to end up in court; certain kinds of interactions may have deteriorated more often than others.

Yet notarial sources have their own limitations. Although the notarial loan was the dominant form of credit, debtors and creditors may not have recorded very small loans, or some loans between close friends and relatives. Women may have been more likely to extend these non-registered loans. Without additional documentation, we can only speak about notarized credit transactions; the world of credit outside the notary's office remains in shadow. Additionally, notarial documents provide little information about the relationship between the parties, unless they were linked by blood or marriage, and no information about individuals who participated in the transaction informally. Brokers who brought borrowers and lenders together, and spouses or family members who provided advice or aid, incurred no contractual obligation, and thus remain invisible in the registers. Notarial contracts only allow us to determine the visible and public ways in which women participated in credit transactions; their involvement behind the scenes remains purely speculative.

Castelló's extant registers contain 2,065 loan contracts between Jewish lenders and Christian borrowers.[27] The table in Appendix 1, which I will

---

[24] Baiges i Jardí, 'El notariat català', 136.

[25] Asunción Blasco Martinez, 'El notariado en Aragón', in *Actes del I Congrès d'Història del Notariat Català*, 214.

[26] J. Massip, 'Els notaris a les "Costums de Tortosa"', in *Estudis sobre història de la institució notarial a Catalunya en honor de Raimon Noguera*, ed. Josep Maria Sans i Travé (Barcelona, 1988), 55.

[27] None of these registers are Libri Iudeorum, notarial manuals dedicated primarily to transactions involving Jews. Although 100 Libri Iudeorum from Castelló have survived, the earliest dates from 1305. See Llop i Jordana, 'Libri Iudeorum', 49.

consult throughout the essay, provides a breakdown of Jewish loans in Castelló between 1260 and 1300, categorized by the identities of the borrowers and lenders. For both types of actors, I have created six categories: men acting independently; women acting independently; married couples acting in tandem; groups consisting exclusively of men; groups consisting exclusively of women; and groups consisting of both men and women.[28] The numbers represent the total number of loans in each category.

Jewish women creditors in thirteenth-century Castelló d'Empúries

The gendered credit system in Castelló provided Jewish women with few opportunities to act as lenders within the dominant notarial credit system. The vast majority of lenders were men: single male lenders made 81 percent of Jewish loans to Christians, and groups of men made an additional 12.5 percent of loans. Women acting independently extended 3.9 percent of Jewish loans, while groups involving women account for an additional 2.6 percent of loans. The overall picture of Jewish women's lending accords with evidence from elsewhere in the Western Mediterranean; Jewish women acting independently account for a nearly identical percentage of Jewish loans in Perpignan.[29]

Individual Jewish women rarely became prominent professional lenders, although a number of Jewish men in Castelló earned a significant amount of income through lending. Only thirteen women made two or more independent loans. Out of these women, only three can be considered professional lenders. These three women – Reina Bedoç, widow of Baró Ferrer; Belaire, widow of Astrug Salandí; and Dolça, widow of Astrug Vides – extended nearly half of women's independent loans, despite only acting as lenders for the last five years of the forty-year period under study.[30]

All three of Castelló's most prominent Jewish women lenders entered the credit market only as widows. Widowed creditors account for nearly three-quarters of women's loans, likely because widowhood allowed them independent control over financial resources.[31] Women with still-living husbands lent less frequently, although some families in Castelló encouraged women's lending. Two sisters-in-law, Dura, wife of Abraham Cordoví, and Bonadona, wife of Issach Cordoví,

---

[28]   I have included the category 'Unknown' in the borrowers for cases where the name of the Jewish lender appears clearly, but the name of the borrower is fully or partially illegible due to damage. This allows me to include all loans made by Jews to Christians even when the borrower's identity cannot be determined with certainty.

[29]   Winer, *Women, Wealth, and Community*, 88.

[30]   See e.g. AHG Ca 7, fol. 26r, where Reina makes a loan of 17 sous to a Christian couple; AHG Ca 364, fol. 27v, where Belaire makes a 220 sous loan to a Christian couple from Santa Maria de Roses; AHG Ca 18, fol. 29r, where Dolça accepts partial repayment from a Christian man for a 135 sous loan.

[31]   Winer describes a similar state of affairs in Perpignan. Winer, *Women, Wealth, and Community*, 99–103.

each made three independent loans.[32] Dura also participated in another six group loans, acting alongside her husband Abraham or her sons Baró and Jucef.[33] Some women may have worked behind the scenes to help with their husbands' lending businesses; such activities could have ranged from administrative aid to brokering relations with new debtors. Indeed, considering the business acumen displayed by some widows, it seems likely that many developed such financial expertise during their marriages. Nevertheless, especially as wives, and even as widows, Jewish women rarely acted formally and publicly as creditors.

Although Jewish women had difficulty entering the credit market as lenders, upon entry they could compete in the largest sector of the market: extending loans of middling size. As the chart (Figure 1) demonstrates, 36 percent of all Jewish loans were for sums between 20 and 50 sous. Jewish women extended these moderate loans at almost the same rate as Jewish men – this category accounts for 37 percent of Jewish women's loans.[34] The work of scholars such as Stephen Bensch, Joel Colomer, and Irene Llop i Jordana corroborates this picture of Jewish credit in thirteenth- and early fourteenth-century Castelló as dominated by small-scale loans to modest artisans in Castelló and the inhabitants of the surrounding villages.[35] The counts of Empúries sought loans from Christians or from Jews of nearby Girona, rather than the Jewish community of their own capital city, until the early fourteenth century.[36]

Despite the predominance of middling loans, Jewish women's lending remained less profitable than that of Jewish men. Jewish women lenders made smaller loans more frequently than their male counterparts, and they made large loans less frequently. Loans between 10 and 20 sous account for 16.5 percent of all loans, but 21 percent of women's loans. More dramatically, only 2 percent of all Jewish loans, but 10 percent of women's loans, were for minor sums of less than 10 sous. When we turn to larger loans, we find that 15.5 percent of Jewish loans were for sums between 50 and 100 sous, and another 16.5 percent were for

---

[32] See e.g. AHG Ca 414, fol. 2r–v, where Dura makes a loan of 300 sous; AHG Ca 419, fol. 14v, where Bonadona makes a loan of 16 sous.

[33] See e.g. AHG Ca 3, fol. 107v, where Dura, Abraham, and their son Jucef release a Christian couple from a 200 sous loan.

[34] To give some idea of the purchasing power of these sums, an artisan could make about a sous per day; one could easily live on about 100 sous per year; and the median price for a house or shop in Perpignan falls between 30 and 40 sous. A decent ecclesiastical benefice yielded about 300 sous per year. These figures come from Burns, *Jews in the Notarial Culture*, 9.

[35] Bensch, 'Baronial *Aljama*', 38; Joel Colomer, 'El crèdit a Castelló a principis del segle XIV: Els Ravaia', in *Jueus del Rei i del Comte* (Girona, 2013), 63–64; Llop i Jordana, 'Els Libri Iudeorum', 52.

[36] Bensch, 'Baronial *Aljama*', 32–33; Joel Colomer, 'El crèdit a Castelló', 65. Although the Jews of Castelló remained free of the excessive royal taxation that plagued their brethren in the larger cities of the Crown of Aragon, they also lacked opportunities for economic advancement. Assis offers a detailed discussion of how the *aljamas* of the Crown of Aragon both benefited and suffered from their complex financial relationship with the count-kings. See Yom Tov Assis, *Jewish Economy in the Medieval Crown of Aragon, 1213–1327: Money and Power* (Leiden, 1997), 118–159.

sums between 100 and 200 sous. Jewish women made loans of 50 to 100 sous at almost the same rate as men – 15 percent – but Jewish women's loans diminish when we consider sums of over 100 sous. Only 10 percent of Jewish women's loans were for sums between 100 and 200 sous. Nine percent of Jewish men's loans, but only 7 percent of Jewish women's loans, were for sums of 200 to 500 sous. Finally, while a few Jewish men made very large loans – 4 percent of all loans were for sums of between 500 and 1,000 sous – no Jewish woman made a loan of over 500 sous (see Figure 1).

Although Jewish women in Castelló faced many barriers to lending, the preponderance of small and middling loans allowed them to compete more effectively in the local credit market than their counterparts in larger Catalan cities. Rebecca Winer has argued that Jewish women in Perpignan made loans infrequently because they rarely had sufficient wealth at their disposal. Few Jewish wives managed financial resources independently, and a widow generally had access to less wealth than her late husband.[37] A widowed guardian of her minor children had access to her late husband's entire estate, rather than just her dowry and dower, but even the most successful guardian often found that 'her work was only analogous to a man less prosperous than her husband had been'.[38] However, widowed Jewish lenders in Perpignan found themselves less prosperous than their husbands and fathers not only because they made fewer

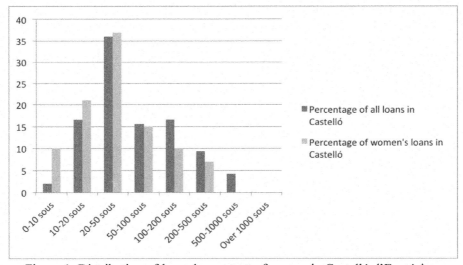

Figure 1. Distribution of loans by amount of money in Castelló d'Empúries

37   Winer, *Women, Wealth, and Community*, 99–102. For the poverty of Christian widows, see Isabelle Chabot, 'Widowhood and Poverty in Late Medieval Florence', *Continuity and Change* 3 (1988), 291–311.
38   Winer, *Women, Wealth, and Commuity*, 102–103; Elka Klein, 'The Widow's Portion: Law, Custom, and Marital Property among Medieval Catalan Jews', *Viator* 31 (2000), 153–155.

loans, but also because they made less profitable ones.[39] In contrast, Jewish women in Castelló likely benefited from the community's reliance on small consumption loans. According to Bensch, the Jewish community's specialization in small-scale credit allowed newcomers to the community to quickly integrate into the local economy.[40] Jewish women, too, likely found that the high demand for small scale credit allowed them to more effectively participate in the economy of Castelló than in the credit markets of other, larger cities.

The Jewish women lenders of Castelló resembled their male counterparts in loan size and in clientele. They lent primarily to the two largest groups of borrowers, Christian men acting alone (51 percent of women's loans) and married couples (26 percent of women's loans). Both of these groups went to Jewish women lenders in almost exact proportion to their presence in the general population of lenders, suggesting that they neither preferred nor avoided women lenders. The same can be said of other mixed gender groups of borrowers, who received 10.7 percent of all loans and 8.8 percent of Jewish women's loans. Groups of male borrowers, however, rarely borrowed from Jewish women. While such groups received 13 percent of all Jewish loans, they received only 5 percent of Jewish women's loans. These groups likely did not avoid women lenders so much as they avoided amateur lenders; Dolça Vides, the most professionalized Jewish woman lender in thirteenth-century Castelló, accounts for all the loans that Jewish women made to groups of Christian men. Christian women debtors demonstrated no preference for Jewish women lenders; rather, Jewish women had disproportionately fewer Christian women clients: while Christian women acting independently received 4.3 percent of all loans, they received only 2.5 percent of Jewish women's loans.

Christian women debtors in thirteenth-century Castelló d'Empúries

The same credit market that limited Jewish women's opportunities to lend also restricted the role Christian women in Castelló could play in securing Jewish credit for their families' needs. Christian women acting alone received only 4.3 percent of loans.[41] The striking similarity here between Jewish women creditors and Christian women debtors suggests that Jewish and Christian families held shared views about the role of women in public credit transactions involving members of the other religious group. Although Christian women may not have interacted with Jewish women through credit transactions, the two groups of women had similar experiences, with Christian women having almost exactly as much difficulty borrowing from Jewish lenders as Jewish women had lending to Christian debtors.

---

[39] Winer, *Women, Wealth, and Community*, 88.
[40] Bensch, 'A Baronial *Aljama*', 38.
[41] Christian women appeared only slightly more often as borrowers, in 7.8 percent of all loans, in Montpellier. See Reyerson, *Business, Banking, and Finance*, 76.

However, Christian women appeared far more often alongside their husbands or adult sons as borrowers than Jewish women did as lenders. Married couples received 24 percent of Jewish loans in Castelló, while other groups including both men and women (usually, either entire families or widows with adult children) represent an additional 11 percent of debtors. In addition, while Jewish women in Castelló never acted together to extend credit to Christians, Christian women jointly incurred debts to Jewish lenders, albeit quite rarely (less than one percent of loans).

Most scholars have interpreted Christian women's role in incurring debts alongside their husbands as primarily a legal safeguard. Creditors ran certain risks when they made loans to married men who acted without their wives' consent. If the husband predeceased his wife, his heirs were required to return her dowry and pay the dower, or *escreix* in Catalan, before satisfying other creditors.[42] Nor could creditors seek repayment from the dotal property of their deceased clients' wives, unless those women had co-signed the debts, or renounced their right to avoid liability.[43] Women could even sue their still living husbands for restoration of their dowries in cases of insolvency or mismanagement.[44] Some couples may have strategically collaborated in this; a suit for the restoration of the dowry could preserve a portion of the family estate against the demands of creditors.[45]

Although this interpretation likely explains the frequency with which Christian women acted alongside their husbands, we cannot rule out the possibility that joint credit transactions allowed women greater control over household finances. While some couples collaborated in dowry restitution suits, Dana Wessell Lightfoot has argued that many of these suits indicate 'the agency of women in protecting their marital property'.[46] Women had opinions about the role of debt in managing the resources of their households, and they willingly challenged

---

[42] Teresa-Maria Vinyoles, *Les barcelonines a les darreries de l'Edat Mitjana (1370–1410)* (Barcelona, 1976), 88.

[43] Women both incurred debts alongside their husbands, which implied liability, and explicitly renounced the senatus consult of Velleius, an institution of Roman law that obviated women from responsibility for their husbands' transactions. Marie Kelleher, *The Measure of Woman: Law and Female Identity in the Crown of Aragon* (Philadelphia, PA, 2010), 59–61; Winer, *Women, Wealth, and Community*, 35–36.

[44] For a particularly extensive examination of dowry restitution, see Dana Wessell Lightfoot, 'Negotiating Agency: Labouring-Status Wives and their Dowries in Early Fifteenth-Century Valencia' (Ph.D. diss., University of Toronto, 2005), 210–266, and *Women, Dowries, and Agency: Marriage in Fifteenth-Century Valencia* (Manchester, 2013), 151–188.

[45] For discussion of this phenomenon in the Crown of Aragon, see Kelleher, *Measure of Woman*, 56; Winer, *Women, Wealth, and Community*, 32–33. For similar household strategies in late medieval and early modern Italy, see Julius Kirshner, 'Wives' Claims Against Insolvent Husbands in Late Medieval Italy', in *Women of the Medieval World: Essays in Honor of John H. Mundy*, ed. Julius Kirshner and Suzanne F. Wemple (Oxford, 1985), 256–303; Francesca Trivellato, *The Familiarity of Strangers: The Sephardic Diaspora, Livorno, and Cross-Cultural Trade in the Early Modern Period* (New Haven, CT, 2009), 261–262.

[46] Wessell Lightfoot, *Women, Dowries, and Agency*, 151.

their husbands on financial matters when necessary. Creditors' preference that wives co-sign their husbands' debts may even have given women a greater role in managing household finances.

Other women who went into debt alongside their husbands and male relatives may have deliberately relied on these men to bolster their own authority to transact.[47] Considering that Jews as well as Christians preferred that women avoid participating publicly in the notarial credit market, Christian women in need of a loan may have found they could avoid censure from their own community and enhance their apparent creditworthiness before male Jewish lenders by acting alongside a man. Marie Kelleher has argued that women who litigated to protect their property rights deliberately sought to portray themselves in gender appropriate ways; transacting alongside men may have been part of a similar performance.[48]

Christian women played a much more significant role as borrowers in Northern Europe; they appear as plaintiffs in 27 percent of one of Jordan's sets of *enquêtes*, and 57 percent of the other.[49] Jordan argues that Christian women in Picardy 'played a crucial role' in handling their families' small-scale credit arrangements, and that since these women tended to borrow from other women, a 'two-leveled credit structure' developed, in which women borrowers and lenders were together segregated in a separate but still visible credit system.[50] Hoyle does not provide quantitative evidence for the prominence of Christian women debtors, but suggests that Jewish and Christian women in England interacted frequently through small-scale loans, in a credit system that bound these women together.[51]

In Castelló, however, those Christian women who did seek loans from Jewish creditors tended to borrow from Jewish men. Individual women debtors went to men or to all male groups in 93.25 percent of cases; they received credit from groups including both men and women in 4.5 percent of cases, and they borrowed from individual women lenders in only only 2.25 percent of cases. Individual Christian women debtors borrowed from Jewish women lenders even less often than the general population.

Gender and the notariate

Other scholars have recognized the sharp difference between the economic prominence of northern and southern Jewish women. Jewish communities and families in the medieval Mediterranean world placed constraints on Jewish

---

[47] Elka Klein has made this argument for Jewish women. See Elka Klein, 'Public Activities of Catalan Jewish Women', *Medieval Encounters* 12:1 (2006), 55–56.
[48] Kelleher, *The Measure of Woman*, 49.
[49] Jordan, 'Jews on Top', 42–43.
[50] Jordan, 'Jews on Top', 55.
[51] Hoyle, 'Bonds that Bind', 127–129.

women's work, only encouraging their public economic activity when necessary for the good of the family or community.[52] Anna Rich Abad traces these constraints directly to the 'rules of patriarchal society and the interests of their own male-dominated community', as well as similar rules in the surrounding Christian society.[53] However, a patriarchal system undoubtedly also existed in contemporary northern Europe. Rebecca Winer links the difference between north and south to the 'Mediterranean sense of honor and shame'. The Jewish community as a whole demonstrated a strong concern for the modesty of Jewish women. Travel, in particular, represented a threat to women's modesty; as a result, even those few Jewish women who did take on a more prominent economic role virtually never engaged in business that required travel.[54] David Nirenberg argues that Jews, Christians, and Muslims in the Crown of Aragon all attempted to assert their honor by controlling the sexuality of their women, and, in particular, preventing miscegenation.[55]

Anxieties about women's honor, as described by Winer and Nirenberg, likely led many Catalan Jewish communities to discourage women not only from economic activities that involved travel, but also from economic activities that brought them into frequent contact with non-Jewish men. Moneylending in Castelló necessarily involved contact with male borrowers – individual men or all-male groups received 58 percent of Jewish loans – as well as the male notary. Similarly, the Christian community of Castelló may have discouraged women from borrowing from Jews without a husband or male relative by their side, precisely because the vast majority of Jewish lenders were men.

The notarial credit system itself played an important role in masculinizing the practices of credit and marginalizing both Jewish women creditors and Christian women debtors. According to both Jordan and Hoyle, northern European women participated in credit arrangements as a natural extension of their other domestic responsibilities. Credit transactions between Jewish and Christian women took place in private homes and involved the pawning of common household objects.[56] In Catalonia, however, most borrowers and lenders finalized their arrangements in the public space of the notary's office. The concept of credit as a formal, public activity, rather than a domestically based business, affected the preferences of both Christians and Jews in Castelló. When Catalan Christian women sought Jewish loans in the public space of the notary's office, they normally went accompanied by their husbands or male relatives, while Jewish women rarely made notarized loans to Christians at all. Whether because they had internalized broader social views of women's honor,

---

[52]   Winer, *Women, Wealth, and Community*, 80.
[53]   Anna Rich Abad, 'Able and Available: Jewish Women in Medieval Barcelona and their Economic Activities', *Journal of Medieval Iberian Studies* 6:1 (2014), 73.
[54]   Winer, *Women, Wealth, and Community*, 97–98.
[55]   David Nirenberg, *Communities of Violence: Persecution of Minorities in the Middle Ages* (Princeton, NJ, 1996), 138.
[56]   Hoyle, 'Bonds that Bind', 128; Jordan, 'Jews on Top', 51.

or because modesty formed a part of their deliberate self-presentation, Catalan women often avoided public activity. Elka Klein points out that at least some Catalan Jewish women sought a greater degree of privacy and separation from public affairs than the community generally granted; in the thirteenth century, two Jewish widows received royal privileges allowing them to take oaths in the privacy of their own homes, rather than venturing into public spaces.[57] Kelleher has found evidence of Christian women acting in accordance with gendered assumptions of female modesty.[58]

The marginalization of women in the notarial credit system had a self-reinforcing effect. Due to either personal preferences or social constraints, women in medieval Europe often transacted with other women. Jordan suggests that interest free loans between women stemmed from pre-existing networks of kinship and friendship.[59] Many women may have built non-kin social networks primarily with other women, and thus sought credit from women rather than from men. While notarial sources normally do not permit us to identify affective relationships between Jewish creditors and Christian debtors, Jewish as well as Christian women may have preferred to transact with women rather than men, even when they did not have a prior relationship. For Jewish women, the notary's office likely seemed an overwhelmingly male, Christian space. The registers of Castelló indicate that when a Jewish woman registered a loan, she faced not only the notary and the debtor, but also a large group of Christian men who passed in and out of the notary's office to register their own transactions and make themselves available as witnesses. Few Jewish women entered this space; they either avoided credit transactions entirely, or participated in peripheral and now invisible ways, by aiding their husbands or by extending their own smaller and less secure non-notarized loans. This absence of Jewish women lenders likely further discouraged Christian women from seeking Jewish credit without the support of a husband or male relative.

Those few Jewish women lenders who entered the credit market had a freer range of borrowing partners than their counterparts in the north. Considering the marginalization of Christian women as debtors, social restrictions on women's ability to transact with men of another religious group would have created severe transaction costs for all would-be Jewish women lenders. However, Jewish women lenders extended credit to men with no apparent problem: 51 percent of women's loans were made to individual men, 35 percent to mixed-gender groups, and 5 percent to all-male groups. The three women of Castelló whom we can consider professional lenders all had a wide range of borrowing partners. Similarly, had Christian women been limited to the small pool of women lenders, they would have experienced severe difficulties in finding sources of

---

57 Klein, 'Public Activities', 49–50.
58 Kelleher, *The Measure of Woman*, 28.
59 William Chester Jordan, *Women and Credit in Pre-Industrial and Developing Societies* (Philadelphia, PA, 1993), 25.

Jewish credit. Women debtors borrowed from individual men or all male groups in 93 percent of cases.

Although women who participated in the Jewish–Christian credit market of Catalonia borrowed freely across gendered lines, Jewish women lacked the opportunity to specialize in a small-scale credit market, while Christian women had less independent control over the credit needs of their households. While this flexibility in choosing borrowing partners had economic benefits, socially, women may have experienced it primarily as an additional challenge, which kept most women out of the notary's office. Some Jewish and Christian women may have relied on an 'underground' system of pawnbroking, separate from the notarial credit system. Even if pawnbroking provided income for Jewish women and a source of credit for Christian women, the marginalization of women in the dominant notarial credit system limited Jewish women to making the smallest and least profitable of loans, and deprived both Jewish women creditors and Christian women borrowers of the added financial security provided by the notaries.[60]

Religion and the notariate

Credit transactions undoubtedly played an important role in Jewish–Christian relations in Europe, but while some scholars have presented credit as an important source of friction, others have argued in favor of amicable credit transactions. Jordan, in particular, presented credit transactions between Jewish and Christian women as contributing to medieval anti-Judaism. Christian women, and their young children who accompanied them, experienced feelings of 'personal humiliation' as they traveled into the unfamiliar space of the Jewish quarter and abandoned their precious possessions as pawns in the homes of Jewish women. They carried these feelings of resentment, Jordan suggests, into future interactions with Jews.[61]

However, scholars of both Northern and Mediterranean Europe have offered more optimistic views. Hoyle points out that by their very nature, both Jordan's *enquêtes* and her English plea rolls only describe credit relationships that have soured. In reality, she argues, Jewish and Christian women likely conducted most of their transactions on pleasant terms.[62] Joseph Shatzmiller, in his study of the Jewish moneylender Bondavid of Draguignan in fourteenth-century Marseille, argues that Jewish lenders cultivated good relations with frequent clients, and thereby earned the respect and good will of the surrounding Christian

---

[60] The nature of woman's work as less profitable, less secure, and less respected accords with findings for Christian women in northern Europe. See Judith Bennett, *Ale, Beer, and Brewsters in England: Women's Work in a Changing World, 1300–1600* (Oxford, 1996); Sharon Farmer, *Surviving Poverty in Medieval Paris: Gender, Ideology, and the Daily Lives of the Poor* (Ithaca, NY, 2005), 117–135.

[61] Jordan, 'Jews on Top', 50–52.

[62] Hoyle, 'Bonds that Bind', 123.

community, as well as a good business reputation.[63] He even describes those who testified in favor of Bondavid as character witnesses as his 'friends'.[64] The testimony he cites undoubtedly indicates, if not necessarily friendship, at least a positive and respectful relationship.

The reality likely lies between the extremes of amity and enmity. Notarial sources say little about affective relationships between the parties to a transaction. Yet court records from Mediterranean Europe associate credit with friendship; as Daniel Lord Smail has argued, 'relationships of credit in Marseille were suffused with friendly emotions'.[65] Smail cites Shatzmiller, but otherwise suggests that most Jewish–Christian loans were impersonal business transactions.[66] However, the powerful links between credit transactions and friendship in the medieval Mediterranean world suggest that Jewish lenders developed cordial, affective relationships with at least some of their clients. While not all loans publicly demonstrated friendship, they indicated the continuity of good business relationships.

Notarial credit documents provide a few important clues to the relationships between Christian debtors and Jewish creditors. First, creditors and debtors finalized most transactions in the notary's office. Christians did not travel to unfamiliar, 'Jewish' domestic space, but to the familiar space of a public official. Professional Jewish lenders, who went to the notary frequently, may have conceived of this space as neutral ground; the notary was Christian, but his office made him a disinterested party. Moreover, the high volume of credit transactions in general, and credit between Jews and Christians in particular, indicates the normalcy of indebtedness and of Jewish–Christian credit relationships in thirteenth-century Castelló.[67] In a society so reliant on credit, recourse to a Jewish moneylender was not shameful, nor was the moneylender a person to be resented; these credit transactions, and the Jews who extended credit, formed a regular part of life in this community.

Most transactions ended on terms acceptable to all parties. Cancellation marks on the documents indicate that most loans were eventually repaid. Documents in which borrowers and lenders renegotiated terms suggest that creditors remained flexible, and accepted a later repayment rather than antagonizing their clients. Finally, most Jewish moneylenders cultivated repeat clients, with whom they likely developed cordial business relationships. Few Jewish women extended credit often enough to become enmeshed in the surrounding Christian community through their credit transactions, but those who did – Reina Bedoç, Belaire

---

[63] Joseph Shatzmiller, *Shylock Reconsidered: Jews, Moneylending, and Medieval Society* (Berkeley, CA, 1990), 71–72.

[64] Shatzmiller, *Shylock Reconsidered*, 104–118.

[65] Daniel Lord Smail, *The Consumption of Justice: Emotions, Publicity, and Legal Culture in Marseille, 1263–1423* (Ithaca, NY, 2003), 135.

[66] Smail, *Consumption of Justice*, 137.

[67] Soldevila i Temporal has noted the same for Castelló in the fourteenth century. Soldevila i Temporal, *Crèdit i endeutament*, 79.

Salandí, and Dolça Vides, the three most active women lenders of Castelló – all had repeat clients.[68]

The non-professionalization of Jewish women lenders hints at further Jewish–Christian interactions outside the notary's office. While some members of the Jewish community of Castelló, mostly men, became publicly known as lenders, a number of women made only one or two loans. How did debtors connect with these potential creditors? The link between borrower and lender, made visible at the moment the notary recorded the transaction, suggests the presence of social relationships that crossed both religious and gender lines. Although few Jewish women developed relationships through credit transactions, the loans they made may reflect relationships between Jewish and Christian neighbors or colleagues that pre-dated the transaction itself.

Conclusions

In Catalonia, credit neither brought Jewish and Christian women together, nor tore them apart. The notarial credit system assigned both Jewish women lenders and Christian women debtors a marginal role. For both groups of women, this gendered credit system proved self-reinforcing. The definition of the notary's office as male space, and the credit transaction in particular as a transaction between men, prevented most Jewish women from extending loans and most Christian women from seeking credit without their husbands or male relatives. The continued absence of all but a few women only reified these definitions. As Judith Bennett argues in her theory of 'patriarchal equilibrium', continuity rather than change often characterizes women's history; the self-reinforcing nature of patriarchal institutions forms an important part of this process.[69] The limitations placed on both Jewish women as lenders and Christian women as debtors in the credit markets of medieval Catalan towns should become part of our picture of the differences between Jewish women's lending in Northern and Mediterranean Europe.

The notarial sources from Castelló reveal neither friendship nor hostility between Jewish creditors and Christian debtors. In part, this neutrality reflects the limitations of a type of source material that rarely describes interpersonal relationships. However, the neutral relationships seen in the notarial registers also suggest that while Shatzmiller's claims of amity might be overly utopian, Jordan's concept of an undercurrent of hostility does not apply to Mediterranean Europe. The normalcy of indebtedness, and the prominence of Christians as well as Jews as creditors, likely prevented most Christians from resenting Jewish moneylenders. The loan documents from Castelló chiefly demonstrate

---

[68]   For example, Dolça Vides made two small loans to Esteve Sunyer of Fortià, his wife Estefania, and his son Ramon Esteve, in 1298. AHG Ca 11, fols. 17v, 77r.
[69]   Judith M. Bennett, *History Matters: Patriarchy and the Challenge of Feminism* (Philadelphia, PA, 2006), 80–81.

constant interaction between Jews and Christians, which often took place in the neutral space of the notary's office; certain moneylenders' long-term relationships with repeat clients suggest that many of these interactions were at least relatively cordial, and that moneylending enmeshed Jews in Christian society. As for northern Europe, the differences between Jordan's and Hoyle's interpretations suggest that only further research can determine whether credit transactions truly engendered greater hostility there than in Mediterranean Europe.

The similar roles of Jewish women as creditors and Christian women as borrowers indicates that Jewish and Christian communities in thirteenth-century Catalonia shared a set of gendered assumptions about the appropriate economic role for their daughters, wives, and mothers. Notably, Jewish women made independent loans almost exactly as often as Christian women received them.[70] The marginalization of women of both religious groups suggests that the 'common culture' shared by Catalan Jews and Christians, to use Elka Klein's term, extended also to concepts of gender and the role of women.[71] The very absence of financial interactions between Jewish and Christian women stemmed from shared Jewish and Christian ideas about their appropriate economic roles.

---

[70] Interestingly, the same can be said of northern France. Jordan, 'Jews on Top', 53.
[71] Elka Klein, *Jews, Christian Society, and Royal Power in Medieval Barcelona* (Ann Arbor, MI, 2006), 2.

Appendix 1: Loans between Jewish lenders and Christian borrowers in Castelló d'Empúries, 1260–1300

Borrowers

Lenders	Single male	Single female	Married Couple	Group (Male)	Group (female)	Group (mixed)	Unknown	Total
Single male	744	71	405	223	12	185	34	1674
Single female	41	2	21	4	3	7	2	80
Married couple	6	0	2	1	1	2	0	12
Group – all male	128	12	60	32	1	21	4	258
Group – all female	0	0	0	0	0	0	0	0
Group – male and female	15	4	12	3	0	6	1	41
Total	934	89	500	263	17	221	41	2065

Source: Arxiu Històric Girona, Girona, secció Castelló, nos. 1–5, 7–12, 14, 16–18, 20–21, 75, 156b, 206, 305, 358, 364, 414, 419, 1944, 2085–2089, 2098.

10

Military Entrepreneurs in the Armies of Edward I
(1272–1307) of England

David Bachrach and Oliver Stoutner

Two important historiographical traditions have combined in fruitful ways to illuminate the participation of the knights and landed gentry in the wars of the English kings from the latter thirteenth century through the fifteenth century. In his survey of warfare in 1980, the prominent French military historian Philippe Contamine argued for the importance what he called the 'sociology of war', making the case that the composition of armies accurately reflected the underlying structure of society.[1] Contamine's 'call to arms' for scholars to investigate the sociological aspects of war was warmly received by specialists in English history. Scholars in this tradition were long accustomed to investigating the gentry not only as a social and political class, but also as a group that played a leading role in military conflicts of the English kings as mounted fighting men. The result has been an outpouring of studies, many prosopographical in nature, that have illuminated the participation of the knights and sub-knightly gentry in war, primarily as mounted fighting men.[2]

---

[1]   Philippe Contamine, *La Guerre au Moyen Age* (Paris, 1980). The text was translated by Michael Jones as *War in the Middle Ages* (Oxford, 1984). For this passage see pp. 238–239 in the English translation.

[2]   Important studies include Nigel Saul, *Knights and Esquires: The Gloucestershire Gentry in the Fourteenth* Century (Oxford, 1981); Philip Morgan, *War and Society in Medieval Cheshire, 1277–1403* (Manchester, 1987); Andrew Ayton, *Knights and Warhorses: Military Service and the English Aristocracy under Edward III* (Woodbridge, 1994); M.H. Keen, *Knights and Men at Arms in the Middle Ages* (London, 1996); Peter Coss, *The Origins of the English Gentry* (Cambridge, 2003); and David Simpkin, *The English Aristocracy at War from the Welsh Wars of Edward I to the Battle of Bannockburn* (Woodbridge, 2008). The crucial monographs by Michael Powicke, *Military Obligation in Medieval England: A Study in Liberty and Duty* (Oxford, 1962) and Michael Prestwich, *War, Politics and Finance under Edward I* (Totowa, NJ, 1972) predate Contamine's study, but they provide important insights regarding the composition of English armies. However, their focus is on institutional structures rather than social, prosopographical or political questions relating to the knightly and sub-knightly gentry. Underlying much of the scholarship in the post-war era on the military role of the gentry is the path-breaking work of K.B. McFarlane, 'Bastard Feudalism', *Bulletin of the Institute of Historical Research* 20 (1943–1945), 161–80, and the enormous volume of discussion that it engendered. Most recently, see Anne Curry, Andy King, and David Simpkin, *The Soldier in Later Medieval England* (Oxford, 2013).

The scholarly focus on the gentry in war has been facilitated by the edition during the nineteenth and early twentieth century of a substantial corpus of documents that shed light on landowners and their participation in royal military service. Paradigmatic in this context is Francis Palgrave's two volumes of *Parliamentary Writs and Writs of Military Summons*, published between 1827 and 1834, which remains a basic work for the analysis of the participation of knights and gentry in war.[3] Indeed, Palgrave and other editors appear to have chosen quite explicitly to focus their attention on those documents that revealed the participation of the wealthier members of society in war, and to have ignored those texts that focused primarily on men who did not belong to the gentry. This is explained in large part by their focus on collecting writs of summons, documents that were issued to the wealthier members of society.

This source bias toward landowners is illuminated in one of the most important collections of published documents relating to warfare in the reign of Edward I (1272–1307), Henry Gough's *Scotland in 1298*.[4] This volume, published in 1888, includes editions of royal documents relating to Edward I's campaign in Scotland in 1298 and has played a central role in subsequent prosopographical studies of the mounted forces who served this king. Gough edited contracts, letters of protection, mobilization orders for knights and other property owners, letters of attorney, summonses to military tenants, the *Falkirk Roll of Arms,* and, perhaps most importantly, horse evaluation rolls.[5] This last type of document records the value of the horses of mounted combatants so that the owners could be compensated if the animals were lost on campaign. As a consequence, horse rolls have proven particularly important for proposopgraphical studies of knights and gentry serving in war.[6] Conspicuous by their absence in Gough's volume, however, are the pay records for the foot soldiers for the 1298 campaign, although he did include the royal commands for the mobilization of foot soldiers.[7] Indeed, almost none of the pay records for the entirety of Edward I's reign have been published and very few have been utilized by scholars for prosopographical research.

The decision by scholars to avoid these pay records is certainly understandable. There are many thousands of individual texts, ranging from voluminous wardrobe books to brief two-line receipts written on scraps of parchment. In contrast to the lengthy lists of names found in documents such as horse

---

3   *Parliamentary Writs and Writs of Military Summons*, ed. F. Palgrave (2 vols. in 4 parts, London, 1827–1834).
4   *Scotland in 1298: Documents Relating to the Campaign of Edward I in that Year*, ed. H. Gough (London, 1888).
5   The horse evaluation roles for the campaign of 1298 are printed in Gough, *Scotland in 1298*, 161–237. Gough also published royal writs summoning foot soldiers to war but did not devote attention to the documents that provide information about these foot soldiers or the men who served as their officers.
6   The most detailed treatment of these documents, including their strengths and weaknesses for prosopographical research is Ayton, *Knights and Warhorses*, particularly 49–137.
7   See *Scotland in 1298*, 57–64.

evaluation rolls, pay records often include references to just a handful or even just one fighting man. As a consequence, it is a tedious task to prise data from these texts, to collate the information about fighting men, and then cross-reference this information with findings with material taken from yet other unpublished documents, in order to create a usable database of individuals who served as mounted troops in the royal army.[8] Nevertheless, despite the laborious process needed to use them, the pay records from Edward I's reign yield in their aggregate an enormous volume of information about very large numbers of mounted fighting men, including those below the level of the gentry, who do not appear in the documents traditionally utilized by scholars.

One important consequence of the scholarly neglect of pay records is the absence of prosopgraphical studies of the many hundreds of men—indeed more than 2,000—below the economic and social status of the gentry, who played a very important role as mounted troops in the armies of Edward I, both on the battlefield and in the holding of captured territory.[9] For the most part, these men were military entrepreneurs, who volunteered to serve in war on horseback for pay. Because of their lack of property, they did not have the legal obligation to serve as mounted troops. Instead they chose to do so, taking financial risks by investing substantial sums of money to purchase horses and equestrian equipment. These men often made a military career in King Edward's service.[10] It is their story that is the focus of this essay.

Military obligation

Property qualifications for obligatory participation in expeditionary military operations were a central element of Anglo-Saxon and early Anglo-Norman military organization.[11] Henry II's assize of arms in 1181 did not alter the basic connection between property and the obligation to perform military service that

---

[8]   This type of painstaking work has been done for English armies during the Hundred Years War by Anne Curry, Andy King, and David Simpkin in *The Soldier in Later Medieval England*.
[9]   It is my intention to publish the full range of prosopographical data for the 2,000 or so *centenarii* and *soldarii* who served in the armies of Edward I. In the present paper, however, I have included just those men whom I have identified from the counties of Yorkshire and Northumberland.
[10]   For an introduction to the service of these men in the armies of Edward I, see David S. Bachrach, 'Edward I's "Centurions": Professional Soldiers in an Era of Militia Armies', in *The Soldier Experience in the Fourteenth Century*, ed. Adrian R. Bell et al. (Woodbridge, 2011), 109–28.
[11]   For the Anglo-Saxon period, the two major traditions that focus, respectively, on governmental control over military service that was based on wealth, and military service based on ties of loyalty to one's lord, are represented by C. Warren Hollister, *Anglo-Saxon Military Institutions on the Eve of the Norman Conquest* (Oxford, 1962) and Richard Abels, *Lordship and Military Obligation in Anglo-Saxon England* (Berkeley, CA, 1988). C. Warren Hollister, *The Military Organization of Norman England* (Oxford, 1965), and Powicke, *Military Obligation*, remain foundational for the relationship between wealth and military obligation under the Anglo-Norman kings.

had been part of English military organization for centuries.[12] However, the assize of 1181 did update this obligation to account for the contemporary military organization and the greater wealth of the population at large, specifically tying mounted military service to the possession, on the one hand, of knights' fees or, on the other, to 16 marks (roughly 10 pounds) worth of property.[13] The government of Henry III (1216–1272) reissued the assize of arms several times, including in 1253, when specific arms requirements were instituted for members of the lower wealth categories for service in the royal army on foot. Wealthier property owners, who were now identified as those with properties valued at 15 pounds, still had the obligation to provide themselves with equipment and horses for mounted military service.[14]

During the reign of Edward I, the royal government devoted enormous energy to enforcing the obligations on both the holders of knights' fees and wealthier property owners to perform mounted military service.[15] This effort is explicable by the unprecedented scale and number of military operations undertaken by Edward I in diverse theaters of war, including Gascony, Flanders, Wales, and above all, Scotland.[16] In this regard, the king issued summons for the holders of knights' fees in 1276, 1282, 1283, 1287, 1293, 1297, 1298, 1299, 1301, and 1303.[17]

Edward's government also issued numerous summonses for wealthier property owners to prepare for military service by purchasing warhorses, or to mobilize for service in the royal army as mounted troops.[18] In May 1282, for

---

[12] Powicke, *Military Obligation*, 54–56.
[13] Powicke, *Military Obligation*, 55.
[14] See the discussion by Powicke, *Military Obligation*, 90.
[15] Edward I renewed the provisions of the assize of arms in the statute of Winchester, which was issued in 1285. See the discussion by Prestwich, *War, Politics, and Finance*, 83.
[16] For Edward's campaigns, see Michael Prestwich, *Edward I* (2nd ed., London, 1997). For Edward's Welsh campaigns, the study by J.E. Morris, *The Welsh Wars of Edward I* (Stroud, 1998) remains valuable. This new edition of the text includes a foreword from Michael Prestwich discussing Morris's role in developing government documents as sources for military history.
[17] *Calendar of Close Rolls 1272–1307*, ed. H.C. Maxwell Lyte and William Henry Stevenson (5 vols., London, 1900–1908), i (*1272–1279*), 410; *Calendar of Various Chancery Rolls: Supplementary Close Rolls, Welsh Rolls, Scutage Rolls. Preserved in the Public Record Office A.D. 1277–1326* (London, 1912), 213, 246, 251–252, 258, 278, 306, 359–360; *Close Rolls 1296–1302*, iv, 76, 78, 127, 132, 200, 201, 203, 219, 306, 374, 480, 488, *Close Rolls 1302–1307*, v, 71; *Calendar of Patent Rolls Edward I A.D. 1272–1307* (4 vols., London, 1893–1901, repr. 1971), here, *Patent Rolls 1281–1292*, ii, 275. Michael Prestwich, 'Cavalry Service in Early Fourteenth-Century England', in *War and Government in the Middle Ages: Essays in Honour of J.O. Prestwich*, ed. J. Gillingham and J.C. Holt (Woodbridge, 1984), 147–58, here 148, argues that there was an additional summons in 1306, for which only fragmentary returns survive. A royal writ to the sheriffs of Bedfordshire, Wiltshire, and nine other counts requires the mobilization of all *homines ad arma* to join the royal army and to arrest those who refuse to serve, but this is not limited to men holding knights' fees, and may be seen rather as a broader mobilization of men equipped with horses and arms suitable for equestrian combat. See C46/2/22. This and all subsequent manuscript references are to documents located in the National Archives at Kew.
[18] For a thorough treatment of this topic, see Powicke, *Military Obligation*, 103–117; and Prestwich, *War, Politics and Finance*, 83–90.

example, a writ was issued to all the sheriffs in England ordering them to see to it that all men in their counties with lands valued at 30 pounds equip themselves with warhorses.[19] In November of that same year, writs were issued to all of the sheriffs of England to mobilize and inspect the equipment and horses of all men in their counties with property valued at 20 pounds or more.[20] In 1297, Edward issued orders for the mobilization of all men throughout England, who did not have knightly status but did possess properties worth 20 pounds or more.[21] In Yorkshire, however, the property qualification for mobilization to serve as mounted fighting man was set at 30 pounds.[22] The next year, in 1298, mobilization orders were issued to all men in Nottinghamshire and Derbyshire with property valued at 30 pounds to mobilize for mounted military service. Men with property valued at more than 30 pounds were to provide mounted troops commensurate with their wealth at a rate of one man for each 30 pounds of income.[23] In 1300, Edward's government ordered sheriffs throughout England to mobilize all men with properties valued at 40 pounds for mounted military service in Scotland.[24]

Voluntary military service on horseback

Detailed investigations of the mobilization of men with knights' fees and wealthier property owners makes clear that the royal government was very successful in obtaining military service that was owed by these strata of English society during the late thirteenth and early fourteenth century.[25] However, the mounted forces provided by these men were insufficient to meet the military needs of the royal government under Edward I, particularly during the final third of his reign when he undertook numerous campaigns to conquer Scotland. Consequently, the royal government routinely sought additional means of maximizing the mounted forces that were available for offensive military operations. To this end, Edward's government substantially increased the size of the royal military household, with more than 500 mounted troops under arms for the Flanders campaign of 1297, and almost 800 mounted troops for the 1298 campaign in Scotland.[26]

---

[19] *Welsh Rolls*, 252. The rationale for this order was that there were too few military quality horses available in England, and the royal government wished to increase the overall supply of these animals by requiring wealthier individuals to purchase them. This is an interesting example of the royal government seeking to use the private market as a means of solving a problem facing the kingdom.

[20] *Welsh Rolls*, 275–276.

[21] In this regard, see C47/2/16.

[22] *Parliamentary Writs and Writs of Military Summons* i, 281.

[23] *Patent Rolls, 1292–1301*, iii, 387.

[24] *Close Rolls, 1296–1302*, iv, 380–381.

[25] The most recent study on this topic by Simpkin, *The English Aristocracy at War*, 23, indicates that over 80 percent of eligible men of knightly status served in the armies of Edward I.

[26] Prestwich, War, *Politics, and Finance*, 52.

A second method employed by Edward I to increase the size of his mounted forces was to ask great magnates to mobilize as many men as possible for service in their military households, usually without royal pay, on the basis of the love and affection that these magnates had for the king.[27] Michael Prestwich has argued that Edward was very successful in obtaining unpaid service of this type and estimated that more mounted troops served without royal pay than there were who served for the king's wages.[28]

Maximizing the turn-out of men holding military tenures from the king, increasing the size of the royal military household, and seeking unpaid voluntary service of this type undoubtedly led to the recruitment of substantial mounted forces. However, even these measures were insufficient to recruit all of the mounted troops required by the royal government. Consequently, Edward I actively sought volunteers to serve as mounted forces in return for royal pay. Moreover, the royal government did not limit its request for volunteers to the knightly class or even to the landed gentry. For example, King Edward issued a letter patent on 16 September 1297 to sheriffs throughout England in which he ordered them to mobilize both knights and anyone else who possessed horses and arms to join the army. The sheriffs were explicitly ordered to offer royal pay for service.[29] Similarly in September 1298, the chancery issued letters to all of the sheriffs in England ordering them to mobilize all men who were capable of mounted military service to join the royal army at Carlisle. This was for a campaign that was planned for 1299 but ultimately did not take place. Once more, the sheriffs were to make a specific promise of royal wages to those who agreed to serve on horseback.[30]

A similar example of recruiting a wide range of men to serve as volunteer mounted troops can be seen in the context of defensive operations along the Scottish frontier in 1303. In this case, letters patent were issued to the sheriffs of the northern counties, including Yorkshire, Cumberland, and Westmorland to mobilize all of the men capable of mounted military service to join the army that the king had ordered mobilized at Wark on Tweed to serve under the command of the royal commander John de Segrave.[31] These mounted troops were serve at their own cost up to the Tweed and for eight days after crossing the river, but thereafter they were to serve for royal pay.[32] The men summoned for mounted military service were to include barons, knights, sergeants, as well as *boni homines* and townsmen.[33]

---

[27] Prestwich, *War, Politics, and Finance*, 69–70.
[28] Prestwich, *War, Politics, and Finance*, 91.
[29] C47/2/16; *Calendar of Patent Rolls, 1292–1301*, iii, 309; and *Calendar of Close Rolls 1296–1302*, iv, 132.
[30] *Calendar of Close Rolls, 1296–1302*, iv, 219.
[31] *Calendar of Patent Rolls, 1301–1307*, iv, 101 and 103.
[32] *Calendar of Patent Rolls, 1301–1307*, iv, 101 and 103.
[33] *Calendar of Patent Rolls, 1301–1307*, iv, 101 and 103. By contrast with the mounted troops, the foot soldiers who were mobilized to serve in the royal army were to begin receiving royal pay as soon as they crossed the Tweed.

The work of scholars such as Michael Prestwich and David Simpkin has made clear that the vast majority of 'fighting knights' and landed gentry served in the military households of the King Edward and his magnates.[34] So the question then arises, who were these additional men whom the king summoned to serve as mounted troops at royal pay? How numerous were they? Moreover, in what capacity did they serve? These questions rarely have been posed by scholars, and certainly have not been answered.

The militarized sub-gentry: *soldarii and centenarii*

There are two types of mounted troops serving in the armies of Edward I, who generally were not part of the royal or magnate military households, and whose service has not received significant attention from scholars. These men were designated in government documents as *soldarii* and *centenarii*; they were also denoted as *constabularii*. The former served as heavy cavalry, much the same as all other *homines ad arma*. The *centenarii* were infantry officers in command of one hundred men. *Centenarii* served on campaign mounted on horses that were equipped with a protective coat, that is *equi cooperti*, and were paid a shilling a day.[35] This was the same rate earned by all of the sub-knightly troops who served as heavy cavalry, including the *soldarii*.[36] It is likely that some *centenarii* were recruited at the same time as, but certainly not in the same manner as, foot soldiers.[37] The personnel who served as *soldarii* and as *centenarii* overlapped to a considerable extent, suggesting that they came from the same social and economic strata.[38] The rate of pay earned by both *soldarii* and *centenarii* was six times higher than that received by the foot soldiers in Edward's army, who received just 2 pence a day for their military service. Consequently, one can see that the investment in a horse that was suitable for war, as well as the protective covering for this horse, offered a man with entrepreneurial instincts the opportunity to vastly increase his earning potential in the king's service.

To give a sense of the ways in which traditional scholarly approaches to the study of the mounted forces in the armies of Edward I have missed *soldarii* and *centenarii*, it is helpful to compare the information provided by the horse inventories produced in 1298 with the information that is available from the

---

34   Prestwich, *War, Politics, and Finance*, 69–70, and 91; Simpkin, *Aristocracy at War*, 112–150.

35   King Edward's government issued letters patent in June 1300 authorizing sheriffs and commissioners of array to recruit an appropriate number of officers (here denoted as *constabularii*) to lead companies of foot soldiers on campaign. See *Calendar of Patent Rolls, 1292–1301*, iii, 519 and 529–530.

36   See the discussion by Bachrach, 'Edward I's "Centurions"', 111.

37   Commissioners of array were commanded by the king to mobilize *centenarii* to command units of 100 horsemen in June 1300 and again in June 1301. Otherwise, it is not clear how *centenarii* were recruited. See *Patent Rolls 1292–1301*, iii, 519, 529–530, and 596.

38   Concerning the overlap in personnel between those serving as *soldarii* and those serving as *centenarii*, see Bachrach, 'Edward I's "Centurions"', 109–128.

pay records for the campaign in Scotland during this year. A total of forty-nine men who served as *centenarii* and thirty-nine men who served as *soldarii* in 1298 are recorded on the two major extant horse inventories, which were published by Gough.[39] It should be noted that these men are not designated on the horse rolls as either *soldarii* or *centenarii*, but can be identified as having served in these roles on the basis of information provided by royal clerks in pay records from this campaign. Thus, for example, a man named John Bagepus appears on one of the horse inventory rolls for the 1298 campaign in Scotland.[40] Separately, John is listed in several royal pay records where he was identified by the king's clerks as a *centenarius* from Cheshire in command of a unit of foot soldiers at Berwick castle, and also as a *millenarius*, that is the commander of 1,000 men, also at Berwick.[41] Adam de Chetewind was listed on the same horse inventory as John Bagepus. He also appears in a pay record from 1298 and is denoted as a *centenarius* who commanded a company of men on foot from Staffordshire.[42] A third individual, Eustace de Parles, is identified in two separate pay records for 1298 as a *soldarius* and also appears on the same horse inventory as John and Adam.[43]

These three mounted fighting men represent exceptional cases. The forty-nine *centenarii* listed in the 1298 horse rolls comprise less than eight percent of 641 *centenarii* who appear in the pay records for this campaign in Scotland.[44] At just over sixteen percent of the total, the thirty-nine *soldarii* listed in the horse rolls comprise a somewhat higher proportion of the 238 *soldarii* who appear in the pay records for 1298.[45] In all, a minimum of 791 men equipped with war horses, i.e. *equi cooperti*, are not accounted for in the calculations of mounted fighting men traditionally used by scholars to assess the fighting strength of Edward I's army in 1298.

There is a smaller but similar discrepancy between the mounted forces traditionally identified in Edward I's army for the Scottish campaign of 1300 and those mounted troops who can be identified using the full array of pay records. The king's wardrobe account for 1300 was published in 1787 by J. Topham, and like Gough's volume, this text has played a crucial role in subsequent investigations of the armies of Edward I, including studies of the military service of the knights and gentry.[46] Topham's edition includes information about 375 *soldarii*

---

[39]   Gough, *Scotland in 1298*, 161–237.
[40]   E101/6/39. This document records the names of mounted men who were not in the royal military household, but whose mounts would be replaced by the royal government if they were lost on campaign.
[41]   E101/6/35; E101/7/2; and E 101/7/7 1r. For the details of John Bagepus' career, see Bachrach, 'Edward's "Centurions"', 113–114.
[42]   E101/6/39 and E101/6/35.
[43]   See E101/6/39; E101/6/35; and E101/7/2.
[44]   See E101/6/35; E101/7/2; E101/7/7; and C47/2/20.
[45]   See E101/6/35/E101/7/2; and E101/7/7.
[46]   *Liber Quotidianus Contrarotulatoris Garderobiae*, ed. J. Topham (London, 1787).

and *centenarii*, who served in the royal army in 1300.[47] However, these men comprise just over half of the 715 men who can be identified serving in these roles during the campaigns of 1300, when the 244 *centenarii* and ninety-six *soldarii* are excluded whose names do not appear in the wardrobe book edited by Topham.[48] It is worth noting that the royal clerks who drew up the *Liber quotidianus* were not as consistent in their use of terminology as the royal clerks who compiled the pay records for Edward I's forces in the field. In the latter, *soldarii* are always separated out as a distinct group of mounted fighting men. By contrast, the clerks who wrote the records that comprised the *Liber quotidianus* sometimes combined the term *soldarius* with other terms used to denote members of military households, such as *scutifer*, creating the compound term *scutiferi soldarii*.[49]

It has been estimated that for his campaign in 1298, Edward I was able to mobilize 3,000 knights and members of the gentry equipped with *equi cooperti* to serve in the royal army.[50] The 870 or so *centenarii* and *soldarii* who served in this campaign, therefore, comprised a fifth of all of the mounted troops in Edward's army. The 715 *soldarii* and *centenarii* serving in 1300 likely comprised a similar proportion of the mounted troops in the royal army in this year.[51] Because of their sheer numbers, therefore, the failure of scholars to account for these men represents a significant lacuna in current knowledge regarding the mounted forces available to Edward I. However, even more importantly, the *soldarii* and *centenarii* played central roles in the conduct of Edward's campaigns, so that accounts that fail to account for their service as mounted men provide a misleading impression regarding the conduct of war in this period.

Soldarii and *centenarii*: the nature of service and social position

The term *soldarius* itself appears to have been adopted for the first time by royal clerks in 1297 to denote a specific category of heavy cavalryman who was different in kind from the *scutiferi, valleti*, and *servientes ad arma*, who are noted in the horse inventories and other types of administrative documents.[52]

---

47   Prestwich, *War, Politics, and Finance*, 69, describes this text as providing 'an absolutely reliable list of all those in receipt of wages on the campaign'.
48   See E101/6/21; E101/8/7; E101/8/18; E101/8/19; E101/8/20; E101/8/23 nos. 2, 4, 5, 7; E101/8/26; E101/9/28; E101/13/34; E101/13/36; E101/13/36; E101/612/25; E101/684/46; and E101/684/52.
49   *Liber quotidianus*, 140 and 145.
50   Prestwich, *Edward I*, 479. Simpkin, *English Aristocracy at War*, 18, accepts these figures as realistic. M. Haskell, 'Breaking the Stalemate: The Scottish Campaign of Edward I, 1303–1304', *Thirteenth Century England VII*, ed. Michael Prestwich, R. Britnell and R. Frame (Woodbridge, 1999), 223–41, here 229, argues that the mounted forces in 1303 were comparable in size to those in 1298.
51   For the campaign in 1300, see Prestwich, *War, Politics and Finance*, 69–71.
52   With regard to the use of the term *soldarius* by royal clerks, see Bachrach, 'Edward's "Centurions"', 113.

The latter three terms were all used interchangeably to denote the men who were equipped with *equi cooperti* and who also served in the military households of English magnates. By contrast, the term *soldarius* was employed by royal clerks specifically to denote those men who had volunteered individually or in small groups to serve as heavy cavalry in Edward I's later campaigns, and who were not members of magnate military households.[53] These *soldarii* played a particularly important role as garrison troops in Scotland and sometimes comprised the majority of the mounted forces who served in fortifications north of the English frontier.[54] Although not every garrison included *soldarii*, when they are present, they are always denoted as a separate group among the heavy cavalry.

The *centenarii*, for their part, provided important leadership in the armies of Edward I to the foot soldiers in both garrisons and in the field. Their leadership was particularly important because many *centenarii* served in multiple campaigns and brought extensive experience to the conduct of military operations. In addition, many of the *centenarii* who originally saw service commanding units of foot soldiers from their home counties, turned to recruiting companies of foot soldiers for long-term service in Edward I's armies, particularly in Scotland. These contract companies, commanded by veteran *centenarii*, provided the bulk of the foot soldiers who served in royal garrisons between active campaigning seasons in Scotland.[55]

So who were these *soldarii* and *centenarii*, who served in such large numbers in King Edward's armies and played such important roles, particularly in his Scottish campaigns? *Soldarii* have received virtually no attention from scholars and have not been identified as a distinct category of mounted forces in the armies of Edward I. By contrast with the *soldarii*, the presence of *centenarii* in the armies of Edward I and his successors has been noted by numerous scholars.[56] However, there has been very little investigation of their social status, wealth, or origins. This is largely the case because the *centenarii* have not been considered within the compass of the mounted forces of royal armies but rather as part of the infantry, which has suffered from significant scholarly neglect.[57]

In his brief discussion of the *centenarii*, during the reign of Edward III rather than Edward I, Michael Powicke concluded that these men must have been drawn

---

[53]   For a discussion of the careers of some of the men who served as *soldarii* see Bachrach, 'Edward's "Centurions"', 111–121.

[54]   The garrison at Kirkintilloch in 1301, for example, included three knights and their eight *homines ad arma*. They were joined by twenty *soldarii*. See E101/9/16 1v. The *soldarii* also comprised a majority of the mounted troops in the garrison at Edinburgh that year. The knight, John de Kingston, had 10 *homines ad arma* with him, and there were an additional 12 *soldarii* serving in the garrison. See E101/9/16 1r.

[55]   See the discussion of the *centenarii* by Bachrach, 'Edward I's "Centurions"'.

[56]   See, for example, Morris, *Welsh Wars*, 96–96, who discusses commanders of 1000 men, that is *millenarii*; Powicke, *Military Organization*, 186; Prestwich, *War, Politics, and Finance*, 106.

[57]   Both Prestwich, *War, Politics and Finance*, 92–113, and Powicke, *Military Obligation*, 118–133, discuss the role played by infantry forces in the armies of Edward I. However, their focus is on the institutional structures that were in place to mobilize these forces and their generally poor fighting ability rather than on prosopographical questions.

from the wealthier classes of property owners.[58] The implication is that if they were mounted, they must have been wealthy. More recently, David Simpkin has argued that although some *millenarii* and *centenarii* in the armies of Edward I were knights, most of these infantry officers came from lower in the social scale than this.[59] The implication again, however, is that these infantry officers were members of the gentry albeit those with smaller landed holdings.

The hypothesis that the *centenarii*, and by implication the *soldarii* as well, were drawn from the gentry can be tested in several ways. First, one can compare the value of the horses that these mounted troops brought on campaign with the value of the horses ridden by both the knightly class and the sub-knightly gentry who served in the royal military household and in the military households of the English magnates in paid royal service. I have been able to identify the value of the horses utilized by 143 *centenarii* between 1296 and 1303 through an investigation of both horse rolls, and a range of pay records. The horse values range from a minimum of 30 shillings to a maximum of 402 shillings. The average price was about 112 shillings. I also have been able to identify the values of the horses ridden by 196 *soldarii*, which range from 20 to 400 shillings, with an average value of 126 shillings.[60] It is noteworthy that the average values of the horses ridden by *centenarii* and *soldarii* represent approximately two years' wages for a common laborer in the late thirteenth century if he worked every day of the year. Given that this level of work is unlikely, it is more probable that the cost represents closer to two and a half years labor.[61]

In contrast to the value of horses ridden by *centenarii* and *soldarii*, the average value for knights' horses in the final third of Edward I's reign was 444 shillings, which is almost 400 percent greater than the horses of the infantry officers and unattached heavy cavalrymen.[62] Similarly, the average prices for

---

58   Powicke, *Military Organization*, 186.
59   Simpkin, *English Aristocracy at War*, 55.
60   For the prices of horses ridden by *centenarii* see E101/5/23; E101/6/19; E101/6/28; E101/6/37; E101/6/39; E101/6/40; E101/7/5; E101/7/7; E101/8/7; E101/8/23; E101/8/26; E101/9/9; E101/9/13; E101/9/23; E101/9/24; E101/10/12; E101/13/7; E101/612/8; E101/612/9; E101/612/12; and *Liber Quotidianus*. For the prices of horses ridden by *soldarii* see E101/5/23; E101/6/19; E101/6/28; E101/6/37; E101/6/39; E101/6/40; E101/7/7; E101/8/7; E101/8/23; E101/8/26; E101/9/9; E101/9/13; E101/9/23; E101/9/24; E101/10/12; E01/10/14; E101/11/16; E101/13/36; E101/612/8; E101/612/9; E101/612/11; and *Liber Quotidianus*.
61   For the wages of daily laborers, see *Building Accounts of King Henry III*, ed. Howard M. Colvin (Oxford, 1971), 12.
62   Useful tables for the average prices of war horses ridden on campaign by knights and the sub-knightly gentry can be found in Ayton, *Knights and Warhorses*, 195–196; and Simpkin, *English Aristocracy at War*, 59. However, these tables do not distinguish between the values of warhorses ridden by knights and gentry, on the one hand, and *soldarii* and *centenarii* on the other. I hope to publish a study on the prices of warhorses during the latter third of Edward I's reign in the near future. For the prices of horses ridden by *milites*, see E101/5/23; E101/619; E101/6/28; E101/6/37; E101/639; E101/6/40; E101/7/; E101/7/7; E101/8/23; E101/8/26; E101/9/9; E101/9/23; E101/9/24; E101/10/12; E101/612/9; E101/612/11; E101/12/8; E101/13/7; and *Liber Quotidianus*.

horses ridden by the members of the royal and magnate military households over this period was 183 shillings, which was almost 60 percent greater than those of the *centenarii*, and 40 percent greater than those of the *soldarii*.[63] When we take into account these substantial differences in the value of the horses ridden by the knights and the members of their military households on the one hand, and the *centenarii* and *soldarii* on the other, it seems reasonable to suggest that the latter had significantly less disposable wealth than the propertied classes who served in Edward I's armies.

A second means of establishing the economic and perhaps the social status of the *centenarii* is through an examination of the surviving property assessments from Edward I's reign. This comparison is possible for the *centenarii* because royal pay records often provide information about their counties of origin. By contrast, the royal clerks did not provide this information about *soldarii*. Tax assessments were conducted on a county by county basis, consequently, determining the county of origin of a particular *soldarius* is not usually possible.[64]

In comparing the names of *centenarii* from individual counties with the names of the individuals whose assets were assessed for taxation in those same counties, it is clear that the great majority of the *centenarii* did not have sufficient non-landed assets to be subject to taxes on moveable wealth. For example, I have been able to identify 124 individuals who served as *centenarii* leading troops from Yorkshire on campaign in the decade between 1297 and 1307.[65] Of these, at most a dozen appear in the tax rolls.[66] However, it should be noted that information produced for tax assessments authorized by parliament during Edward I's reign has survived unevenly. In Yorkshire, only the assessments for 1284–1285, 1301, and 1302–1303 have survived.[67] As a consequence, it is possible that more of the *centenarii* had sufficient moveable wealth in Yorkshire to be liable for taxation than can be demonstrated on the basis of the surviving sources.

The situation is similar in Northumberland. I have been able to identify seventy-four men who served as *centenarii* leading infantry companies from

---

[63] For the prices of the horses ridden by the members of the royal and magnate military households, who were below knightly status, see E101/5/23; E101/6/19; E101/6/28; E101/6/37; E101/6/39; E101/6/40; E101/7/5; E101/7/7; E101/8/7; E101/8/23; E101/8/26; E101/9/9; E101/9/13; E101/9/14; E101/923; E101/924; E101/10/12; E101/13/7; E101/612/8; E101/612/9; E101/612/11; and *Liber Quotidianus*.

[64] However, if a particular *soldarius* also served as a *centenarius* who led an infantry company from a particular county, it is possible to investigate whether this individual held property in that county.

[65] See Appendix I for a list of the Yorkshire *centenarii* and the documents in which they appear.

[66] See Appendix I for a list of the Yorkshire *centenarii* and the documents in which they appear.

[67] For a detailed discussion of royal taxation in this period, see Prestwich, *War, Politics and Finance*, 177–203.

Northumberland between 1298 and 1304. Of these, eleven appear in the lay subsidy roll of 1296.[68] This is a somewhat higher percentage of Northumberland men (15 percent), and only one tax roll has survived from this period as compared with three from Yorkshire. Consequently, it seems reasonable to conclude that a greater proportion of the *centenarii* from Northumberland had sufficient moveable wealth to make them subject to taxation than was the case in Yorkshire. Nevertheless, the percentage was still quite small.

In looking closely at the limited number of *centenarii* who had sufficient moveable wealth in Yorkshire and Northumberland to be subject to taxation it is clear that most of them were men of limited means. For example, Edward Carbonel, who led a company of Yorkshire footmen to Scotland in 1300, paid just 19 pence for the moveable property that he held in the village of Cowesby in northern Yorkshire as part of the lay assessment of one-fifteenth granted to King Edward in 1301.[69] On this basis, it appears that Edward held property assessed at just 24 shillings. Nicholas de Hoperton, who also led a company of foot soldiers from Yorkshire in 1300, paid just 10 pence in taxes for his property in the city of York, indicating that his moveable property was assessed at just twelve and half shillings.[70]

There are, however, some exceptions to the generally small moveable property holdings of the *centenarii*. John de Langton, for example, who commanded infantry companies in 1300 and 1304, and served as a *soldarius* in 1300, 1301, 1302, and 1303, appears to have been a substantially wealthier man than his fellow Yorkshire *centenarii*.[71] John, who also was a citizen of the city of York, paid a tax of 6 shillings and 6 pence on his moveable wealth suggesting that he had been assessed at almost 5 pounds.[72] This assessment is obviously much greater than that of either Edward Carbonel or Nicholas Hoperton.

A similar pattern emerges with regard to the wealth of the men from Northumberland who served as *centenarii*. A very small number of these men, such as William Ribaud were assessed at a high rate. William, who led a company of foot soldiers from Northumberland in both 1301 and 1303, also served as a *valletus* in the military household of the great magnate Robert Clifford in 1300.[73] William held half a knight's fee in Howick from Sir John de Vesci, the total

---

[68] See Appendix II for a list of Northumberland *centenarii* and the documents in which they appear.

[69] For Edward Carbonel's service, see *Liber quotidianus*, 256. For the tax paid by Edward Carbonel in 1301, see *Yorkshire Lay Subsidy being a Fifteenth, Collected 30 Edward I (1301)*, ed. William Brown (Leeds, 1897), 87.

[70] See *Yorkshire Lay Subsidy*, 120, for Nicholas Hoperton's tax payment, and E101/6/21; E101/8/20; and *Liber quotidianus*, 252, for his military service in 1300.

[71] For John de Langton's military service, see E101/9/16; E101/10/5; E101/10/12; E101/11/1; E101/11/15; E101/11/29; E101/13/34; and E101/684/52.

[72] *Yorkshire Lay Subsidy*, 120.

[73] For William Ribaud's military career, see MS ADD 7966A; E101/8/23 7; E101/11/1; and E101/612/9 1303.

value of which was assessed at 20 pounds in 1289, following de Vesci's death.[74] Thus, although he was certainly quite well off, William's property valued at 10 pounds, was not sufficient to make him subject to mobilization as a mounted fighting man at any point in Edward I's reign. William may have been obligated to provide one mounted fighting man of sub-knightly status as his contribution for his portion of the knight's fee that he held from the de Vesci family. An obligation of this type would certainly explain William's service as a *valletus* in 1300. It is worthy of note, however, that despite William's elevated social and economic status, he did not bring very expensive horses on campaign. In 1300, his mount was valued at just 107 shillings by royal clerks, and in 1303 William's mount was valued at just 80 shillings.[75]

William's economic status, however, was unusual among the Northumberland *centenarii* who were assessed in the 1296 lay subsidy roll. More common was the situation of John de Glanton, who served as the commander of a company of Northumberland foot soldiers in 1303.[76] He was assessed for moveable property valued at just under 2 pounds in Longframlington.[77] Robert Scot, who led a company of Northumberland foot soldiers in Scotland in 1301, was similarly assessed for moveable property valued at just under 2 pounds, in his case in the liberty of Tynemouth.[78]

Conclusion

Scholars investigating the composition, social status, and political activity of the knightly class and the broader sub-knightly gentry from the late thirteenth through the late fourteenth century have observed that men of these social and economic statuses were militarized to a significant degree.[79] The present study indicates that the militarization of the population penetrated even more deeply into English society. The vast majority of the *centenarii* and *soldarii* who served in the armies of Edward I possessed insufficient property to be assessed for the numerous lay subsidies granted to the king. Among the relatively few men who did have sufficient property to be assessed, most fell well below the threshold that would have required them to serve as mounted fighting men in the king's army. Consequently, the more than 2,000 *centenarii* and *soldarii* who served in Edward I's armies constituted what might be considered a militarized sub-gentry.

---

[74]   *The Northumberland Lay Subsidy Roll of 1296*, ed. C.M. Fraser (Newcastle upon Tyne, 1968), 142. One knight from Northumberland, William de Fenton, did serve as a *centenarius* leading companies of foot soldiers. See MS ADD 7966A and E101/12/16. For William de Fenton's properties in Northumberland, see *Northumberland Lay Subsidy Roll*, 16, 36, 54, 81, 92, 160, 164, 167, and 168.
[75]   E101/8/23 and E101/612/9.
[76]   E101/10/28.
[77]   *Northumberland Lay Subsidy Roll*, 161.
[78]   *Northumberland Lay Subsidy Roll*, 98.
[79]   For a detailed survey of this scholarly tradition, see Andy King, 'The English Gentry at War, 1300–1450', forthcoming in *History Compass* 12.10 (2014), 759–769.

Men of this economic and social stratum chose military service, sometimes as a career, and they did so on a voluntary basis. In effect, they were military entrepreneurs who invested in expensive equipment, including warhorses as well as the protective coverings for these animals, so as to qualify to serve as either heavy cavalry or infantry officers in the armies of Edward I, and thereby benefit from the much higher wages earned by men serving on horseback in the king's armies. These investments, even given the relatively inexpensive mounts that they brought on campaign, were far greater than the value of the moveable property that they can be seen to have possessed and represented potentially years of earnings. Moreover, unlike their better off contemporaries among the gentry and knights, most of the men who served as *centenarii* and *soldarii* did not receive a guarantee from the crown that their mounts would be replaced if lost in combat. Consequently, the economic risks undertaken by these *centenarii* and *soldarii* were concomitantly greater than those of men who possessed greater economic resources.

That large numbers of men with few obvious economic resources undertook military service in the armies of Edward I, can no longer be in doubt. But this raises other questions, which will undoubtedly require considerable additional research to answer. Where did these men obtain the initial capital to purchase a warhorse so as to volunteer for military service? Was credit available to men who were willing and able to take up a military career? Did these individuals benefit from the patronage of wealthy patrons, who sought to increase the number of men available for mounted military service? Were there sources of wealth not subject to the taxes on laymen during Edward I's reign? The answers to these questions, however, must await another day.

Appendix 1: Yorkshire *Centenarii*, 1297–1307

Benedict Stubb, E101/13/34; *Liber Quotidianus*, 254
Edmund Carbonel, *Liber Quotidianus*, 256; *Yorkshire Lay Subsidy,* 87
Edmund de Coseby, E101/11/15
Edmund Dorel, E101/11/15
Edmund de Reygate, *Liber Quotidianus*, 236; MS ADD 7966A
Edmund de Wateby, E101/8/20; *Liber Quotidianus*, 247, 249, 251
Edward de Watery, E101/612/25
Elias de Couton, *Liber Quotidianus*, 244
Eustace de Walleswode, E101/8/20; E101/11/15
Galfrid de la Mare, E101/6/37; E101/6/37; E101/6/39; E/101/9/13 (1301);
     E101/9/30; E101/10/12; E101/10/14; E101/11/15
Gilbert Mateby, E101/11/15
Gilbert de Quiky, E101/6/21; *Liber Quotidianus*, 251, 252, 254
Gilbert del Ruy, E101/8/20
Gocelin de Alta Ripa, E101/6/21
Godfrey de Alta Ripa, *Feudal Aids*, 114;[1] E101/7/2; E101/8/20; E101/13/34
Henry Clericus, E101/8/20; *Liber Quotidianus*, 250, 252
Henry de Lascy, *Liber Quotidianus*, 236, 252, 254; E101/6/21; E101/8/20; MS
     ADD 7966A
Henry de Leycester, *Liber Quotidianus*, 270
Henry de Manfeld, E101/6/21; E101/612/25; E101/8/20; MS ADD 7966A;
     E101/12/16
Hugh de Baskerville, E101/13/34; MS ADD 7966A; E101/7/13; E101/12/16
Hugh Dacone, E101/612/25; *Liber Quotidianus*, 245
Henry Histerton, E101/13/34
Hugh de Merton, E101/6/40 1298; E101/6/21; E101/612/25; E101/8/20
Hugh de Montgomery, E101/11/15
Humphrey le Coynier, *Liber Quotidianus*, 256
John Beybridge, E101/11/15; E101/13/16
John de Bristol, E101/8/20; E101/13/34; *Liber Quotidianus*, 248; MS ADD
     7966A; E101/7/13; E101/12/16; E101/12/17
John Bradley, *Liber Quotidianus*, 247; *Yorkshire Lay Subsidy,* 70
John de Cotenesso, *Liber Quotidianus*, 146; E101/13/34; MS ADD 7966A;
     E101/9/9
John cum Avibus de Wakefield, E101/6/21
John Faunt de Wakefield, E101/6/21
John de Greensworth, MS ADD 7966A

---

[1]   *Inquisitions and Assessments Relating to Feudal Aids with other Analogous Documents Preserved in the Public Record Office A.D. 1284–1431* (6 vols., London, 1899–1920), vi: *York and Additions.*

Appendix 2: Northumberland *Centenarii*, 1298–1304

Adam de Rothebur, E101/11/15

David Manwell, E101/6/37; E101/8/7; *Liber Quotidianus*, 242

Edward de Comingham, MS ADD 7966A

Galfrid de Bakerville, *Liber Quotidianus*, 247, 252, 253, 255

Galfrid de Gosewik, E101/10/28

Gilbert de Babington, E101/8/20; *Liber Quotidianus*, 247

Gilbert Modi, E101/13/34; C47/2/20; *Liber Quotidianus*, 221, 236; MS
    ADD 7966A; E/101/9/13; E101/9/30 17; E101/10/14; E101/10/28 no. 28;
    E101/12/16; E101/12/17

Henry de Benteley, *Liber Quotidianus*, 221, 257; MS ADD 7966A; E101/9/30
    17; E101/10/14; E101/8/20; E101/13/34; E101/9/9; E101/9/16; E/101/9/13;
    E101/9/9; E101/12/16

Henry de Eaton, E101/12/16

Henry de Felton, E101/8/23 4; E101/13/34; MS ADD 7966A; E101/7/13

Henry de Gatesby, E101/13/34; E101/12/16

Henry de Stanney, E101/6/39; E101/8/20; *Liber Quotidianus*, 142, 252, 255;
    E101/8/26; E101/8/20

Hugh de Aldeburgh, E101/7/7; E101/8/7; MS ADD 7966A; E101/9/9; E101/10/12;
    E101/612/9 1303

Hugh Bentley, MS ADD 7966A

Hugh le Porter, E101/612/9; E101/11/15

John de Benton, MS ADD 7966A; E101/9/9; E101/9/24; E101/10/12

John de Chitby, MS ADD 7966A

John de Clanton, E101/10/28

John de Clinevest, MS ADD 7966A

John Coldstrother, E101/8/20; *Liber Quotidianus*, 247; E101/9/30 20v;
    Northumberland Lay Subsidy Roll, p. 23 no. 60; E101/9/16; E101/10/12
    (1302); E101/10/5; E101/11/1; E101/12/35

John de Crapington, E101/13/34; *Northumberland Lay Subsidy Roll*, p. 137 no.
    320

John de Dalton, E101/6/40; E101/8/7; *Liber Quotidianus,* 222; MS ADD 7966A;
    E101/6/37 *Northumberland Lay Subsidy Roll*, p. 28 no. 73

John de Engeleys, MS ADD 7966A

John de Glanton, E101/10/28; *Northumberland Lay Subsidy Roll*, p. 161 no. 376

John de Hanwick, MS ADD 7966A

John Herle, E101/9/28; E101/13/34; E101/7/13; MS ADD 7966A; E101/12/16

John de Hogh, *Liber Quotidianus*, 242; MS ADD 7966A; *Northumberland Lay
    Subsidy Roll,* p. 178 no. 411 and p. 63 no. 146

John de Houk, E101/6/37; E101/13/34; E101/12/16

John de Pinkerton, E101/13/34; E101/612/9; E101/12/16

John Sharpton, E101/8/20

John de Trollop, E101/8/20; E101/8/26

John de Witeby, E101/8/20; E101/13/34
Peter de Midford, E101/8/20; E101/13/34
Peter de Riselaye, E101/10/28
Ralph de Castello, E101/11/15
Richard de Bilton, E101/6/40; E101/8/20; *Liber Quotidianus*, 221; MS ADD
    7966A; E101/9/16; E101/9/30 20v; E101/10/5; E101/11/1; E101/11/15;
    E101/13/34; E101/612/9; E101/684/52
Richard Dessingham, MS ADD 7966A
Richard de Felton, MS ADD 7966A
Richard Galou, MS ADD 7966A
Richard Hoggel, *Liber Quotidianus,* 242
Richard de Ludlowe, E101/6/39; E101/13/34; MS ADD 7966A; E101/7/13
Richard de Wetwange, MS ADD 7966A; *Northumberland Lay Subsidy Roll*, p.
    112 no. 267
Robert de Bollesdon, *Liber Quotidianus*, 250; E101/8/20; E101/13/34; E101/11/15
Robert Herle, E101/13/34; MS ADD 7966A; E101/10/28; E101/12/16
Robert de Newcastle, *Liber Quotidianus,* 221; E101/11/15
Robert de Runhull, MS ADD 7966A
Robert de Scocie, MS ADD 7966A *Northumberland Lay Subsidy Roll*, p. 98 no.
    232
Roger de Berwick, E101/8/23 7; E101/13/34; MS ADD 7966A
Roger Delwyk, E101/12/16
Roger de Langdon, E101/7/8; E101/11/15 (1303–1304)
Simon de Farneys, E101/10/28
Simon de Fue, MS ADD 7966A
Simon de Melton, E101/8/20; E101/13/34; *Liber Quotidianus,* 142; E101/10/28;
    E101/12/17
Stephen de Duddene, E101/11/1; E101/612/9 1303
Thomas de Alnewik, E101/10/28 1303
Thomas Baroun, *Liber Quotidianus,* 242; *Northumberland Lay Subsidy Roll*, p. 38
    no. 106 and p. 156 no. 338
Walter Crushenny, MS ADD 7966A
William de Aspele, E101/8/7; E101/13/34; MS ADD 7966A; E101/12/16
William Babington, E101/6/39; E101/8/20; E101/13/34
William Bilton, E101/11/15
William de Coggesdon, MS ADD 7966A
William de Crinton, MS ADD 7966A
William de Dalton, E101/6/39; E101/612/9; E101/11/15 *Northumberland Lay
    Subsidy Roll*, p. 32 no. 87 and p. 43 no. 110; E101/6/39; E101/684/52; *Liber
    Quotidianus,* 222; E101/10/5; E101/11/1
William de Erington, E101/10/28 1303; E101/13/34 (1300); E101/10/28;
    E101/12/16; *Northumberland Lay Subsidy Roll*, p. 78 no. 182 and p. 171 no.
    398
Dominus William de Felton, MS ADD 7966A; E101/12/16; *Northumberland Lay*

Subsidy Roll p. 16 no. 44, p. 36 no. 102, p. 54 no. 118, p. 81 no. 193, p. 92 no. 221, p. 160 no. 376, p. 164 no. 384, p. 167 no. 390, and p. 167 no. 391
William le Grant, E101/8/20; *Liber Quotidianus,* 242; E101/13/34; MS ADD 7966A; E101/12/16; *Northumberland Lay Subsidy Roll*, p. 85 no. 203
William de Hedon, MS ADD 7966A; E101/7/13; E101/12/16
William de Herle, E101/6/39; MS ADD 7966A
William Hodon, E101/13/34; MS ADD 7966A
William Ribaud, MS ADD 7966A; E101/8/23 no. 7; E101/11/1; *Northumberland Lay Subsidy Roll,* p. 142 no. 336
William Wellington, MS ADD 7966A